IMAGES
of America

ASHEVILLE'S RIVER ARTS DISTRICT

ON THE COVER: Asheville's former Southern Railway passenger depot was a lively place in the days of Asheville-native, author Thomas Wolfe's youth. (Courtesy North Carolina Collection, Pack Memorial Library.)

IMAGES
of America

ASHEVILLE'S RIVER ARTS DISTRICT

Rob Neufeld and Henry Neufeld

ARCADIA
PUBLISHING

ISBN 978-0-7385-5426-6

Published by Arcadia Publishing
Charleston, South Carolina

Printed in the United States of America

Library of Congress Catalog Card Number: 2008923154

For all general information contact Arcadia Publishing at:
Telephone 843-853-2070
Fax 843-853-0044
E-mail sales@arcadiapublishing.com
For customer service and orders:
Toll-Free 1-888-313-2665

Visit us on the Internet at www.arcadiapublishing.com

I dedicate this book to students of history—that is everyone I encounter in my research; and to history itself, which is simply the things we care about and want to hold.

Contents

ACKNOWLEDGMENTS

A photograph is a precious thing, and the people who allow them to be scanned and borrowed for publication are making great gifts. Many of the individuals who lent their photographs also have stories. It is the sign of the preciousness of photographs that they do come with stories. Collecting photographs is not like collecting items for Goodwill. You sit awhile. You listen. You understand the photographs' importance, and, of course, you gather stories that make the use of them in a book appropriate. The donors of the photographs in this book are acknowledged in the captions. I am very grateful to them, as well as to those who told stories about others' photographs. The librarians in the North Carolina Collection at Pack Memorial Library in Asheville—Ann Wright, Zoe Rhine, and Betsy Murray—have been especially helpful. The breadth of that collection, the curatorial care that the librarians exercise, the ability of the librarians to tap their personal knowledge, and the ease of getting material from the library are commendable. Regarding access, I can't help but feel another kind of gratitude for the many providers who responded to some tight deadlines. There was so much to collect, so many places to go—sometimes the squeeze was on. Scott Dedman, Mountain Housing Opportunities executive director; Jolene Mechanic, Flood Gallery and Fine Art Center director; Hartwell Carson, RiverLink river keeper; Greta Reisel Browning, archivist, Special Collections, Appalachian State University; Marty Black of Cotton Mill Studios and The Potters' Mark; Courtney Tiberio of Urvana LLC; Gail McCarthy of Highwater Clays; Howard Hangar; and Andrea Clark all came through when it would have been understandable if they had not. The Asheville *Citizen-Times* made an exception for me in giving me free access to their photographs, partly because I've been writing a weekly local history feature for the newspaper for several years. You may also notice that Henry Neufeld, my son, who is 17 years old at the time of this book's completion, has applied his eye for drama and detail to many of the photographs in this book. A photo history is not any easier thing to do than a text-only book. My wife, Bev Robertson, the Mars Hill College library director, can attest to that—and thank God we were able to have some quality time with side-by-side laptops on some particularly overwhelming days.

INTRODUCTION

The River Arts District is this book's title and offering, but I give you more. The one-mile-by-half-mile area dubbed the River Arts District encompasses—in addition to the arts scene—three significant neighborhoods, a river, many industries, the railroad, and new developments.

The arts scene has gained fame of late. Its renaissance during the last 20 years represents the district's resurgence, but the story is larger thematically, as well as geographically. The West End/Clingman, Southside, and West Asheville communities in the area have gone through noteworthy downs and ups, and the up story of the artists also involves community.

You can take this book around with you on your drive or walk to experience history as a living thing. In addition to historical photographs and text, this book includes now-and-then photographs, contemporary photographs, and, I hope, a few insights. It even includes a couple of renderings of the future. In an area as dynamic as the River Arts District, history keeps happening in discernible ways.

The history of the River Arts District is dramatic and therefore not without its tensions. Its occupants are dealing very well with the pressures of prosperity. In the West End/Clingman neighborhood, two diverse neighborhoods have united to maintain their quality of life in the face of threats of decline and development.

In the River Arts District, there is a nonprofit organization, Mountain Housing Opportunities, that has taken an activist role in rehabilitating and building affordable homes and safe communities. RiverLink, another exemplary organization, has been a major force in creating parks, caring for the river, and developing attractive mixed-use urban projects.

When touring the arts district, it is not just the artists you can see. In fact, try not to be just a tourist. There are organizations with causes that visitors can connect with or at least appreciate while in town.

One book is too short to fully convey the excitement of the arts community because there is a story at every stop. At the extreme ends of the district, for instance, are many wonders. To the south, in Riverview Station (the former tannery), modest masters focus on their crafts in large, unglamorous spaces as if they are members of medieval guilds. To the north, in the Phil Mechanic Building (a former buildings' supplies wholesaler), Jolene Mechanic nurtures an international avant-garde with a social mission.

I had commented to Marc Mandon, a fine furniture-maker in Riverview Station, "You know, I think there are four types of artists in the River Arts District." He looked at me skeptically. I went on. "There are the bohemians. There are the artists who are established and who just want to make art. There are the artists who just want to make art but are adapting well to commercial opportunities. And there are the people who have come here because of the commercial opportunities."

"That's fair," Marc said.

"What are you," I asked, "somewhere between two and three?"

"No," he responded, "somewhere between one and two." I'm not sure how you can be a bohemian furniture-maker, but there you go.

There are a few themes that emerge prominently in the history of the district: the power of the river, the effects of low rents, and community. Floods happen periodically and perhaps contribute to low rents. Low rents have attracted industry in the past and, more recently, have attracted pioneer artists. Modern trends may counter the low-rent factor.

Industries had also located by the river because of transportation, especially the railroad. Lately, transportation has become problematic.

Finally, there is the theme of community. I am overwhelmed by this theme. Southside, the African American community that had thrived in the southeast quadrant of the district, had been decimated in the late 1960s and early 1970s by urban renewal, which had been intended to improve living conditions. There is no story that more clearly demonstrates that community does not depend upon plumbing but instead depends upon social relations.

I wanted to include a contemporary photograph of the gentlemen who congregate in Green's Mini-Mart in Southside. I have rarely encountered such a wise and informed group of people. They bridge historical eras. However, I had to be mindful of how many contemporary photographs I included in this book. Arcadia has allowed me to create a guide as well as retrospection—and thus present history in what I consider to be the most vital sense. I think readers will appreciate this.

Community has been a critical component in the river artists' existence. The River District Artists, an incorporated group, promotes and looks out for the interests of the artists as a whole. There are also mini-communities in each building, and there is the notion of community at the heart of the district's phoenix-like manifestation. It is fascinating.

This book is not only a history of Asheville's River Arts District, but also a tour. Thus it begins at a place that represents a historical turning point—the site of the Asheville Cotton Mill, built in 1887. By that time, industrialists had constructed four major factories near the French Broad River and the newly established railroad. Country people came for paying jobs. Many lived in factory houses.

The site is located on Riverside Drive just east of the I-240 overpass—the southwest corner of a one-mile long, bow-tie-shaped expanse that has recently become famous for the artists who have colonized its central portion; it is also important for the vibrant communities it has harbored.

The factory is not what it used to be. In 1995, during the early stages of the River Arts District's renaissance, an arsonist set fire to the mill, leaving only the east-most portion available for restoration.

One

THE HISTORICAL HEART

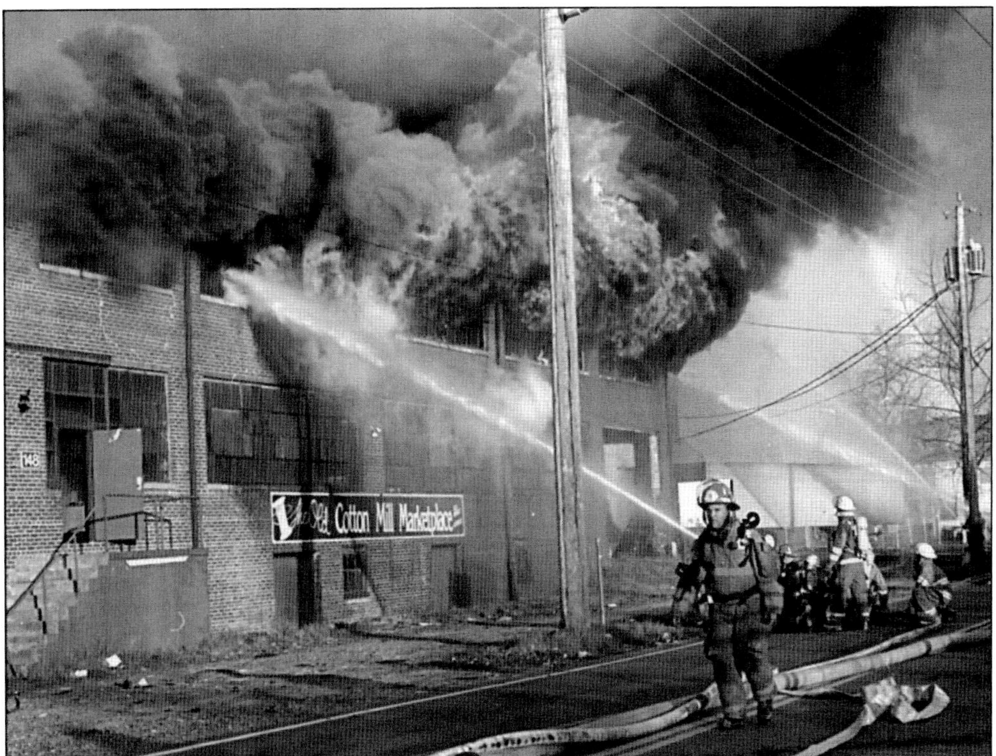

COTTON MILL FIRE. On April 2, 1995, fire destroyed most of what had been a 122,000-square-foot facility. Clyde Savings Bank had sold it to the Preservation Society of Asheville and Buncombe County on generous terms in 1993. The society called it "the key structure in the area's redevelopment." (Courtesy Asheville *Citizen-Times*.)

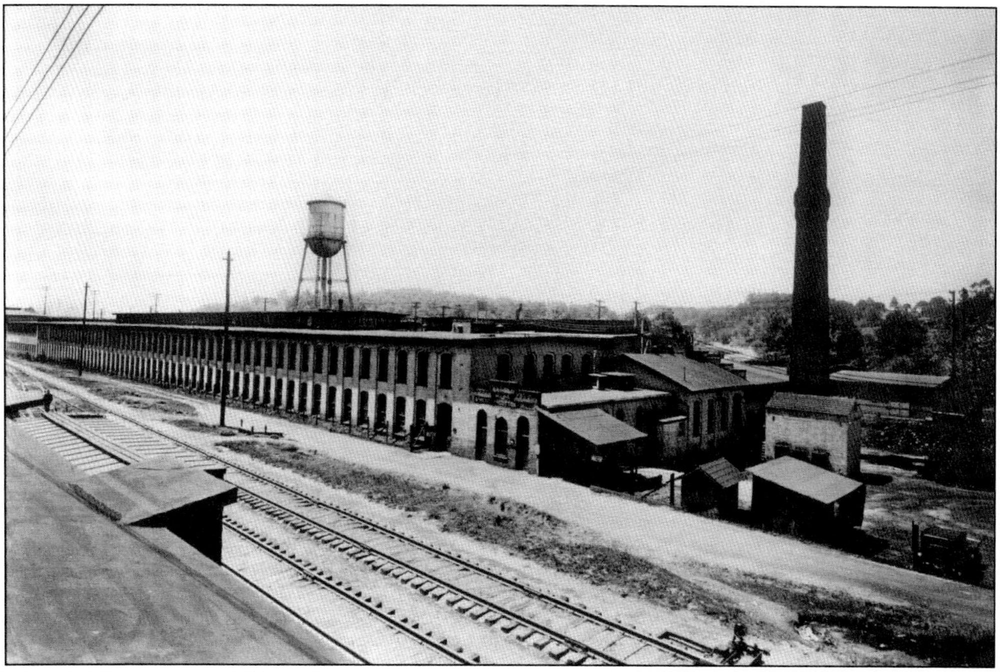

The 1953 Closing. When the preservation society purchased the Asheville Cotton Mill in 1993, it had stood vacant for 40 years. The Cone Mills Corporation of Greensboro, owners since 1889, had closed it down. Post–World War II efforts to modernize the plant to produce synthetics had failed. (Courtesy Preservation Society of Asheville and Buncombe County.)

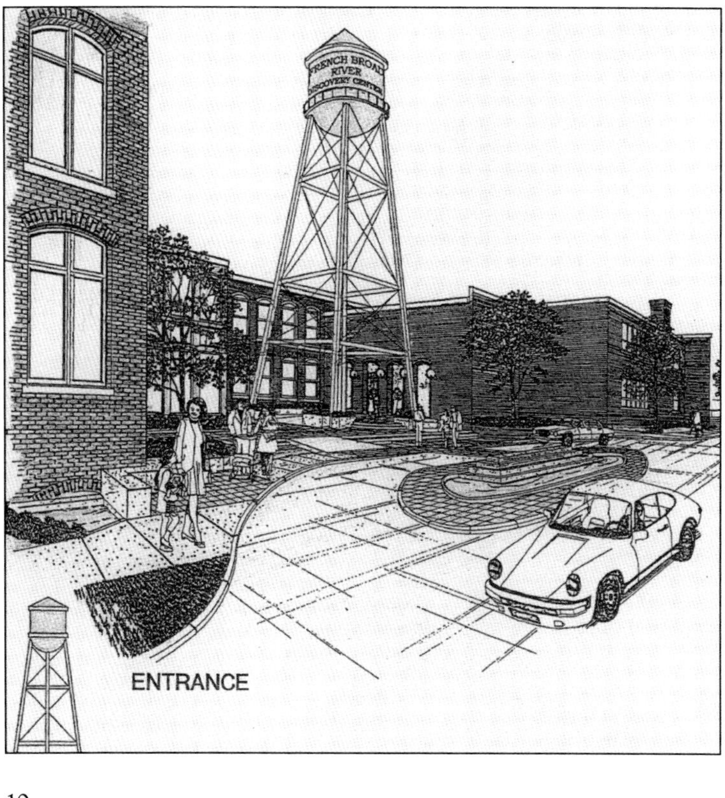

Discovery Center. The renaissance in the River Arts District looks back to 1992, when RiverLink, a nonprofit, created the "Riverfront Plan" and bought Warehouse Studios (see Chapter 3). It worked with the preservation society on a renovation that would include small shops and a textile museum. An artist's rendering (right) features the water tower, which was to become the symbol of the district. (Courtesy Preservation Society of Asheville and Buncombe County.)

TOWER REMOVAL. In March 1993, Clyde Savings Bank, the holder of the Asheville Cotton Mill property, told RiverLink and the Preservation Society of Asheville that tearing down the tower was cheaper than repairing it. A subsequent inspection revised the cost of renovation downward. The structure needed reinforcement of one leg, sandblasting, and painting. By the time the preservation society had bought the mill, it had already upped the value of the tower as "the most notable landmark feature along the waterfront," according to its own reports. The tower became a symbol, as reflected in promotional materials produced by the preservation society. The April 2, 1995, fire ended the water tower's chance for survival, and it was dismantled. Ironically, the purpose of the water tower was to supply a fire-retarding sprinkler system from a 50,000-gallon tank. (Right, courtesy Preservation Society of Asheville and Buncombe County; below, courtesy RiverLink.)

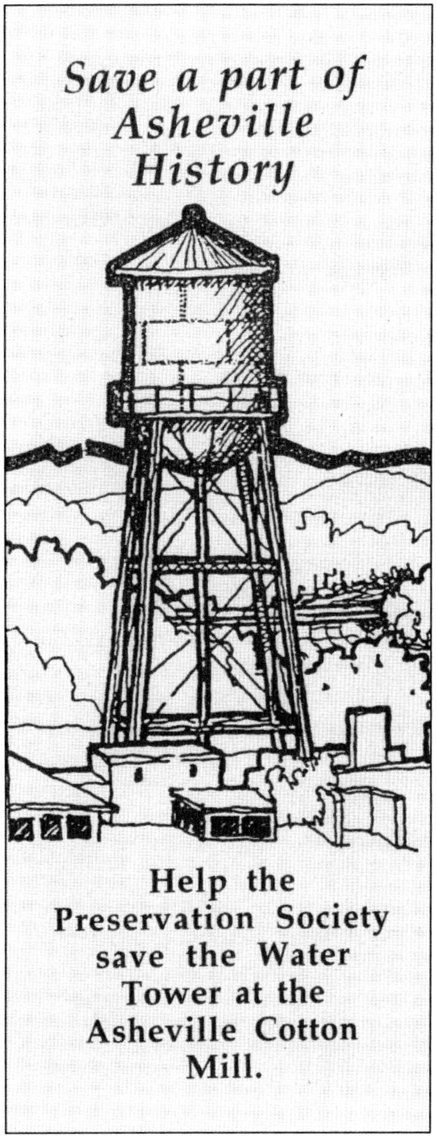

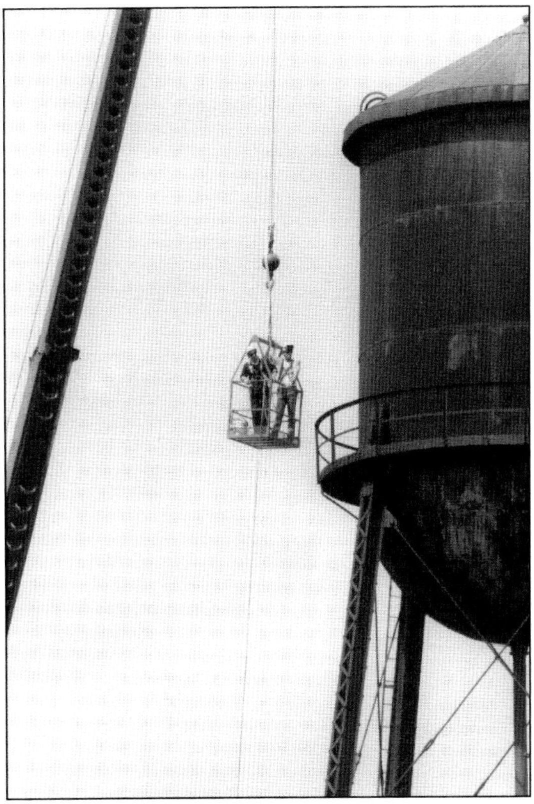

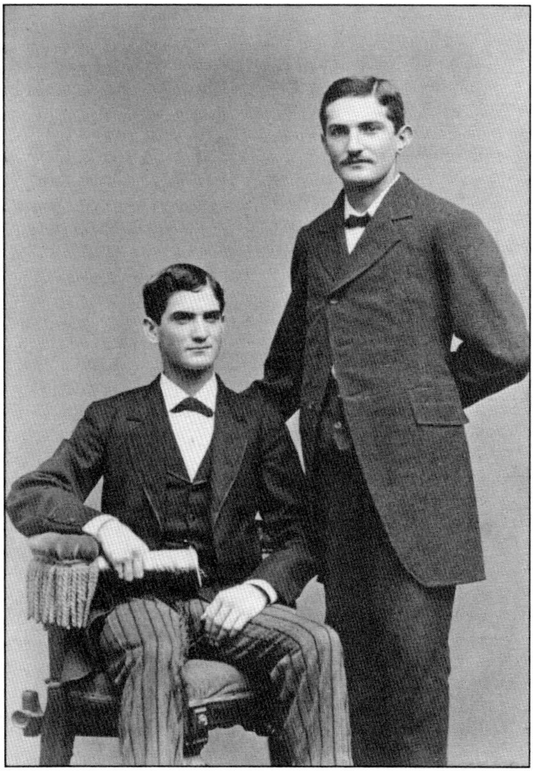

THE CONE BROTHERS. When Moses and Ceasar Cone reorganized C. E. Graham Manufacturing as Asheville Cotton Mills in 1893, they had already established the basis of a Southern textile empire. The Cone brothers' two big ideas were to create a cloth that was more attractive than the coarse plaid produced in Asheville and to create a region-wide selling agency for Southern textile mills. Cone Export and Commission Company was formed in 1891. Two of the Cones' best-selling fabrics were denim and soft flannel. In 1945, their mills merged under Proximity Manufacturing Company, and in 1948, the name changed to the Cone Mills Corporation. (Courtesy Cone Family Collection, W. L. Eury Appalachian Collection, Special Collections, Appalachian State University.)

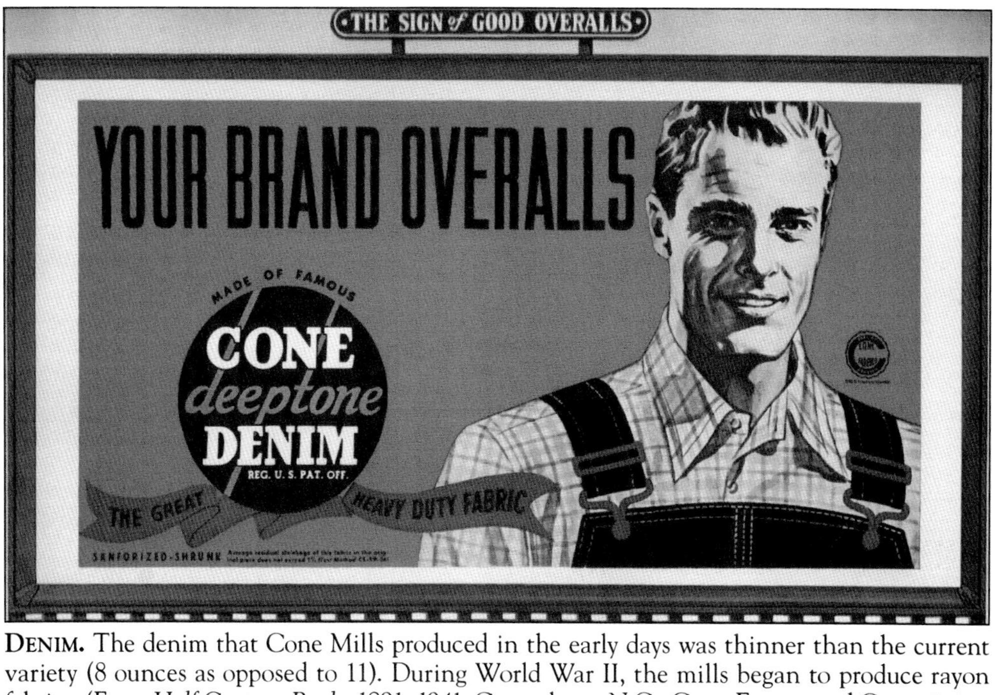

DENIM. The denim that Cone Mills produced in the early days was thinner than the current variety (8 ounces as opposed to 11). During World War II, the mills began to produce rayon fabrics. (From *Half Century Book, 1891–1941*, Greensboro, N.C.: Cone Export and Commission Company, 1941. Part of Cone Family Collection, W. L. Eury Appalachian Collection, Special Collections, Appalachian State University.)

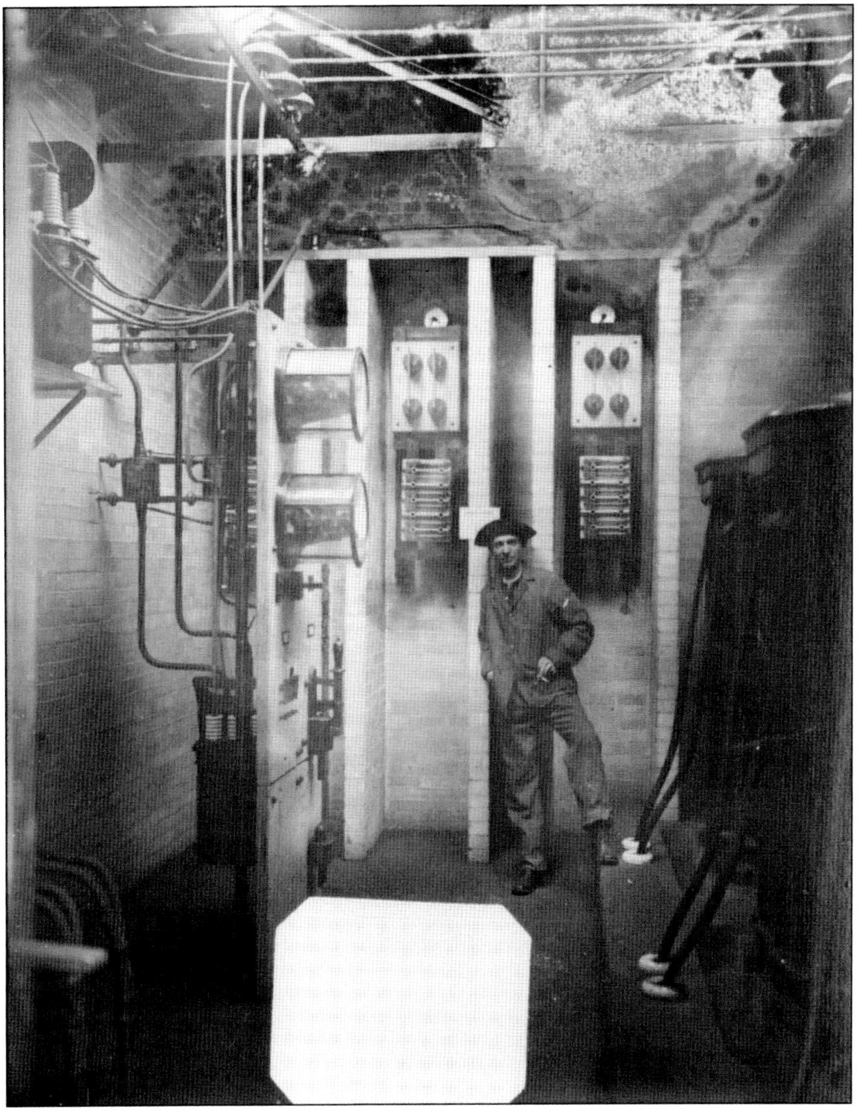

COTTON MILL WORKERS. The Asheville Cotton Mill employed an average of 300 workers through the years. It shifted production to the war effort during World Wars I and II, turning out denim and experiencing high volumes within a 70-year history of ups and downs. The mill provided cash-paying jobs as well as community. The cotton mill engine room was located on the north side of the factory behind the coal shed and in front of the offices. Extending to the right were the large rooms that represented the production process: weaving and spinning, twisting, carding, beaming, and picking. In a separate building on the same lot, cloth was dyed. Across the tracks stood a large warehouse and several factory houses. Factory housing, recreation centers, bathhouses, schools, and daycare centers contributed to community. Community stands out as a major theme in the area. All of the neighborhoods, black and white—West End, Clingman, Factory Hill, and Southside—nurtured children despite the low standard of housing and, in some cases, rough lifestyle. Inevitably, it seems, modern efforts to improve the urban landscape have severely damaged each neighborhood, sometimes for purposes that did not aim to benefit residents. Finally, all of the communities show signs of resurgence. The River Arts District is a study in community. (Courtesy North Carolina Collection, Pack Memorial Library.)

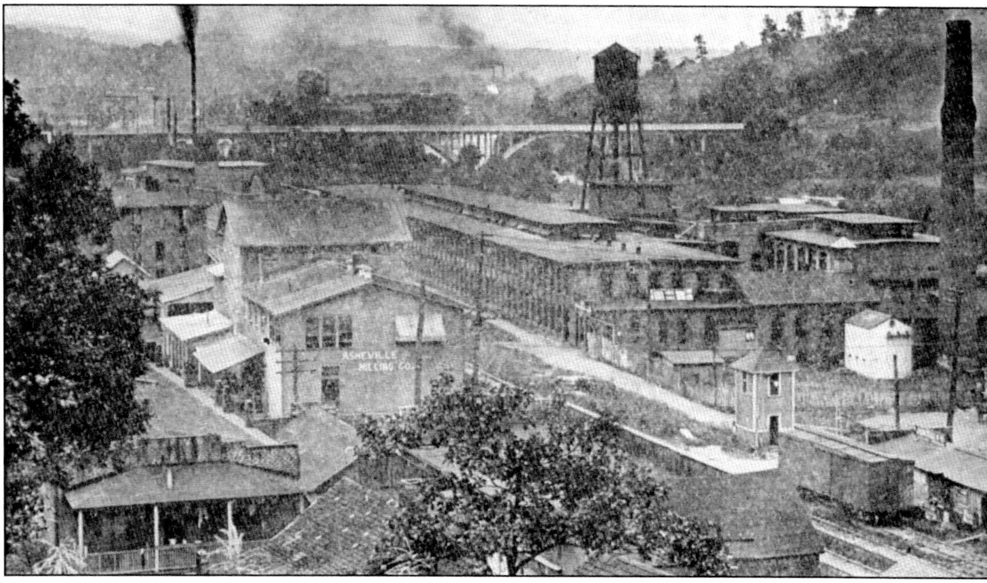

COTTON PROCESS. The smokestack stood near the engine room. The water tower was situated in the middle of the complex near the opener and picker rooms, where the manufacturing process began with a great deal of cotton dust. Once the cotton was cleaned, fluffed, and made into sheets, it was sent to the carding room, where the material was combed and transformed into skeins. A packet of skeins—or "slivers"—were thinned, twisted, and spun to create yarn or thread. Grey cloth—called greige—was the result of a process called beaming, creating the warp out of hundreds of threads, and weaving, interlocking the weft threads. Bleaching and dyeing completed the process. (Photograph from *The Child that Toileth Not*.)

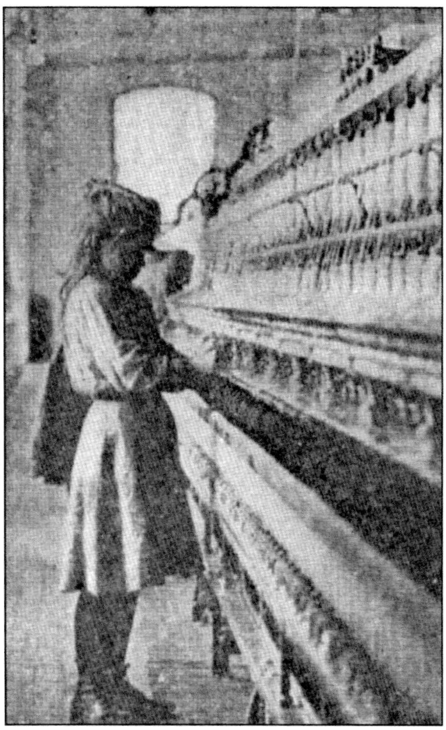

CHILD LABOR. This photograph comes from Thomas Robinson Dawley's book entitled *The Child that Toileth Not*. In 1907, a U.S. Congressional commission sent Dawley to report on child labor abuses in Southern textile mills. Dawley's first stop was the Asheville Cotton Mill. Having trouble locating whistleblowers, he enlisted a charity worker who admitted knowing few mill workers on relief because "the mill management preferred taking care of their own poor." However, there was a widow with five children who had left her farm to work at the mill and applied for relief during the interim. Dawley recorded her testimony in dialect. "I reckon we'll git on all right now," she said. "Three o' th' kids got jobs in th' mill. Sure they don't earn much, but they don't wourk mor' 'an half the time. . . . Th' wourk 'tain't nothin' like wourkin' on th' farm. I got no rest when I war a kid." Dawley's caption for the photograph of the child spinner noted: "I find that the employment of such a child is exceptional, and then she is only employed as a 'learner.'" (Photograph from *The Child that Toileth Not*.)

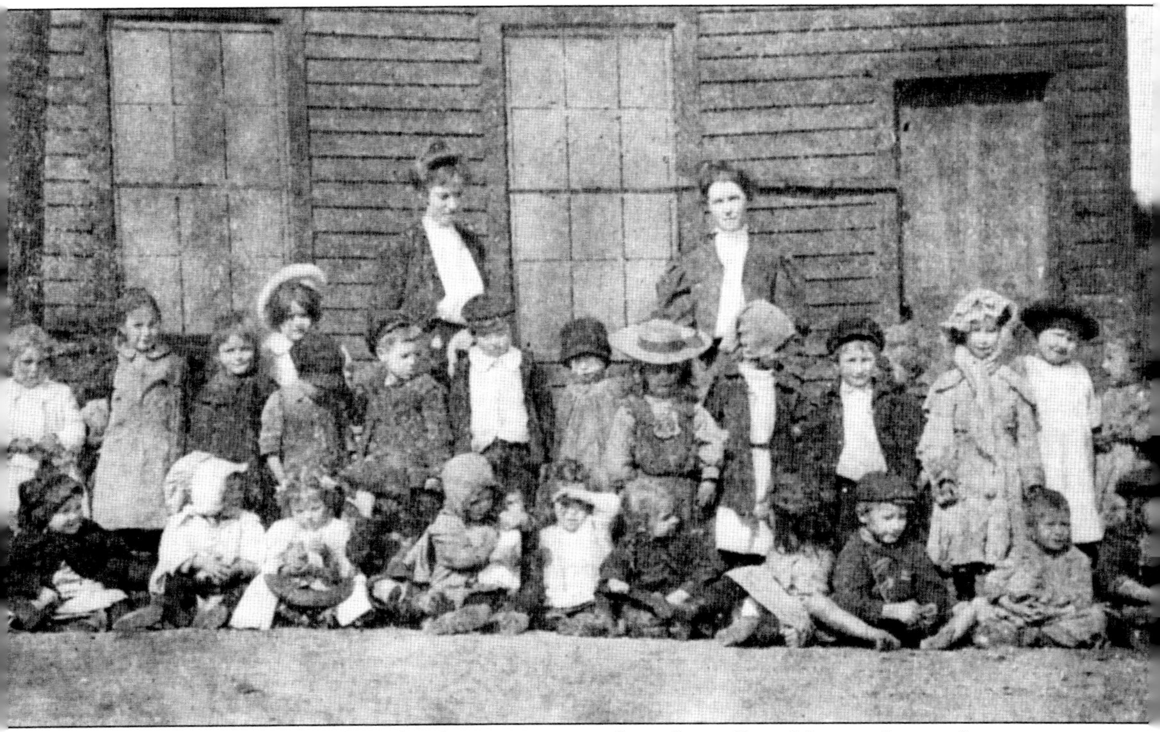

Mill Village Life. Poor farm families came to work at the mill and live in factory housing. The community also included higher-paid mill workers; merchants and others in the service sector; railroad employees; and individuals who depended on the mill for temporary work on the way to other careers. Poverty did not mean a lack of community. A WPA interview reveals that 10-year-old Dick Jones staged variety shows in his apartment-house basement, re-enacting movies that only he had had the privilege to see. The unidentified matriarch of another family admitted, "If it wasn't for [movies], I don't know what I'd do." She put some of their cash toward yard beautification, planting petunias and phlox in discarded gas tanks her husband had hauled from West Asheville. "We just wasn't borned to have money," a mill-working woman said. Mill workers often sought ways out of their plights. Mr. and Mrs. Albert Farlow had come from farm families that had never gone hungry, but the promise of pay drew them to mill towns. "Workin' in the mill now is just slavery," Mrs. Farlow told a WPA interviewer. Her "moment of grace" came when a federal worker taught her how to read and write at age 40. "She put her arm around my shoulders and took my hand to show me," Farlow said with emotion. "When she put her arm around me, the tears come into my eyes, and kept comin'." The cotton mill ran a kindergarten, taking care of the children of women who had just come from farms and were being taught how to make fabric. (Photograph from *The Child that Toileth Not*.)

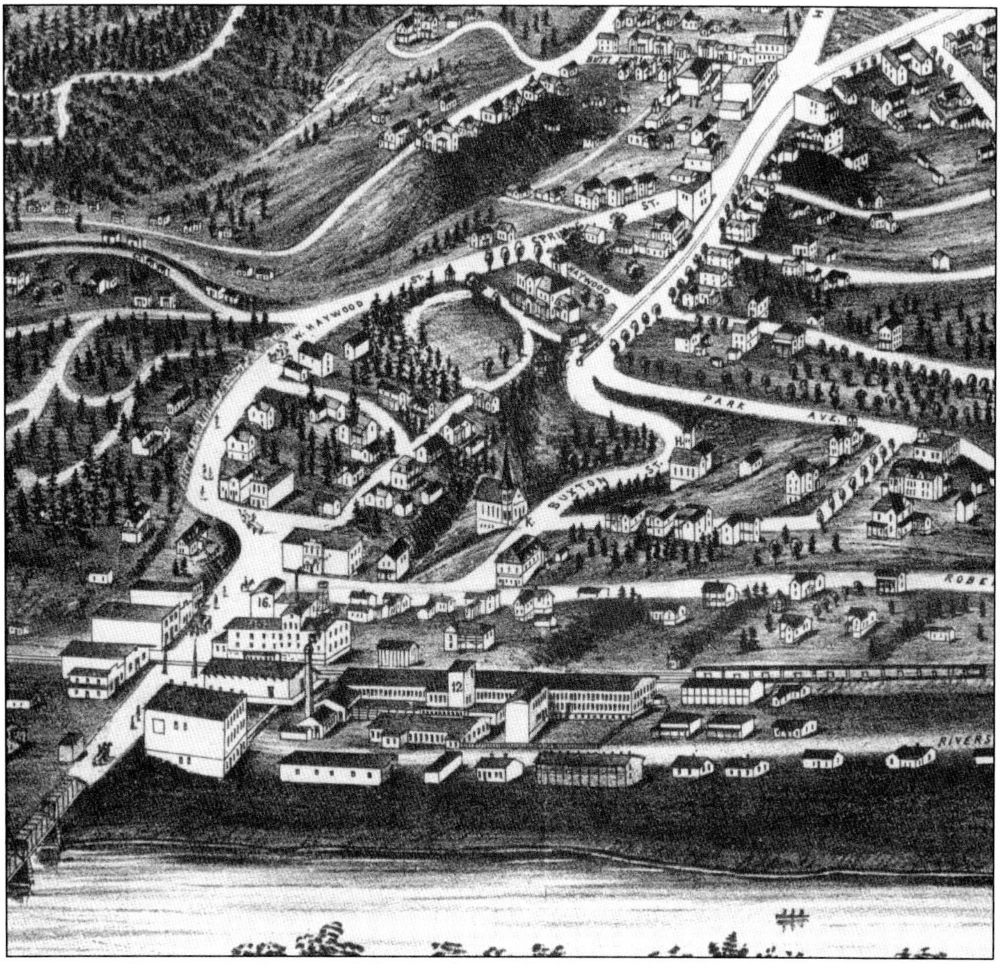

1891 MAP. By 1891, the framework for the district had been largely set. An electric streetcar line (top center) came down the middle of Patton Avenue to Park Avenue. It served the larger homes atop the hill (now part of the West End/Clingman neighborhood), the factory homes (called Chicken Hill or Factory Hill), and the factories. The Asheville Ice Factory and Asheville Milling Company were located at Roberts and West Haywood Streets. The Asheville Cotton Mill, which is what people were already calling Graham Manufacturing Company, spreads out below what had been the Western North Carolina Railroad (and now is Norfolk Southern). (Courtesy North Carolina Collection, Pack Memorial Library.)

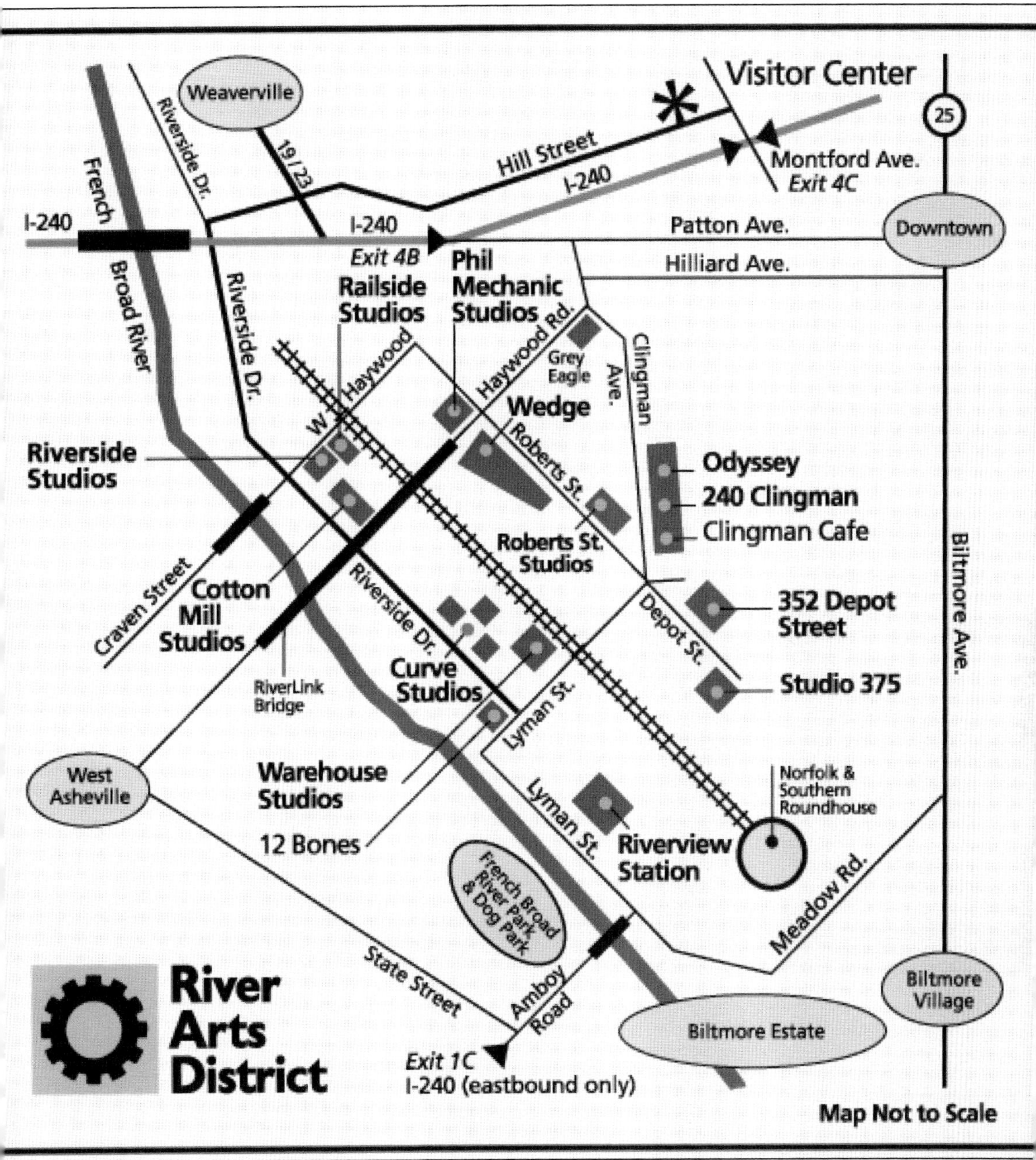

Guide to the River Arts District. Wendy Whitson, a Warehouse Studios artist, created this map (go to any studio for a handout). Notice the changes since 1891. West Haywood Road now comes down the hill to Roberts Street and stops; it then picks up again at the end of Roberts Street. When the former West Haywood Street had been chopped by I-240, the name was also given to what had been Buxton Street. The Park Avenue part of the West End neighborhood has survived in large part but was cut off at its southern end by the conversion of Clingman Avenue to four lanes. (See Chapter 9 about the historic and resurgent West End /Clingman neighborhood.)

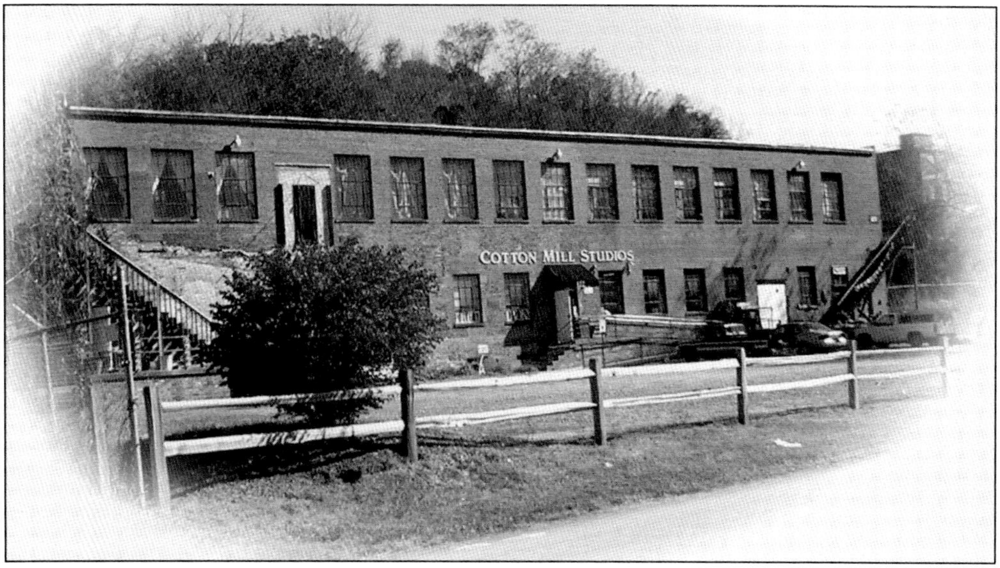

THE NEW SOUTH. Cone Mills closed the Asheville Cotton Mill down in 1953 and sold its property to William B. Dillard, who planned to divide it up and lease space to a variety of concerns. The low-rent, low-maintenance pattern prevailed until the vision of the New South emerged. The modern vision strives to attract money to historic preservation, nostalgic design, communities of artists, parks, and village life. The surviving southern portion of the mill has become Cotton Mill Studios, whose owners, Eileen and Marty Black, have been instrumental in enhancing the promotional efforts of the River District Artists. (Courtesy Marty Black.)

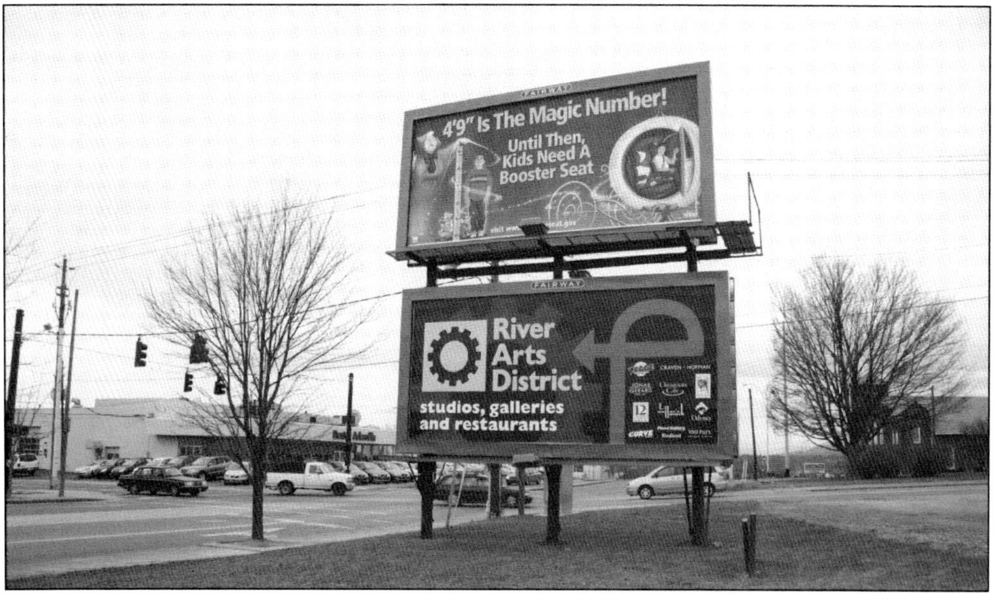

DIRECTIONS. One of the key efforts of the River District Artists is this billboard, which features the group's symbol, a wheel cog, and clearly directs travelers from busy Patton Avenue down Clingman Avenue to "The Wedge" (Chapter 4), Roberts Street (Chapter 3), and Riverside Drive. To the right on Riverside Drive is the cotton mill, and to the left (south) is Warehouse Studios (Chapter 5). Further south are Depot Street (Chapter 7) and the tannery area (Chapter 6). (Photograph by Henry Neufeld.)

COTTON MILL STUDIOS. After the 1995 fire, the preservation society sold the cotton mill site to RiverLink. Subsequently, the south portion with its surviving building was sold to Jonathan Nilsson. In the summer of 2002, potter Eileen Black scoped out the building with a realtor "and walked out breathless," she said. "It was such a clear moment that this [her new business] was meant to be." She and her husband, Marty, an electrical engineer, bought the building six months later. For many years, Eileen had worked in Greensboro, serving as the founding president of the Carolina Clay Guild and selling her wares throughout the country. Two critical connections brought her to Asheville: Highwater Clays, a leading supplier of clay (see Chapter 4), and New Morning Galley, one of the galleries that had represented her work. The Blacks' renovation of the cotton mill building led to several artists, including themselves, operating as The Potter's Mark, Limited. Eileen immediately played a role in the River Arts District, working with Pattiy Torno (see Chapter 5) and others, using memberships to upgrade the River Arts District Studio Stroll guide and other promotions. Eileen Black (right) works on a piece made of her favorite clay, Loafer's Glory, which was obtained from Highwater Clays. The white board behind her keeps track of her orders. (Right courtesy Rob Neufeld; below, courtesy Marty Black.)

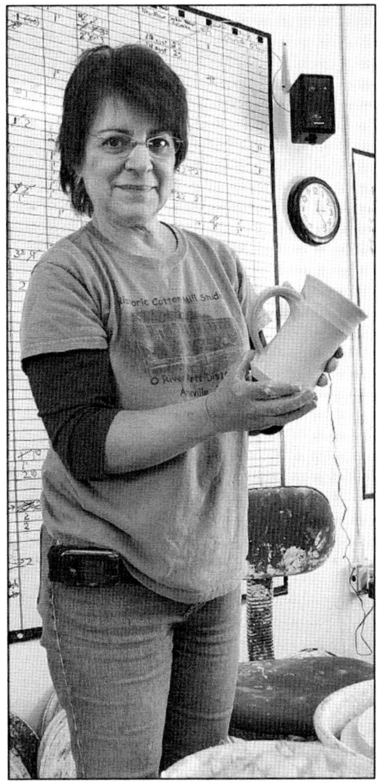

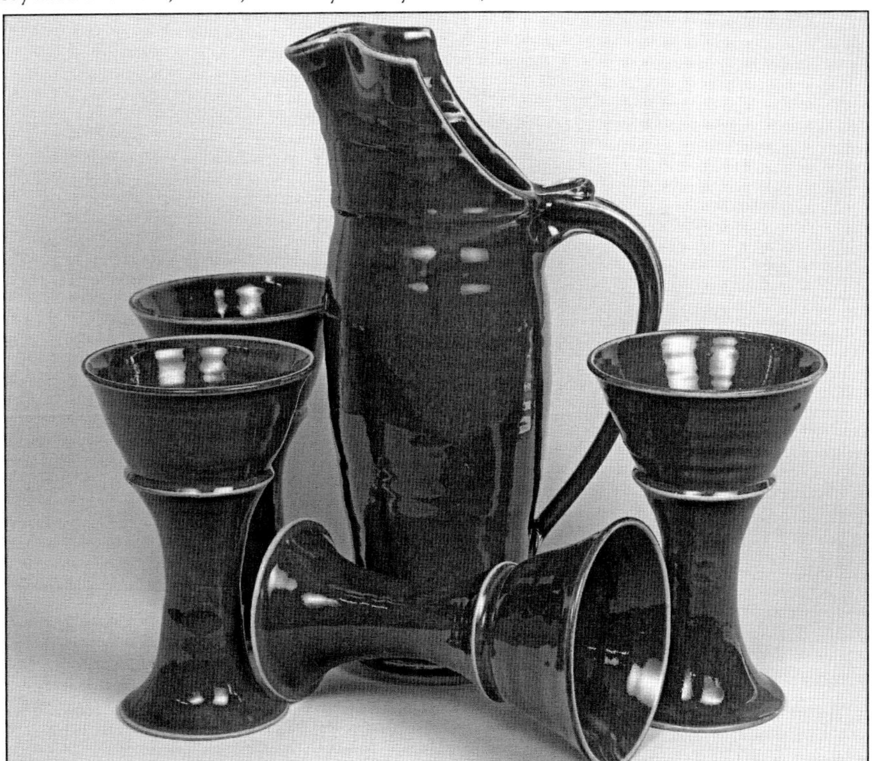

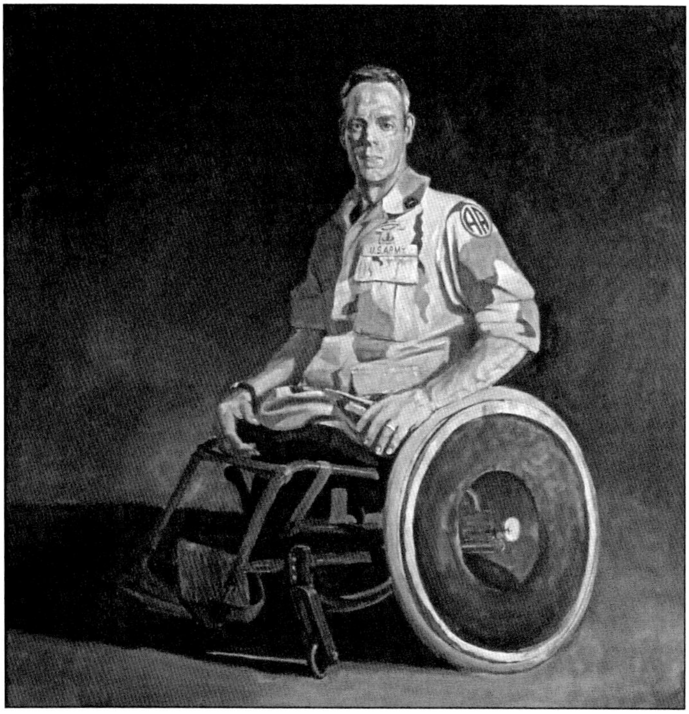

SKIP ROHDE. One of the artists in Cotton Mill Studios is Skip Rohde, an oil painter who creates narrative paintings with messages that reflect current politics. Pictured is a work that forms part of his collection entitled "Meditations on War." (Courtesy Skip Rhode.)

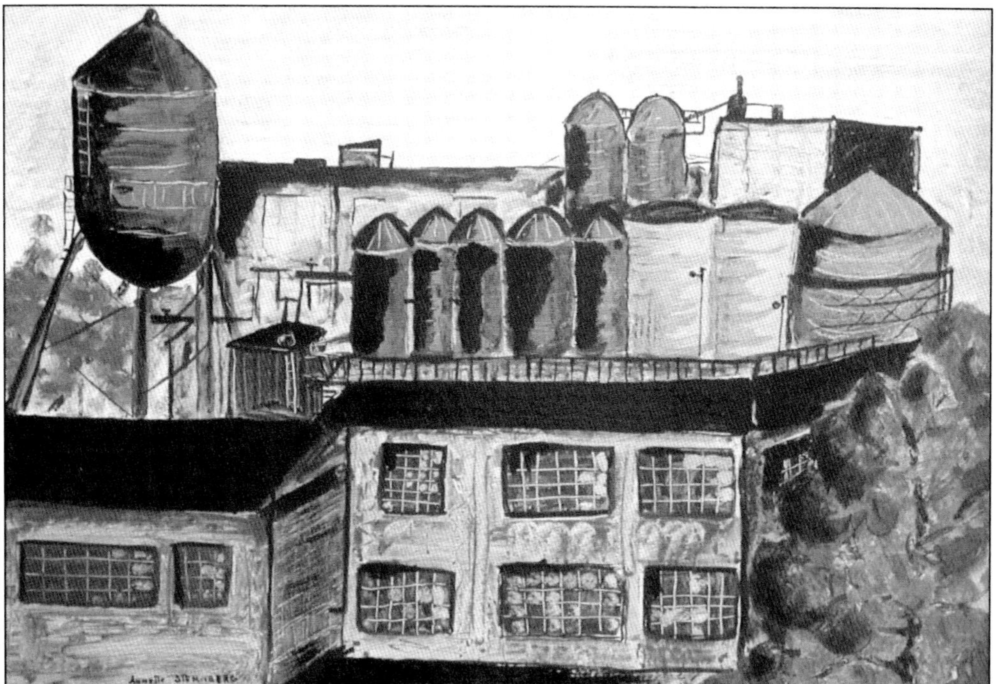

STERNBERG ART. Annette Sternberg's painting of the Asheville Cotton Mill and the Earle-Chesterfield Mill, completed a half century ago, introduces us to the next site located up West Haywood Street from the river. Sternberg is the late mother of Jerry Sternberg, an influential riverside scrap-metal businessman and developer (see Chapter 7). (Courtesy Jerry Sternberg.)

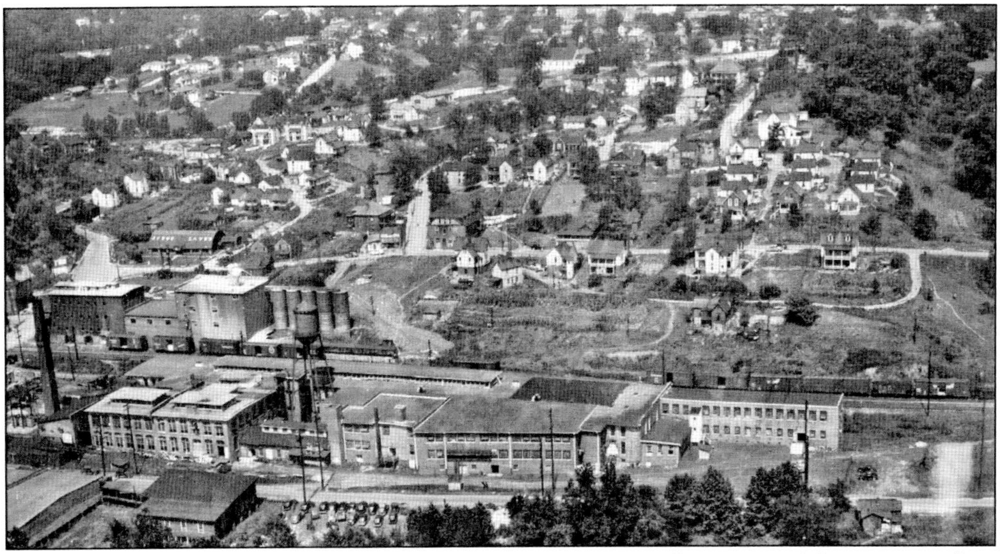

INDUSTRIAL DISTRICT. This 1940s photograph affords an excellent view of the cotton mill in the foreground, the Earle-Chesterfield Mill behind it to the left, and the West End/Clingman neighborhood (see Chapter 9) above. Beginning in 1905, the Earle-Chesterfield Mill made flour and feed from mountain-grown grain. In the mid-1950s, it added a chicken hatchery before closing in 1971. Notice the dusting of flour on the rooftops. The factory burned down in a 1995 fire that jumped to the cotton mill. Whit Rylee, a developer renovating the surviving hatchery and mill structures, calls the neighborhood that his company, Urvana LLC, is creating the "Chicken Hill Co-Operative." Residents of the West End/Clingman Avenue neighborhood (WECAN), which encompasses the Park Avenue area above Roberts Street, object to that name on the basis that much of the Chicken Hill housing (also called "Factory Hill") was wiped out by I-240 and that the catchy name does not reflect the true spirit of their diverse neighborhood. (Courtesy North Carolina Collection, Pack Memorial Library.)

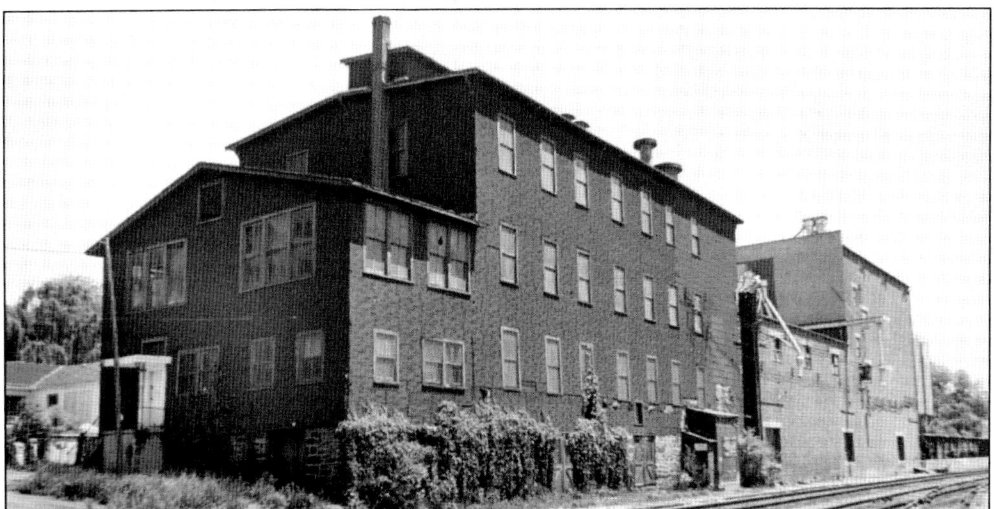

EARLE-CHESTERFIELD MILL. The mill originated as the Asheville Milling Company in 1880. This photograph by Mary Jo Brezny was published in the 1981 edition of *Cabins and Castles* and was donated to the Pack Memorial Library. (Courtesy North Carolina Collection, Pack Memorial Library.)

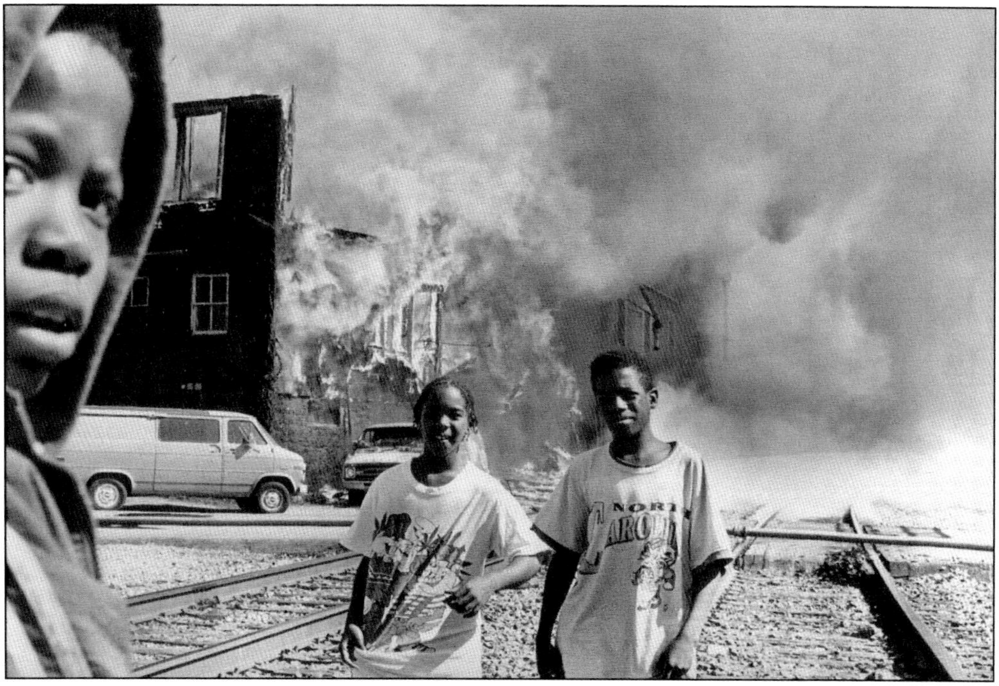

MILL FIRE. The Earle-Chesterfield Mill burned down in 1995. (Photograph by Lisa Gustafson, courtesy Gail McCarthy.)

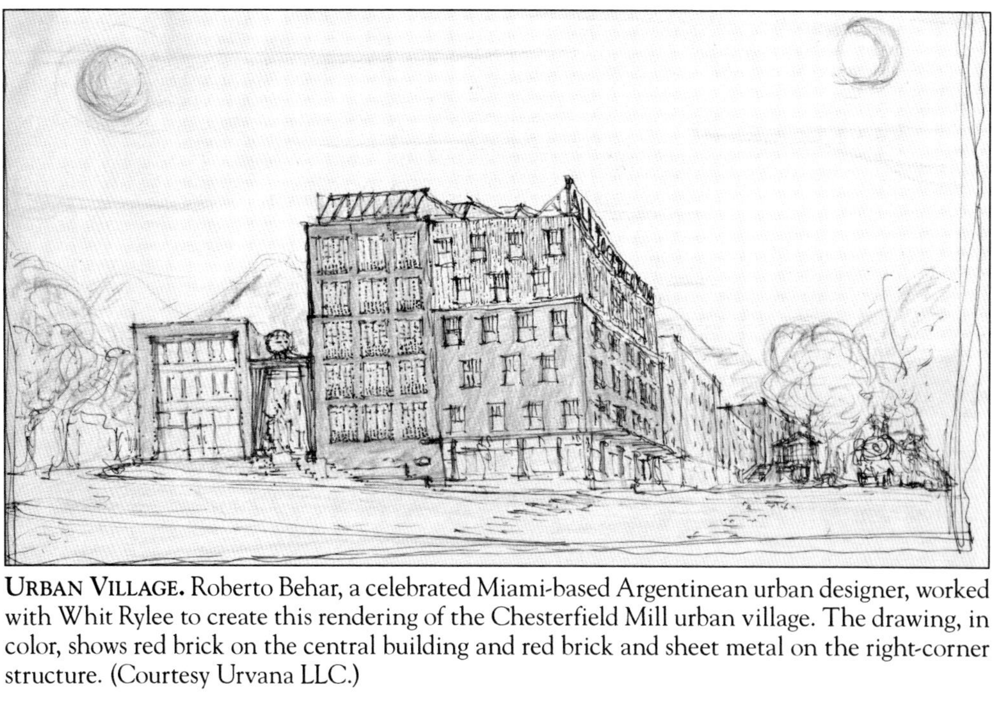

URBAN VILLAGE. Roberto Behar, a celebrated Miami-based Argentinean urban designer, worked with Whit Rylee to create this rendering of the Chesterfield Mill urban village. The drawing, in color, shows red brick on the central building and red brick and sheet metal on the right-corner structure. (Courtesy Urvana LLC.)

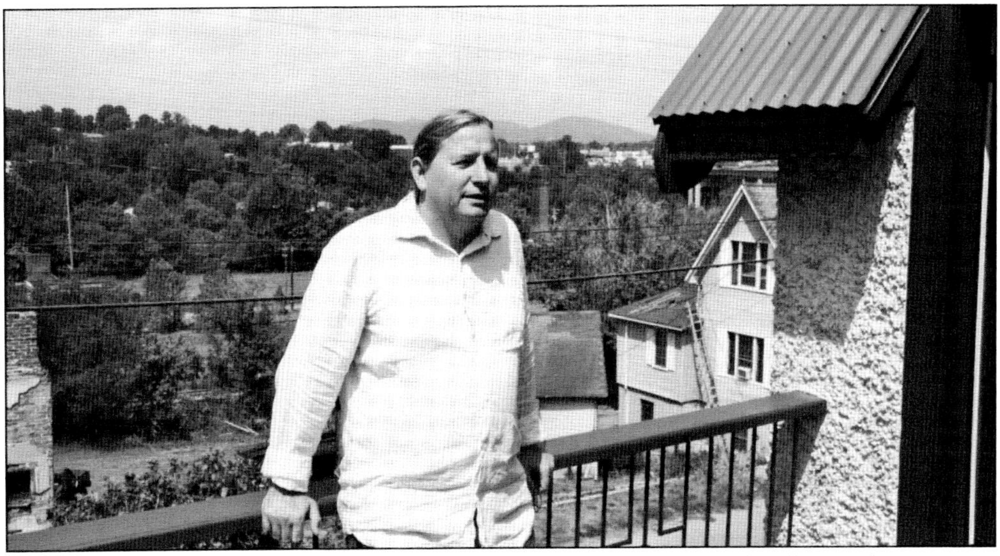

WHIT RYLEE. Growing up in Sarasota, Florida, Whit Rylee participated in his mother's pioneer vision for Laurel Park. Her renovations won Downtown Improvement awards. Rylee found Western North Carolina when his elementary school principal, Owen Woodyard, took Whitt and other boys camping in Brevard. Rylee moved to West Asheville in 1998 with his eye on Montford, but gentrification had inflated prices there. One day while bicycling to town, he rode up West Haywood Street rather than the steeper Club Street and saw a "for sale" sign on the Parsonage, a 1907 arts-and-crafts house in disrepair. Rylee helped Gail and Brian McCarthy of Highwater Clay renovate it and garnered the project a Griffin Award from the Preservation Society of Asheville and Buncombe County. (Photograph by Henry Neufeld.)

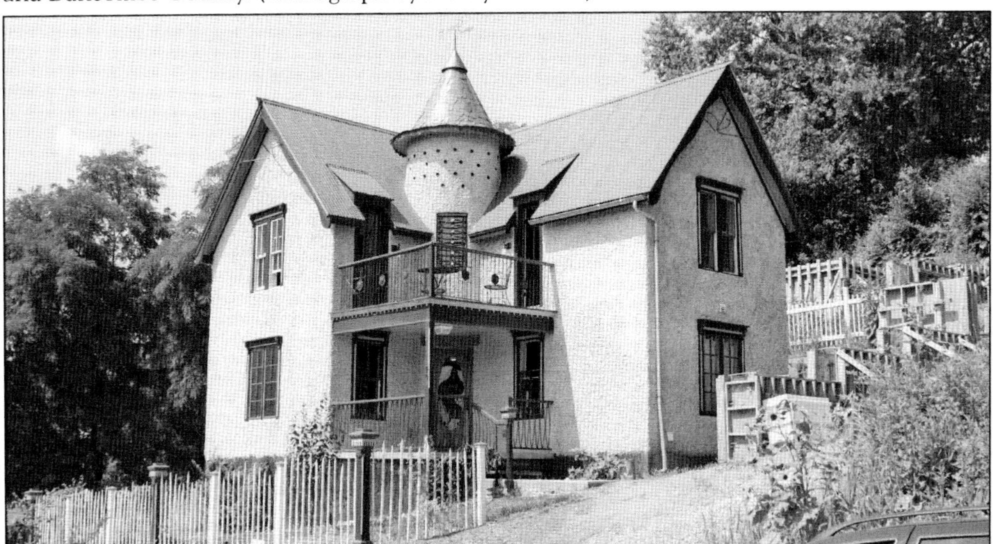

OLIVER'S HOUSE. The residence of Whit Rylee and his son, Oliver, is notably surfaced with pink stucco. Located at 40 Roberts Street, it serves as a model home for what Rylee calls the Chicken Hill Co-Operative. Rylee intentionally incorporates design elements associated with Chicken Hill (the L-shaped plan); the industrial neighborhood (corrugated metal roof); and 19th-century Asheville Victoriana (the Queen Anne tower). (Photograph by Courtney Tiberio, courtesy of Urvana LLC.)

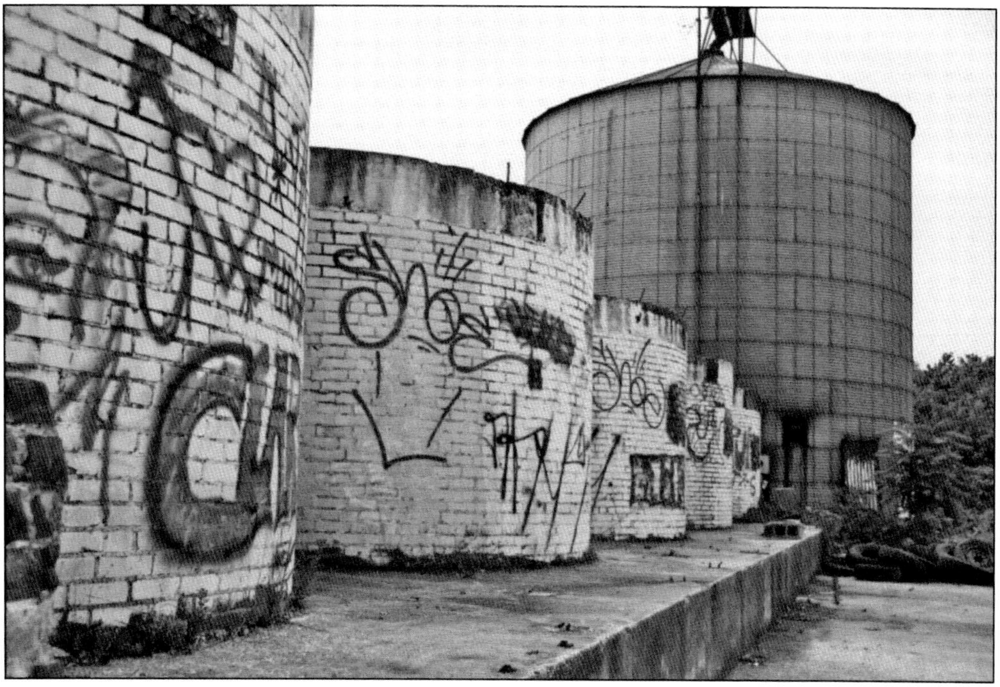

SILOS OF THE FLOUR MILL; BOWLING ALLEY. One of the most remarkable transformations on the drawing board for Chesterfield Mill is the building of a bowling alley and the incorporation of truncated silos as alcove lounges. (Above, photograph by Henry Neufeld; below, drawing by Adib Cure, courtesy Urvana LLC.)

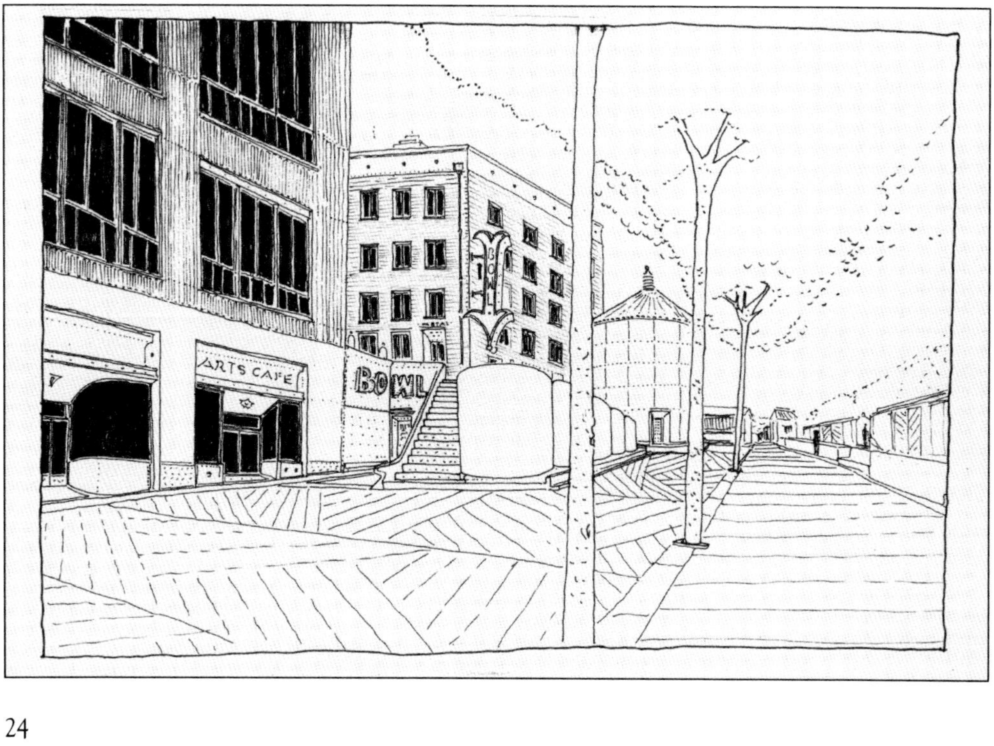

CHICKEN HILL BOYS. Max Price, pictured here with his younger brother, Glenn, grew up on Factory Hill, where many raised chickens. The Prices always had eggs, an ingredient in Mrs. Price's biscuits. Max's dad, Roy, baptized new family members by placing their feet in the dough. The house had no bathing facilities and no heat in the bedrooms. Max and his friends were free to roam—to the river for a swim, to the YMCA for the Clean Life Club, and downtown. One day in 1941, they went to see Santa Claus in Pritchard Park. Santa asked "Stormy" Bishop, "What can Santa bring you, little boy?" Stormy replied, "I don't want nothin', you old son of a gun. I told you what I wanted last year, and you didn't bring me nothin'." (Courtesy Max Price.)

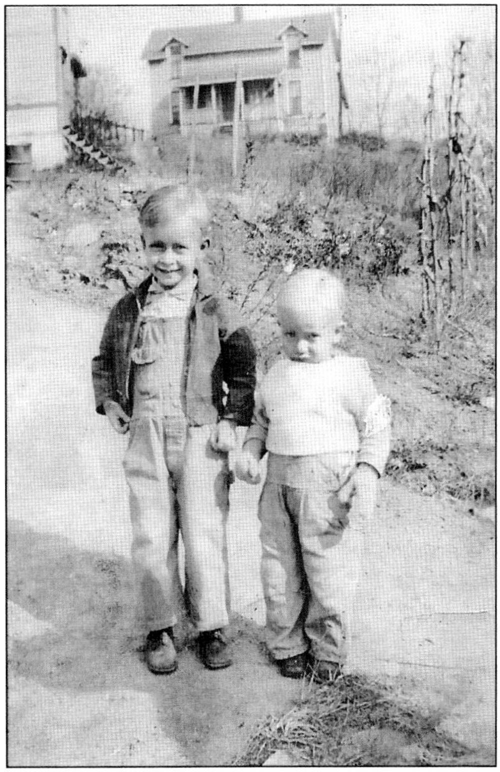

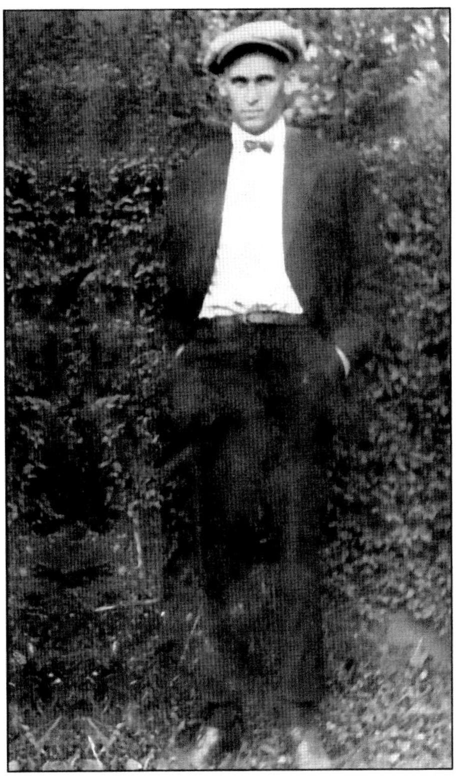

ROY PRICE. Roy was a card fixer at the Asheville Cotton Mill during the Depression. He maintained the machines that combed the cotton. Arriving home, he brushed lint from his clothes. His children found it harder to shed being called "linthead" in school. "After watching my dad come and go," said Max Price, "I knew I would do almost anything to keep from working in the mill. He was exhausted coming home, covered with lint." After Roy's first wife, Dollie, died in childbirth during a labor strike in Marion, Roy went to Detroit, returning to Western North Carolina two years later when he got a job in the cotton mill. He married Lillie Laddie Lewis, a farm girl, moved to 7 Factory Hill in 1932, and conceived Max. (Courtesy Max Price.)

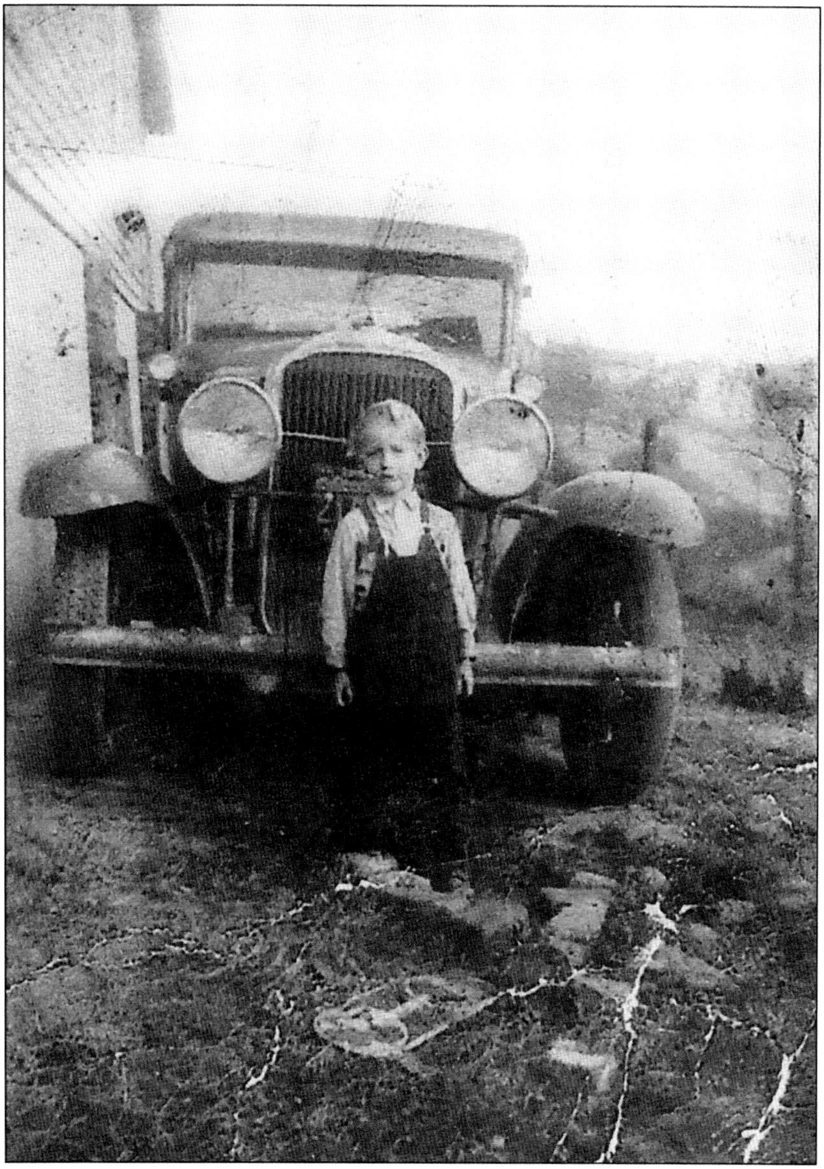

MAX AND THE BUICK. In 1939, Roy Price bought a 1931 Buick for $60. He drove it for several years, though it became less and less reliable. During cold months, he had to siphon off the radiator water and pour it back in the next day. He also had to start the engine with a crank. In 1948, Roy junked the car because the state started requiring inspections that the old Buick would never pass. The roads on Factory Hill were dirt. Every spring, workers would take clinkers from the mill's boiler and cover the streets to give vehicles traction. The overalls in which Max poses were one of two pairs bought for him for the year. He would wear one pair for a week at a time. His mother made him shirts from flour sacks. They had a telltale blue stripe going through them. Max became an achiever in high school and was president of the Junior Optimists Club. He joined the army and got a degree from the University of North Carolina–Chapel Hill on the G.I. Bill when he returned from Korea. His career as a cost accountant for various corporations enabled him to raise his children successfully along with his wife, Jean Lane Price. (Courtesy Max Price.)

Two

RIVERSIDE

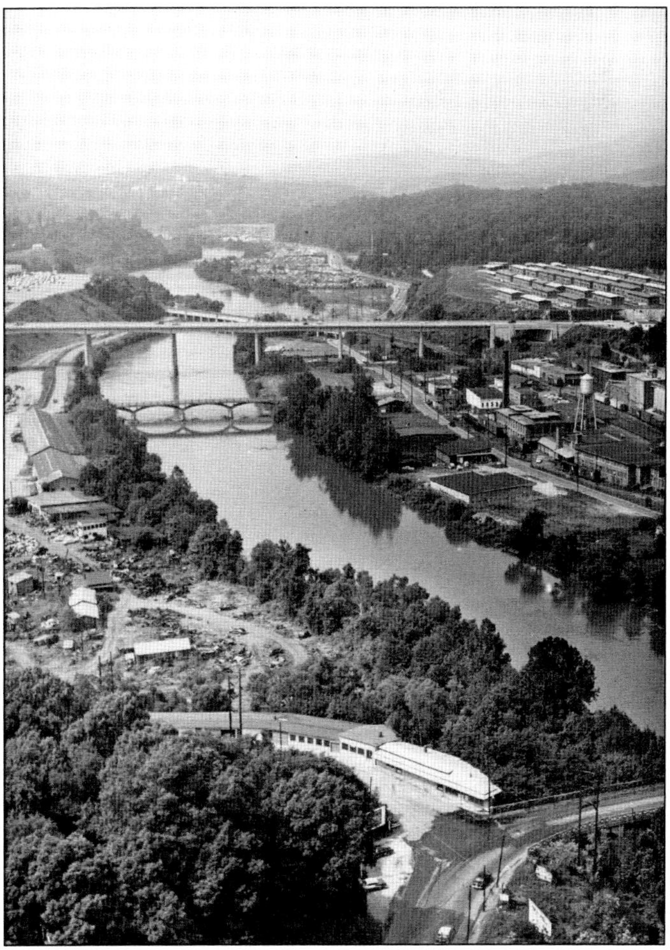

THE RIVER. Between the Smoky Park Bridge (top) and the West Asheville Bridge (bottom) lies undeveloped flood zone land and factory sites that border the railroad. In Jean Webb Park, under the West Asheville Bridge, boaters launch their crafts. Across the river, south of the West Asheville Bridge for a mile, RiverLink established the French Broad River Park in 1994. According to RiverLink, it was the first greenway in the city of Asheville and is part of a plan to create a continuous 17-mile greenway named after author Wilma Dykeman. (Courtesy North Carolina Collection, Pack Memorial Library.)

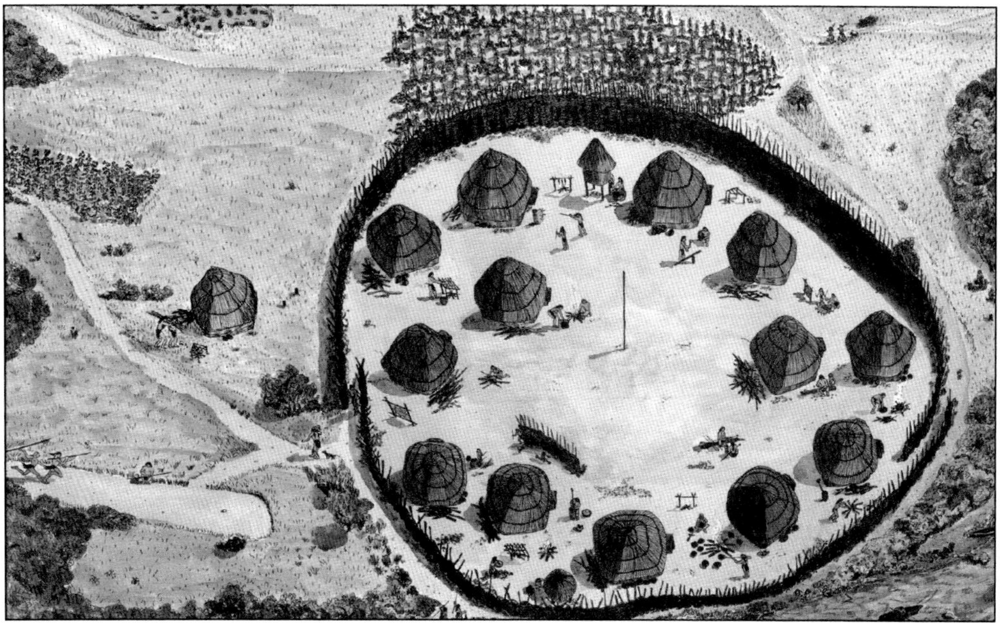

THE CHEROKEES. Eight miles upriver from the River Arts District, local Native Americans inhabited a site for about 8,000 years on what is now the Warren Wilson College campus. One thousand years ago, the Cherokees lived a middle-class life with sturdy settlements, many possessions, farmland, and graveyards. (Courtesy Archaeology Department, Warren Wilson College.)

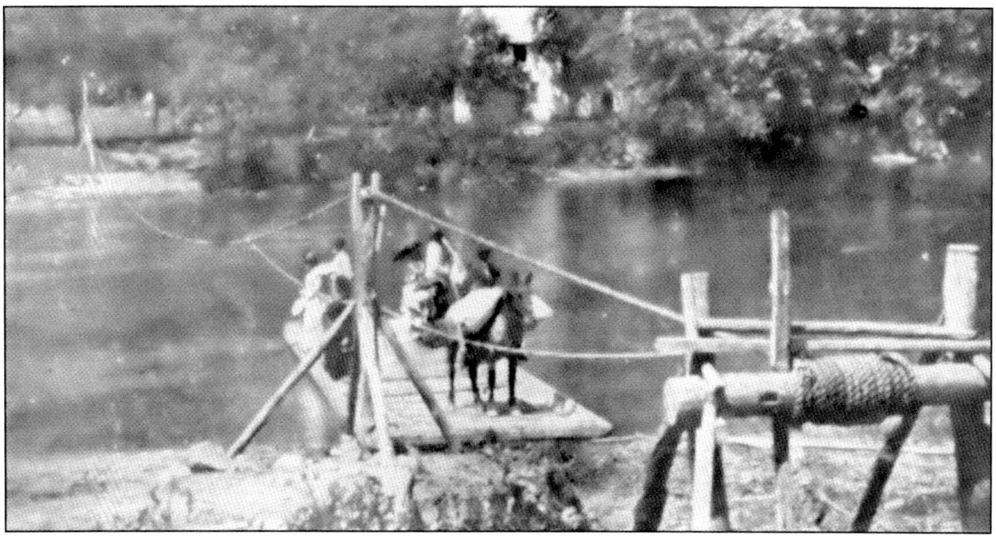

ALEXANDER'S FERRY. The Cherokees' village was located on the Swannanoa River, which feeds into the French Broad River at the Biltmore Estate. Recently, another Cherokees' site was uncovered on the Biltmore Estate. The French Broad does not provide much in the way of arable bottomland in Asheville (though James McConnell Smith's and William McDowell's plantation reached down to the river from their big house on what is now the Asheville-Buncombe Technical Community College campus). The river in this section also does not afford good fording spots. Smith's (or Sam's) Ferry, constructed like Alexander's Ferry further downriver (pictured above), offered an early crossing. It was rope-guided because the river lived up to its Cherokee name, Tah-kee-os-tee, "racing waters." (Courtesy Pack Memorial Library.)

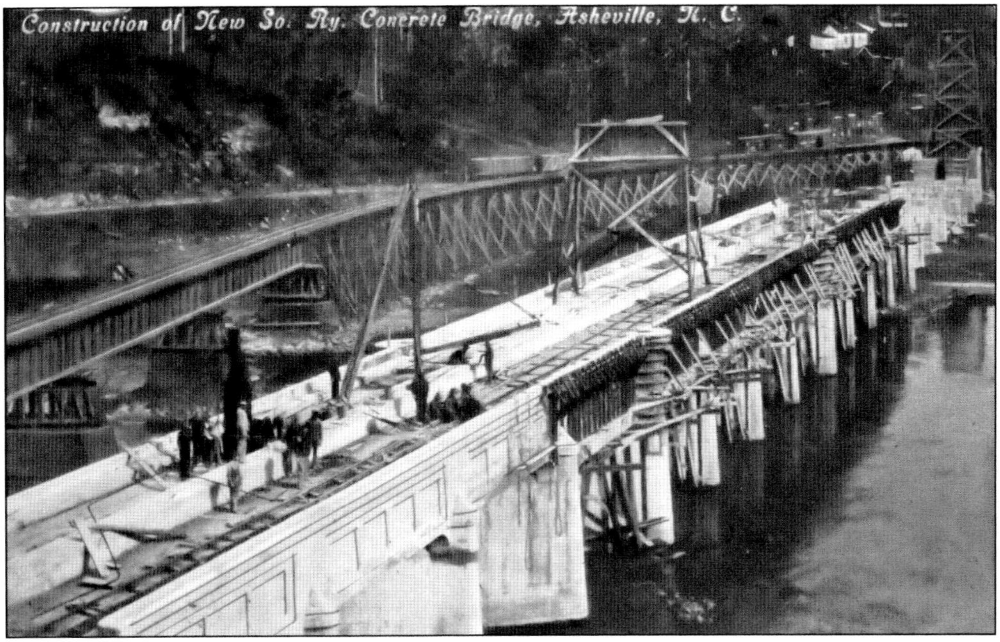

THE BRIDGES. Today four bridges cross the river within the River Arts District: the Southern Railway Bridge; the Smoky Park Bridge (below), carrying I-240, which was built in the early 1950s; Smith Bridge, crossing from Craven Street, which was built after the 1916 flood that had destroyed the 1833 span; and West Asheville Bridge, leading to Haywood Road in West Asheville. (Both, courtesy North Carolina Collection, Pack Memorial Library.)

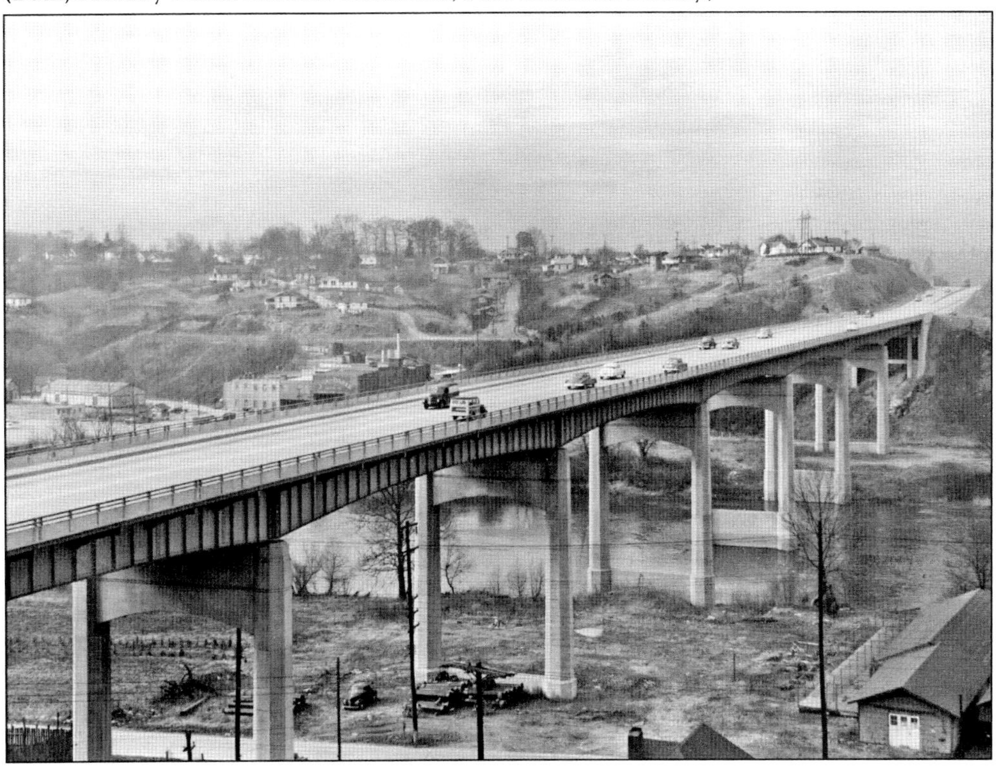

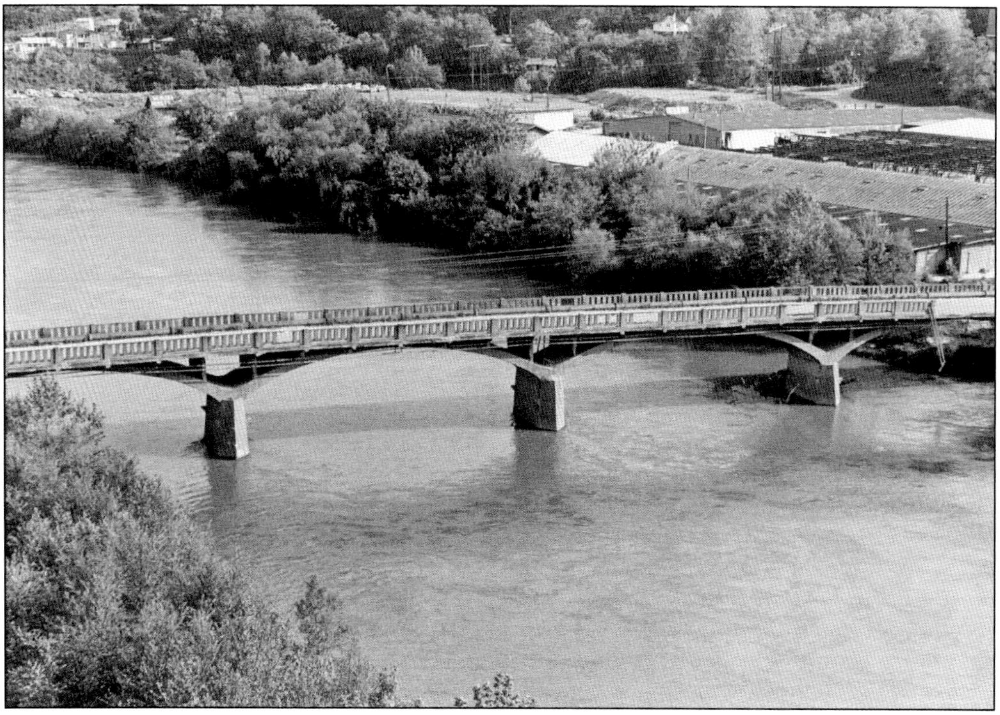

SMITH'S BRIDGE. Smith's Bridge connects Craven Street to West Asheville and leads to Tuten and Penland's auction house, the old Western Carolina Stockyard, and John Bell's Main Auto Parts (See Chapter 10). (Courtesy North Carolina Collection, Pack Memorial Library.)

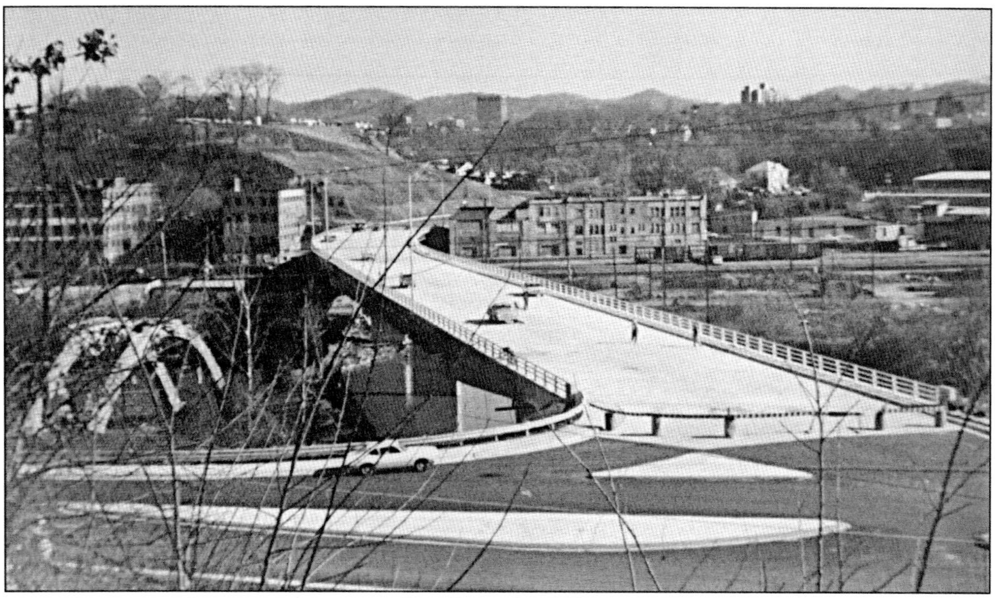

WEST ASHEVILLE BRIDGE. The West Asheville Bridge follows Haywood Road across a controversial road-widening project to West Asheville's main street. Attention now is being paid to neighborhoods and artists' buildings more than highway construction. There is also talk of traffic-calming devices such as a traffic circle at Haywood Road and Roberts Street. (Courtesy North Carolina Collection, Pack Memorial Library.)

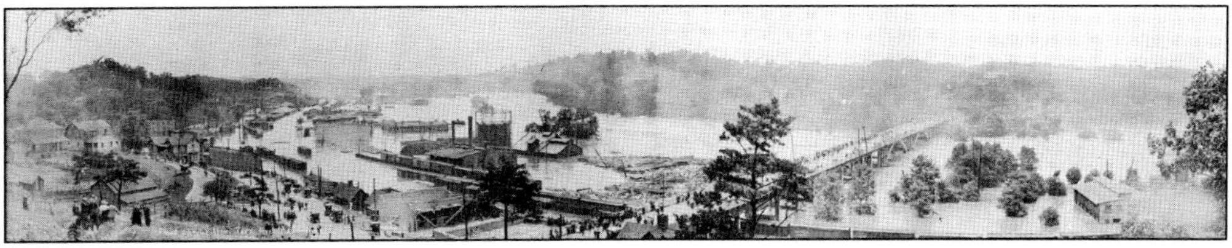

FLOOD OF 1910. The Southern Railway yards and Asheville's Electric Company gas house and power house were inundated on August 31, 1910. The photograph was taken by famed panoramic photographer Herbert W. Pelton. (Courtesy North Carolina Collection, Pack Memorial Library.)

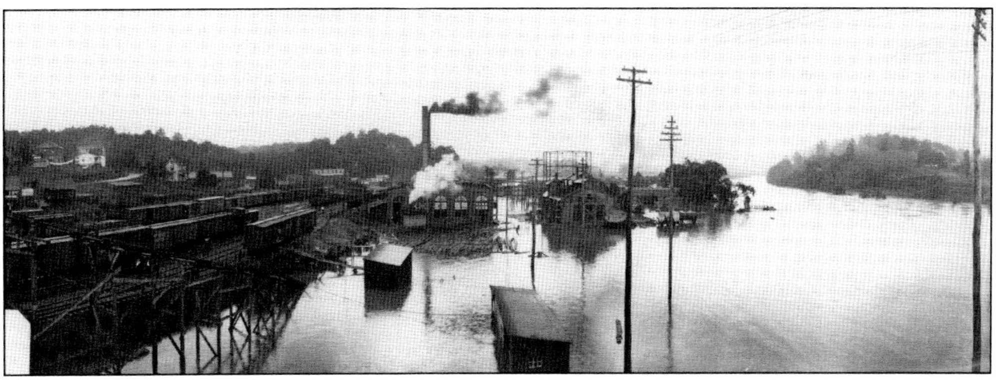

FLOODS. The flood of 1916 (pictured) is considered the worst on record in Western North Carolina, but that is only for one area—the high-value Southern Depot, cotton mill, and Biltmore section. The flood of August 30, 1940, was the worst one to ever pass through the Pigeon River Valley in Haywood County. Certain businesses in the River Arts District experience flooding once every 10 years on average. Societal reactions to floods vary. Before industrialization, floods did less damage and restored the soil for crops. In the modern, urban world, insurance companies step in, as they did in January 1974 with the passage of a federal law requiring municipalities to enforce flood plain management if they wanted to receive other benefits, such as mortgages for public buildings. (Courtesy North Carolina Collection, Pack Memorial Library.)

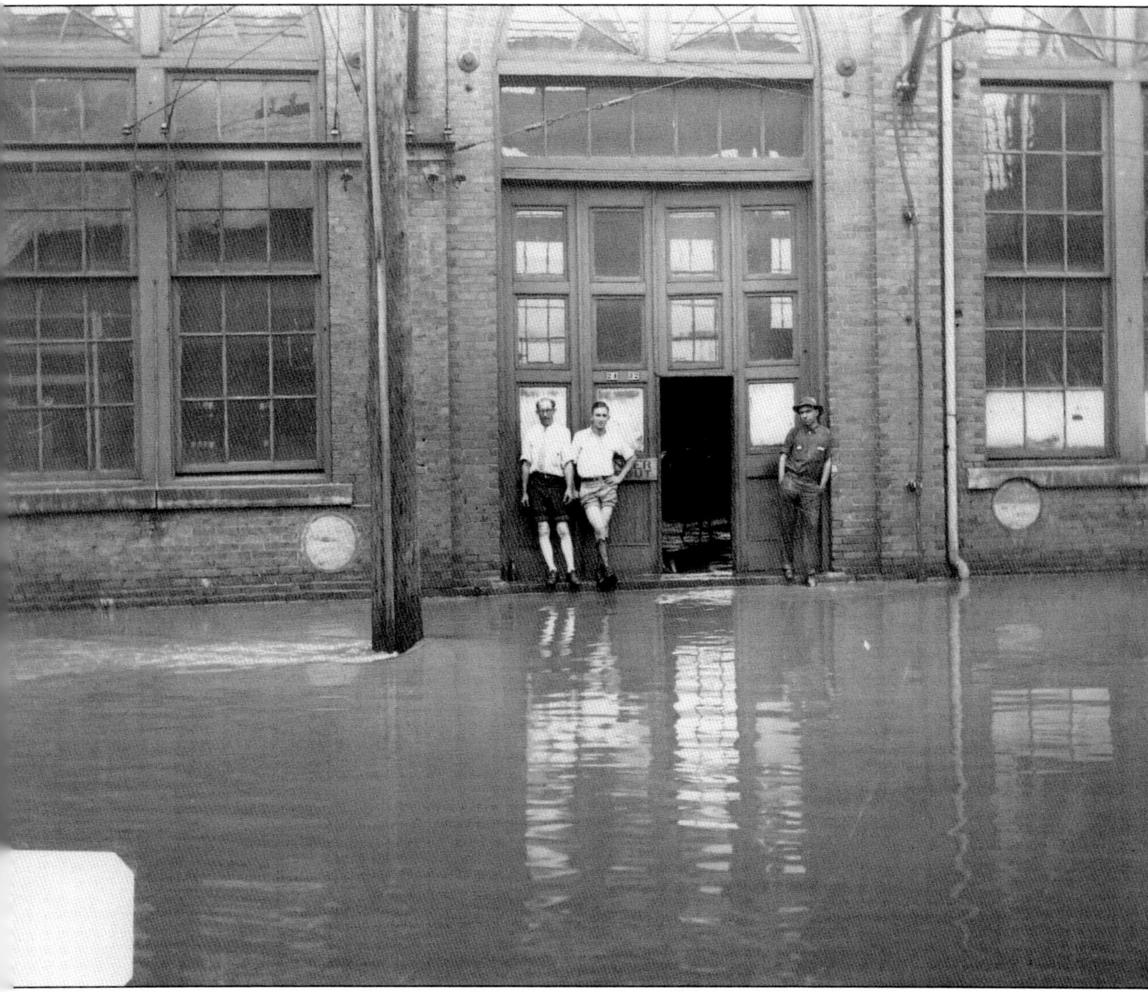

CAROLINA POWER AND LIGHT FLOODED. The flood of August 15, 1928, put the power company out of business for a while. It was located on Avery Street between West Haywood Road and the Southern Railway. (Courtesy North Carolina Collection, Pack Memorial Library.)

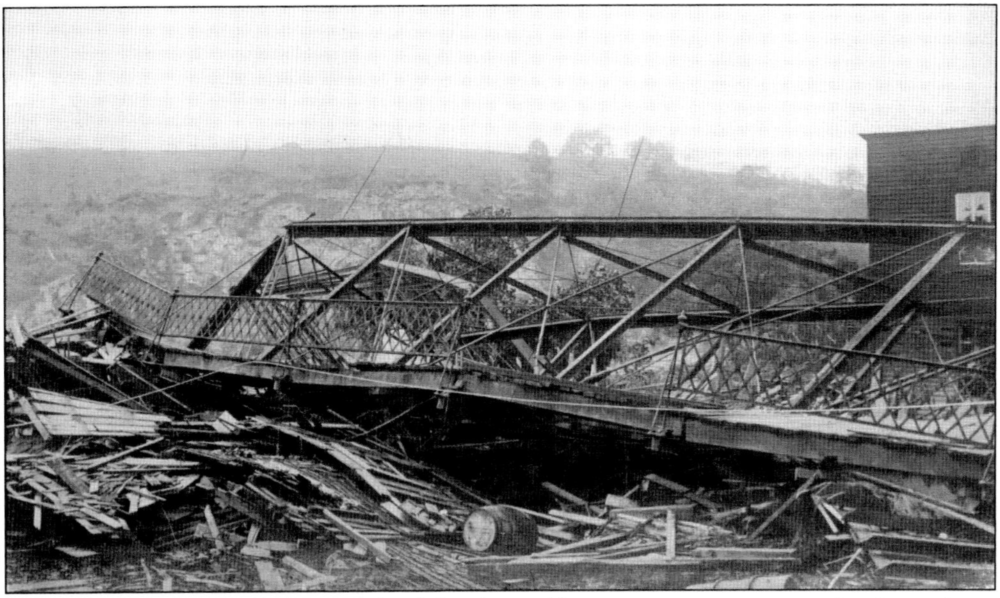

THE POWER OF FLOODS. The 1916 flood, heightened by two converging storms that burst dams, caused water to rise 15 feet in one hour in the river district. In Biltmore, 60-year-old J. C. Lipe, his daughter, and two nurses left his home a little too late. They were washed away but held onto tree trunks. The nurses were torn away and drowned. Before losing his grip, Lipe tied his daughter, Kathleen, to a tree trunk with his coat. More than eight hours later, rescuers lowered Kathleen, semi-conscious, into a boat. Many bridges were destroyed and had to be rebuilt. (Courtesy North Carolina Collection, Pack Memorial Library.)

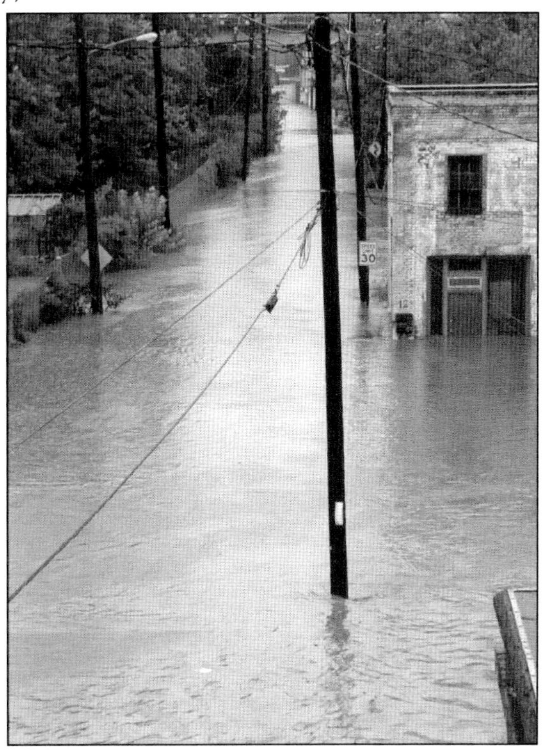

2004 FLOOD. The flood of September 9, 2004, turned Riverside Drive into a canal. Hurricane Frances poured 23 inches of rain on the mountains. Together with Hurricane Ivan, which followed, it caused $300 million of damage in the region. (Courtesy Barbara Fisher.)

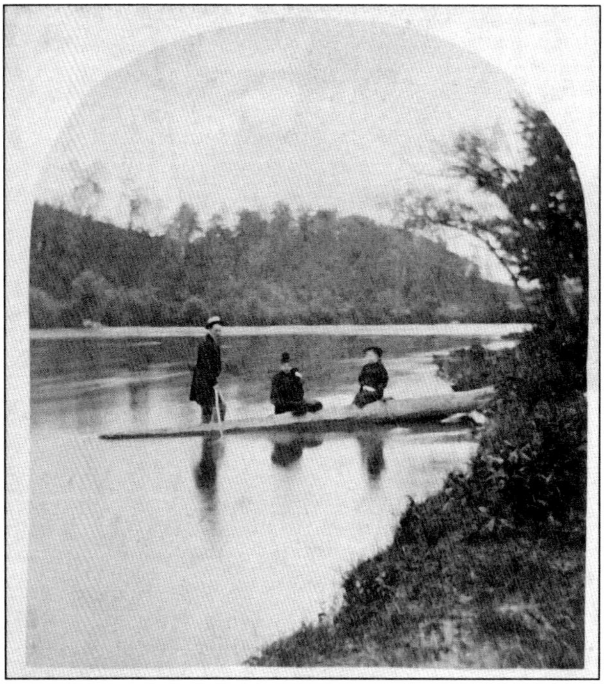

Paddlers. Before the 1916 flood destroyed Riverside Park in Montford (a mile and a half downriver), people could drift leisurely in lagoons. Today paddlers can follow an easy route from the Recreation Park on Gashes Creek, Hominy Creek Park, and Bent Creek Park (across from the Arboretum) to two stops: Jean Webb Park and Woodfin Park (just short of the Craggy Dam). Southern Waterways on Amboy Road (near the French Broad River Park) provides canoes and livery. An early-20th-century stereo view shows a well-dressed trio taking off from a bank below Smith's Bridge on the French Broad River. (Courtesy North Carolina Collection, Pack Memorial Library.)

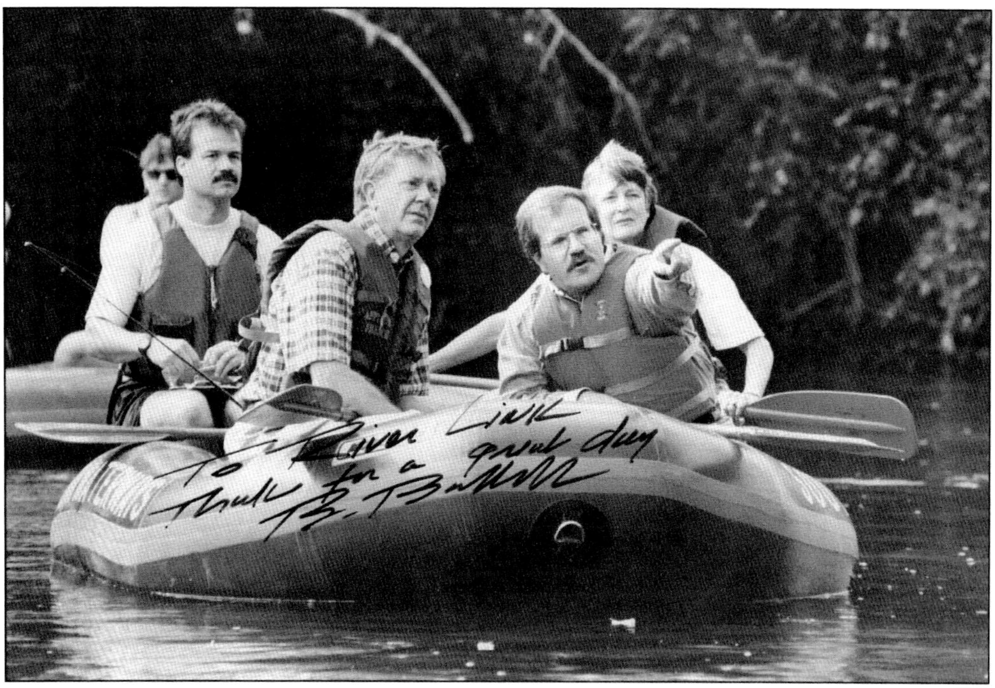

American Heritage River. In 1995, Bruce Babbitt, then secretary of the interior, was invited by RiverLink to tour the French Broad River, which was up for consideration as an American Heritage River. Pictured from left to right are an unnamed security guard, David Donnell (of Southern Waterways), Babbitt, Bill Alexander (of the Biltmore Estate), and Jean Webb. The initiative would streamline federal support to communities without imposing new regulations. Still, property owners feared losing local control. (Courtesy RiverLink.)

Source of the Water. Wilma Dykeman (1920–2006) was the author of *The French Broad.* As Dykeman noted, the distinctive feature of Western North Carolina is moving water, falling plentifully on mountaintops, gurgling in streams, and rushing to the French Broad River. Her first spoken words, growing up at the head of Beaverdam Creek in Asheville, were "water coming down." Dykeman's first novel, *The Tall Woman*, concludes with the heroine going to clean out her spring. Delicious drinking water, medicinal mineral water, and soft water for industrial uses have been primary motivators for settlers in the French Broad River Valley. RiverLink has named its developing 17-mile greenway the Wilma Dykeman RiverWay. The photograph below by George Masa (1881?–1933), considered the premier artist of the mountain landscape during the efforts to create a park in the Great Smoky Mountains, dramatizes the river's origins. (Right, courtesy Wilma Dykeman; below, courtesy North Carolina Collection, Pack Memorial Library.)

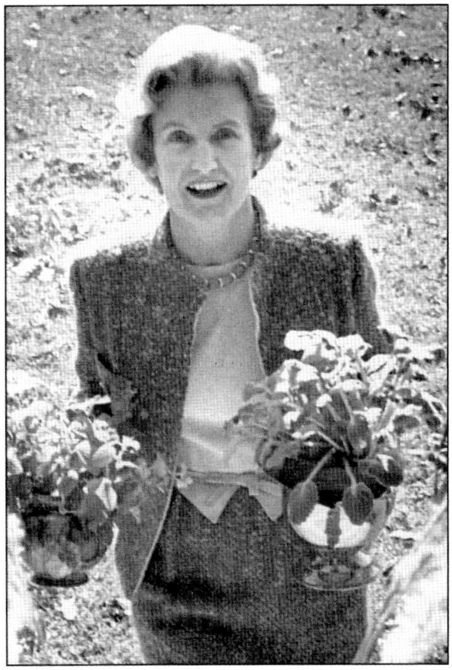

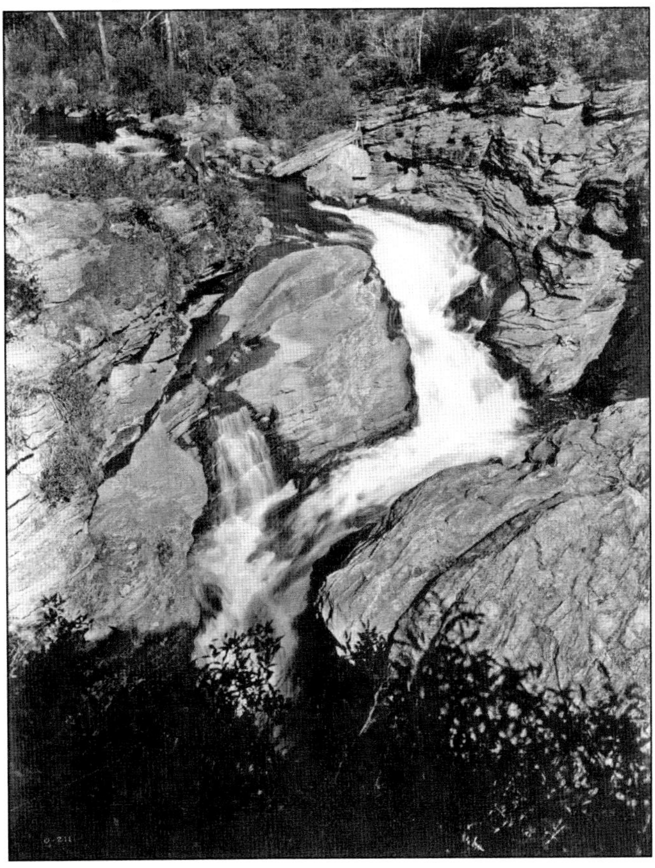

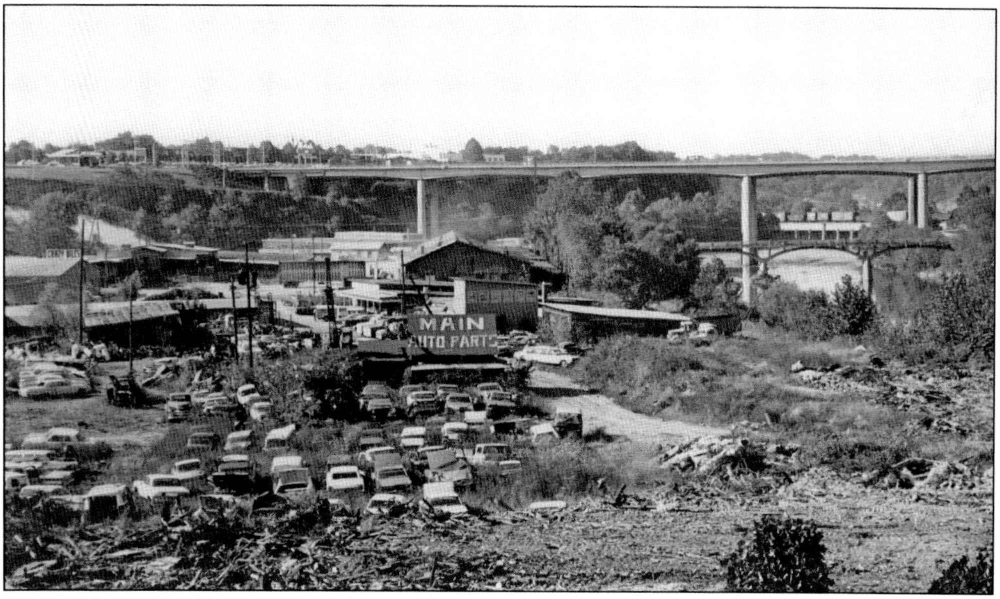

SCRAP YARD. The River District Artists Web site states that after the stock market crash in 1930, the "neighborhood fell into disuse, allowing the scrap yards to multiply." Jerry Sternberg (below), whose grandfather Sigfred started the family's metal and hide scrap business in the river district in 1900, noted that until the establishment of scrap yards, people were dumping used automobiles on the sides of roads and in ravines in large numbers. The photograph of Main Auto Parts in 1977 (above) was taken by Bill Sanders for the Asheville *Citizen-Times*. (Above, courtesy Asheville *Citizen-Times*; below, photograph by Rob Neufeld.)

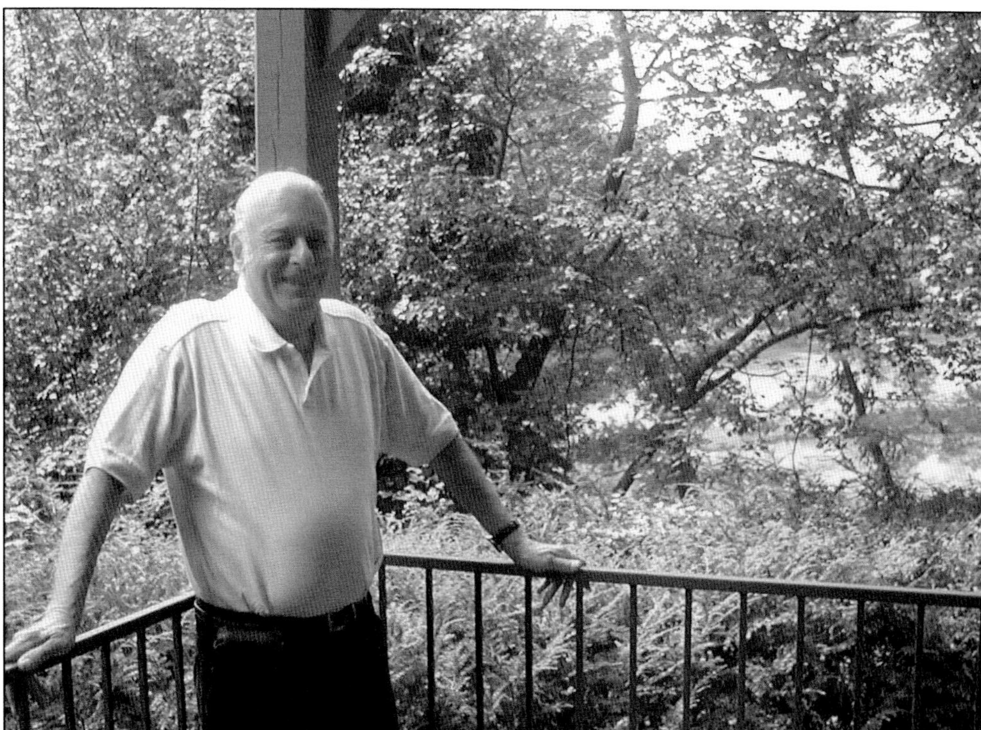

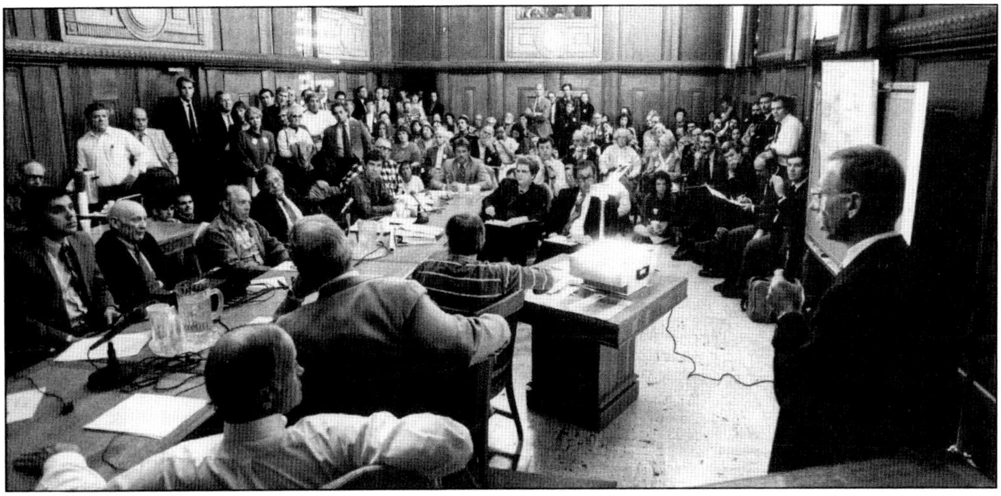

Drinking-the-French-Broad Advocates. Consultant David Dukes advocated using the French Broad River for drinking water in an October 30, 1990, meeting at the Asheville City Hall. (Courtesy Asheville *Citizen-Times*.)

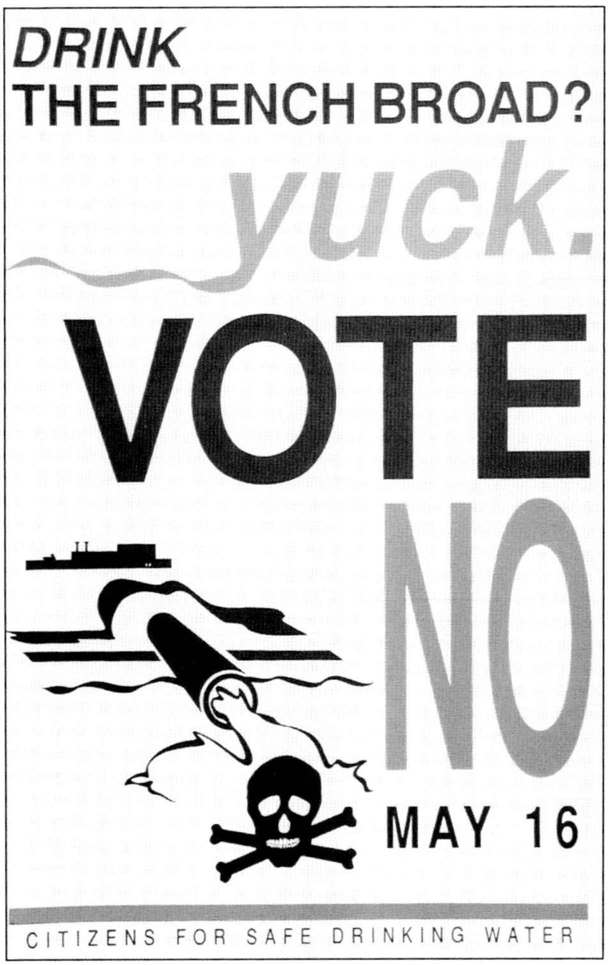

Drinking-the-French-Broad Opponents. A bond referendum to construct a water supply intake and treatment plant on the river failed to pass, and the Asheville-Buncombe Water Authority began seeking alternative water supply sources. Citizens for Safe Drinking Water organized the opposition. Government agencies were active in promoting the effort, as was RiverLink, whose leaders believed the re-use would improve the water quality in general. A greatly enlarged water source, some thought, would also enable greatly increased development. (Courtesy the author's collection.)

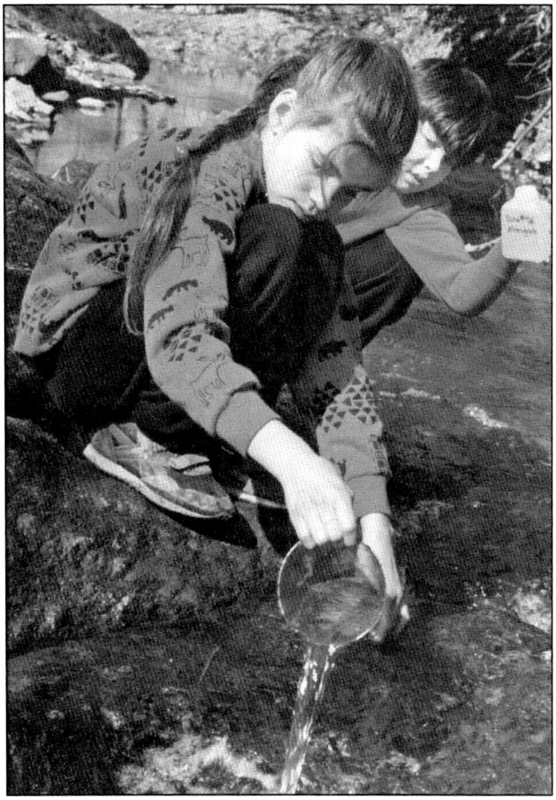

WATER-QUALITY TESTING. Megan Foley and Andy Nelson participated in the newly formed Voluntary Stream Monitoring Network in February 1990. Today the volunteer watchdog group operates under the Environmental Quality Institute at UNC–Asheville. Development and sedimentation have rendered 90 of the 116 miles of the river within Western North Carolina impaired, with one of the most polluted stretches being within Buncombe County. Sediment smothers the eggs of aquatic life and gives pollutants something on which to affix. (Courtesy Asheville *Citizen-Times*.)

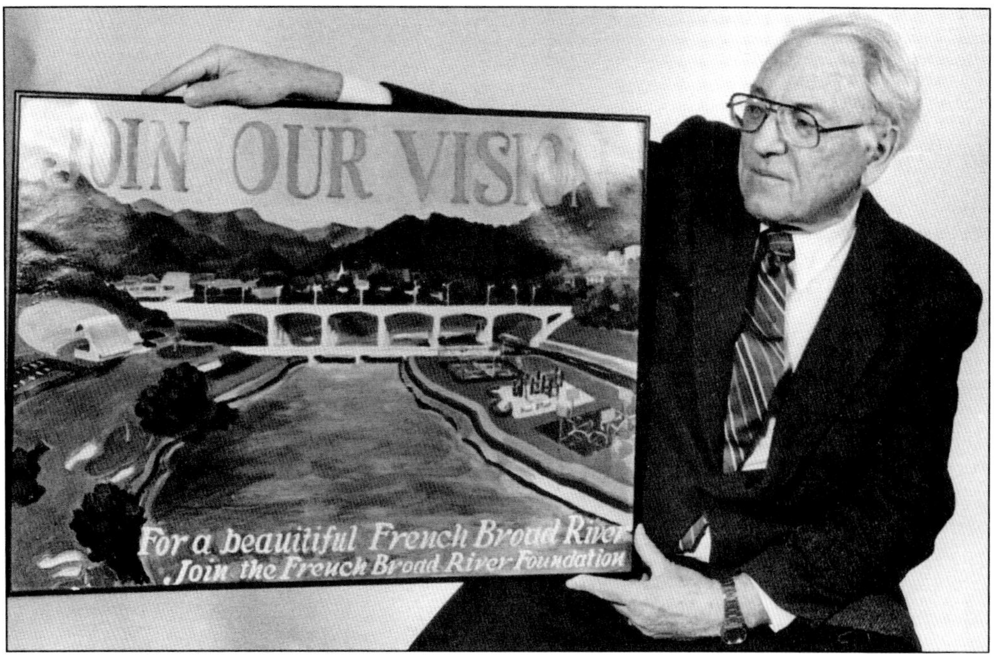

AWARENESS CAMPAIGN. In 1989, James Morgan won the senior citizen poster and slogan contest from the French Broad River Planning Commission, which soon became RiverLink. (Courtesy Asheville *Citizen-Times*.)

THE PLANNING PROCESS AND THE PATTON AVENUE SPINE. "Charrette"—a brainstorming and collaborative designing session—became a favorite word in leaders' vocabulary in the late 1980s when local and visiting planners, excited about Asheville's potential, adopted the architects' method of brainstorming, drawing, and caucusing to turn community input into bold designs. The 1989 riverfront charrette was an outgrowth of a larger community-involving effort, the "2010 Asheville City Plan." The 2010 plan fostered the French Broad Riverfront Planning Committee, whose members later formed RiverLink, a nonprofit agency. The integration of mixed urban usages, linkages to other parts of the city, natural areas, and recreational opportunities was a part of the vision from the start. Patton Avenue was identified as a primary linkage, with several nodes, or green spots, along the way. Pictured below, Angelo Abate (left), North Carolina State University landscape architecture professor, and Asheville architect Carroll Hughes (right) participate in the 1989 four-day charrette to create a vision for river district planning. (Courtesy Asheville *Citizen-Times.*)

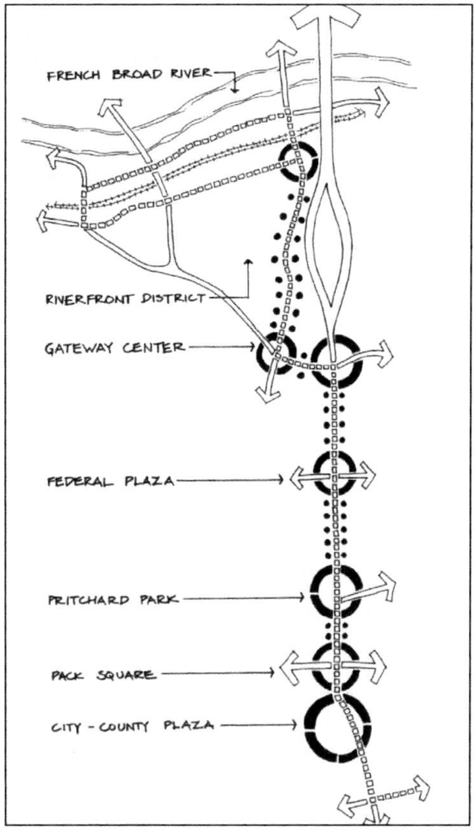

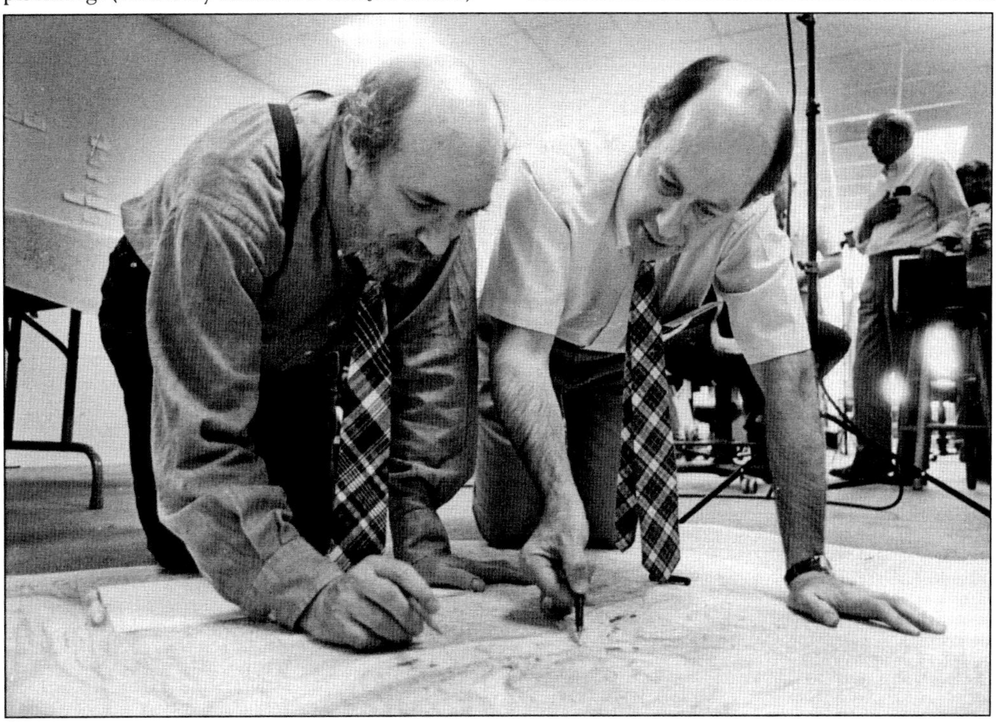

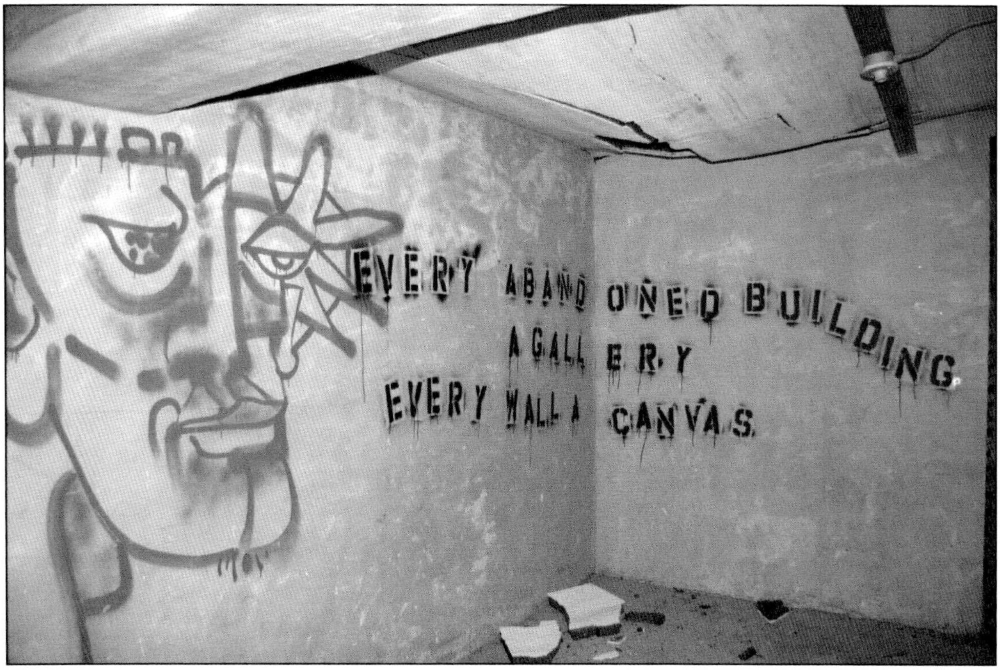

ICE HOUSE ARTISTS. The production of ice was a major industry in pre-refrigeration society. The abandoned icehouse on Riverside Drive has become a huge canvas, inside and out, for a talented group of hobo artists whose graffiti mark the building as well as the nearby railroad bridge. (Photograph by Henry Neufeld.)

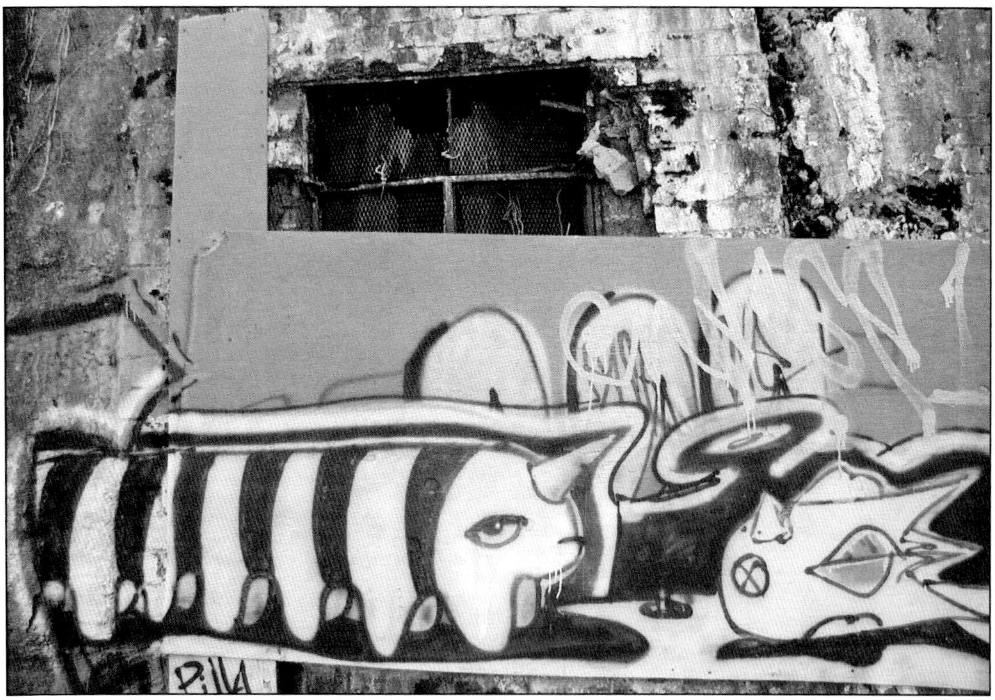

ICONIC HORNED CATERPILLAR. The art will not last here. The building site is slated for improvement. (Photograph by Henry Neufeld.)

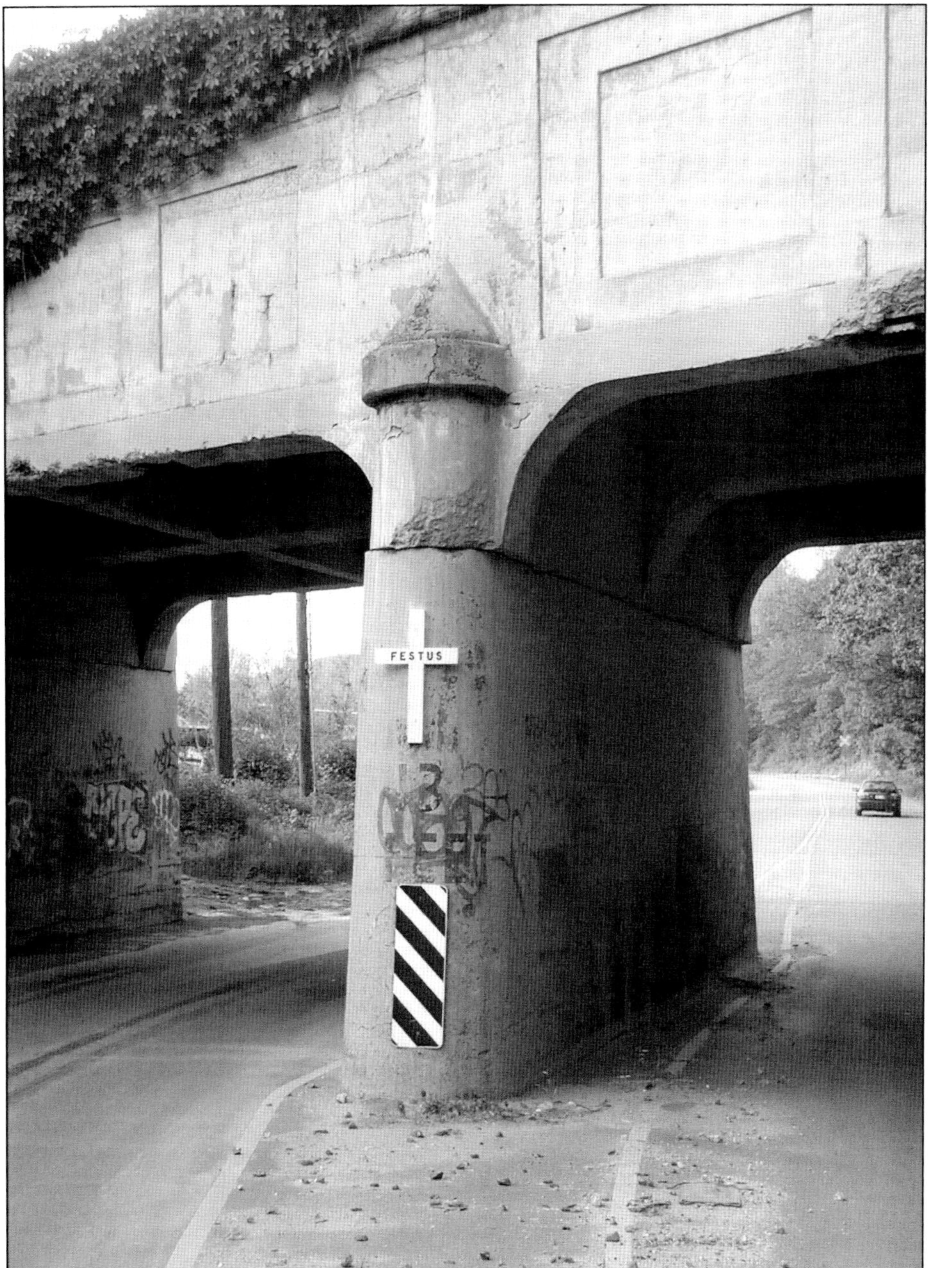

FESTUS MEMORIAL. On a pier of the railroad bridge, a cross bearing the name "Festus" honors the memory of David Allen Walker. On the night of August 31, 2002, Walker, nicknamed Festus by his middle school football coach years before, died when his truck slammed into the monstrous structure. His friends Mark McIntosh, Kerry Putnam, and others created the memorial. In addition to their mother's memory books and a trust fund helped by the Biltmore estate, David's former employer, Walker's children each have a quilt that their great-grandmother Mary Walker made out of David's Tennessee Volunteer T-shirts. Glimpsing her work-in-progress at Christmastime, David's son Cameron said, "I can't wait to take it to bed. It'll feel like his arms are wrapped around me." (Photograph by Rob Neufeld.)

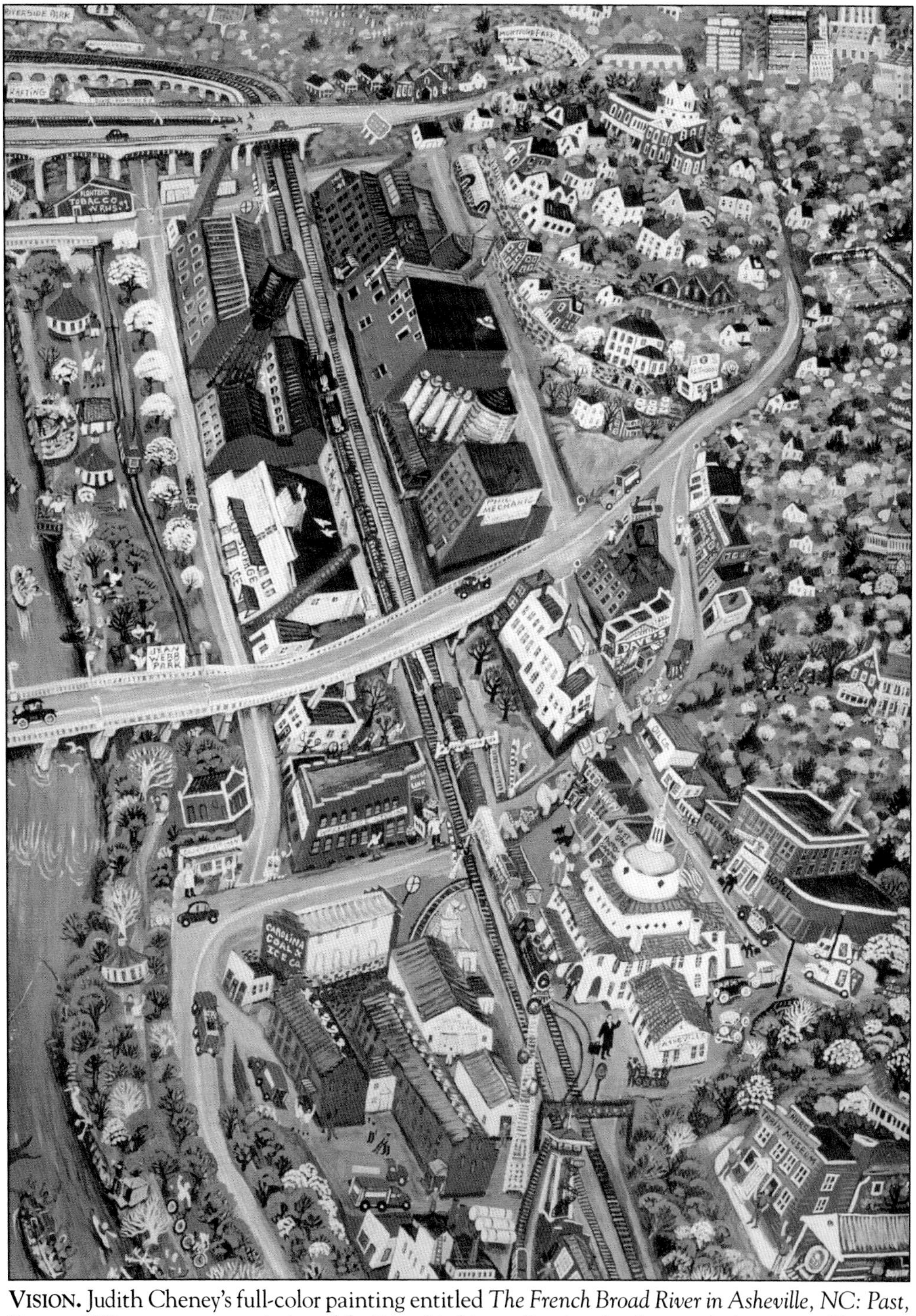

VISION. Judith Cheney's full-color painting entitled *The French Broad River in Asheville, NC: Past, Present & Future* was commissioned for RiverLink's application for the river's American Heritage River status. The painting was made into posters. The strip along the river is verdant parkland in the vision. Roberts Street (the next area covered in this book) is depicted between factories of the past, and a vibrant West End neighborhood is also clearly depicted. (Courtesy RiverLink.)

Three

ROBERTS STREET

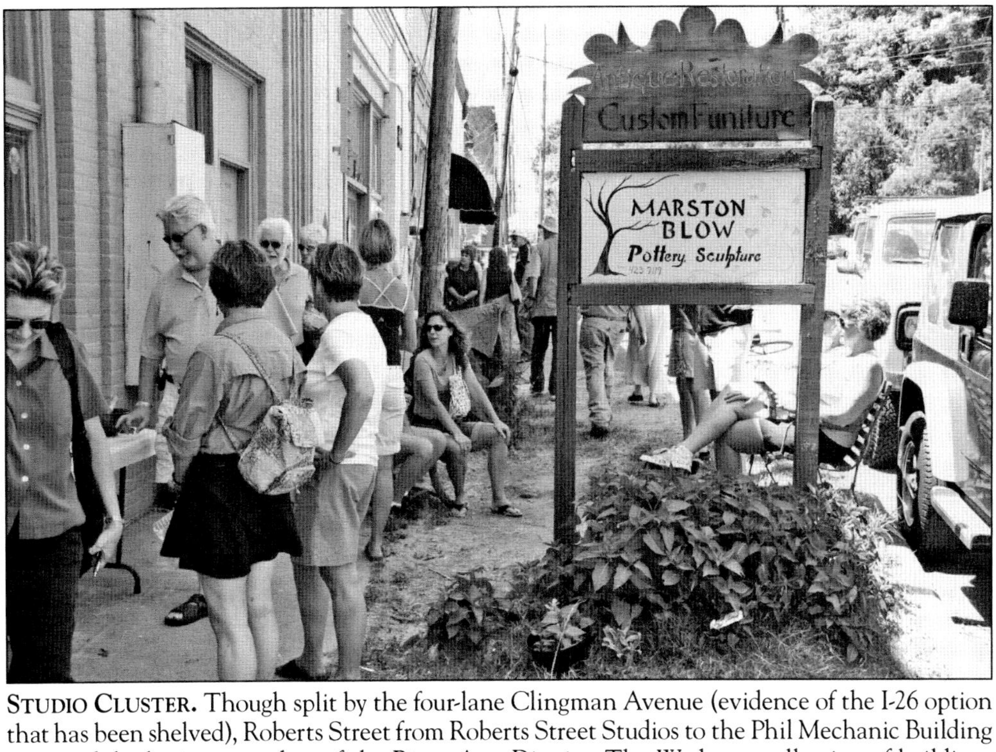

STUDIO CLUSTER. Though split by the four-lane Clingman Avenue (evidence of the I-26 option that has been shelved), Roberts Street from Roberts Street Studios to the Phil Mechanic Building is one of the busiest stretches of the River Arts District. The Wedge, a collection of buildings on the west side, is home to eight river district artists and the Terpsicorps Dance Studio. Part of the attraction of this site is the scrap-yard-decorated steps that lead down to more artists' spaces along the tracks. Before the 1920s, the block provided lots for laborers' homes. The present buildings have gone through a dramatic evolution, housing the Farmers Federation; industrial warehouses; Afram, Inc., the first African-American-owned industry in the region; Future of Tradition, a pioneer street performance group; and various river district artists. (Photograph by Henry Neufeld.)

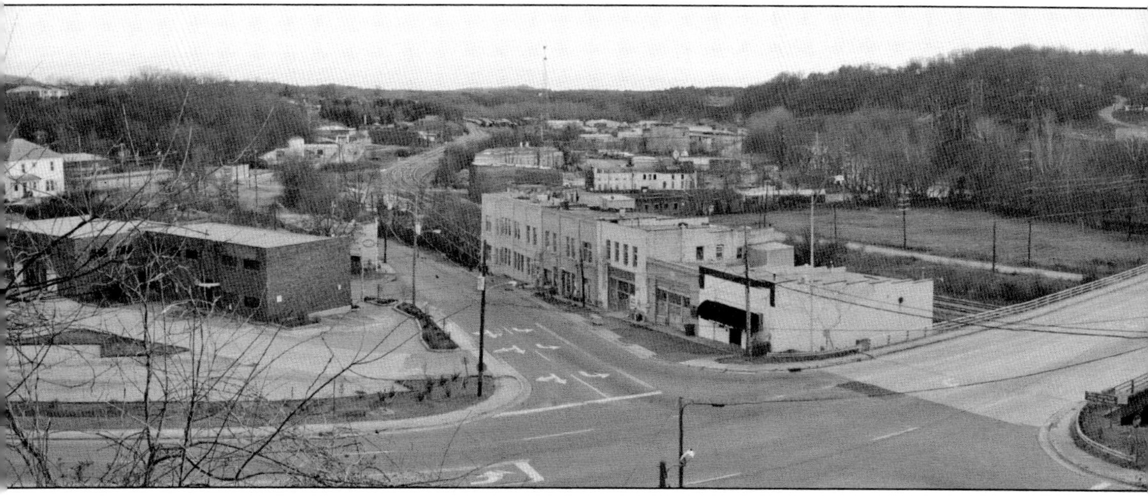

Roberts Street Panorama. The conglomerate, broken, and resurgent aspects of the Roberts Street area are clearly seen in this panorama. The Wedge buildings provide a solid mini-district. The West Asheville Bridge cuts a wide swath. The vital, multi-use Phil Mechanic Building is at the head of the languishing north piece of Roberts Street. The railroad parallels the river. The lawn behind the Wedge complex had been the site of mill workers' homes. In the left foreground is AVL Technologies, a new industry that has pressed into the short south piece of Park Avenue, cut

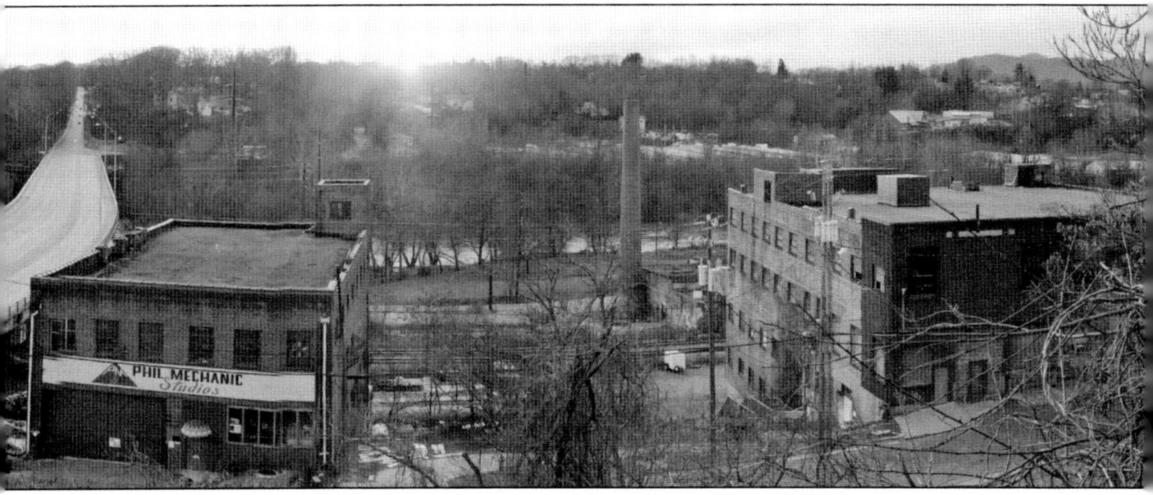

off from its northern neighbors by a rerouted and widened Clingman Avenue. AVL Technologies is a leading producer of vehicle-mounted satellite antenna systems, which has helped armored troops in Iraq communicate with supply centers. The big white house, above on the left, is the last healthy vestige of south Park Avenue, which presides over what had been a major setting for the cult movie classic *Thunder Road.* (Photograph by Henry Neufeld.)

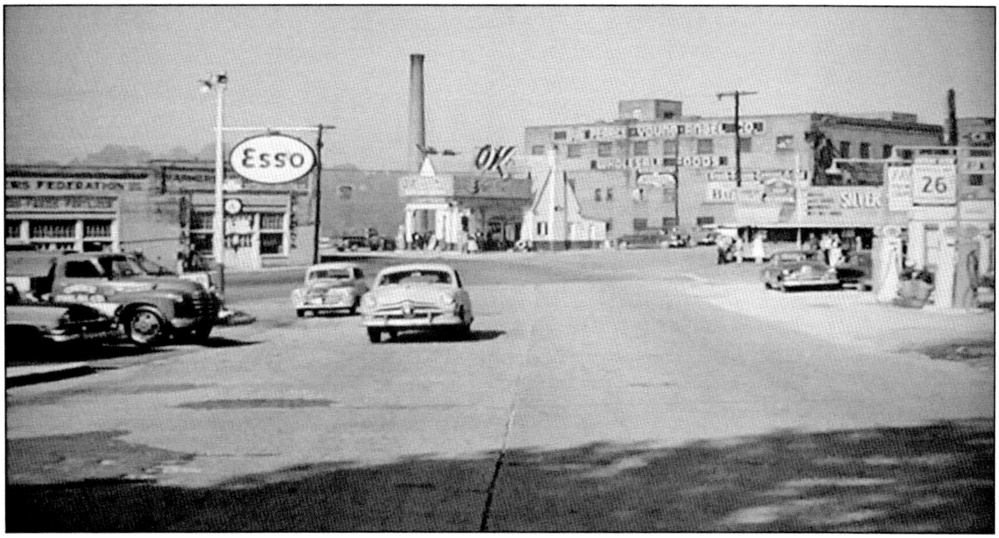

THUNDER ROAD COUPE. In a scene from the 1958 movie *Thunder Road*, Robert Mitchum (playing bootlegger Lucas Doolin) drives his 1950 Ford coupe up what had been East Haywood Street. He is fleeing both Carl Kogan, a crime boss, who is muscling in on independent moonshiners, and Troy Bassett, a U.S. Treasury agent. *Thunder Road* has achieved legendary status in Asheville because of the historic battle between mountain whiskey-makers and the federal government, which taxed and persecuted mountain men out of proportion with other distillers. Bootleggers were experts at outfitting cars to hold secret caches of liquor and at evading agents on mountain roads. Thus bootlegging developed into one of America's most popular sports, stock car racing. (Courtesy MGM.)

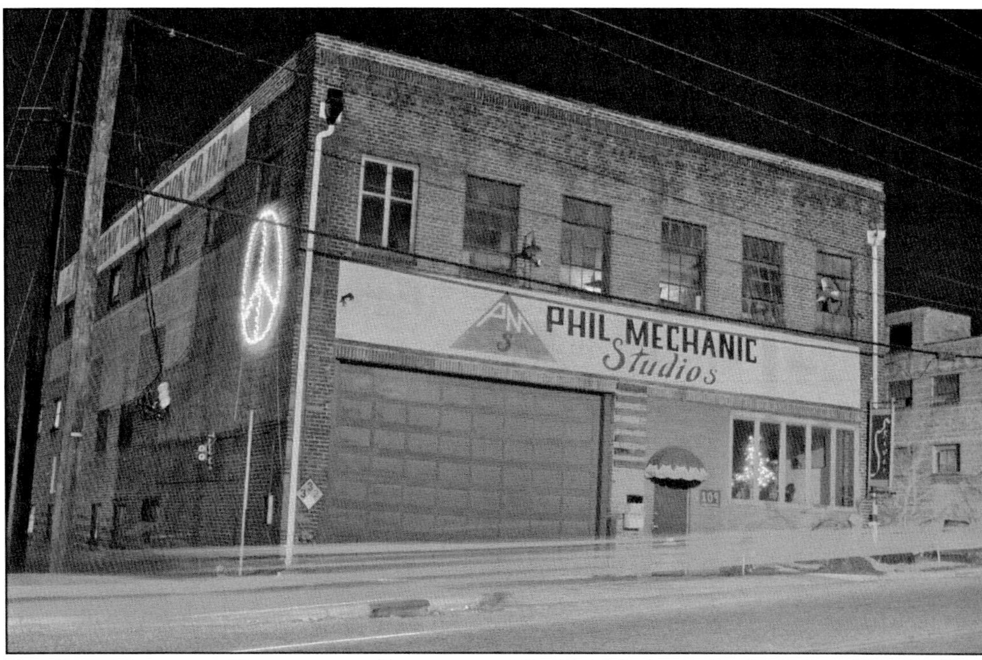

THE PHIL MECHANIC BUILDING AT CHRISTMAS. The Phil Mechanic Building (the large building in the top right of the movie still) now houses the Flood Gallery and Fine Art Center and Blue Ridge Bio-Fuels. (Courtesy Jolene Mechanic.)

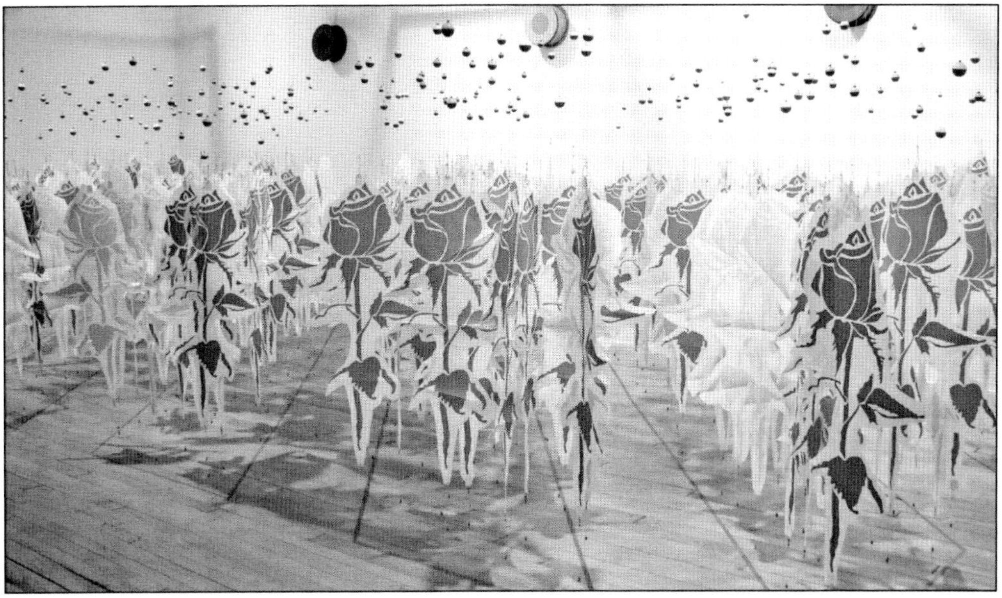

DOMESTIC LOVE TOKENS. The Phil Mechanic Building houses the Flood Gallery and Fine Arts Center, a nonprofit art organization that generates avant-garde art in all media (including performance and poetry). It includes the city's only regular exhibitions of installation art, such as Mark A. Guilbeau's and Rian Kerrane's "Domestic Love Tokens," involving silk-screen prints on butcher paper, fishing tackle, and sound. Each rose is 45 inches high. The work has traveled to the Florence Biennale. (Courtesy Jolene Mechanic.)

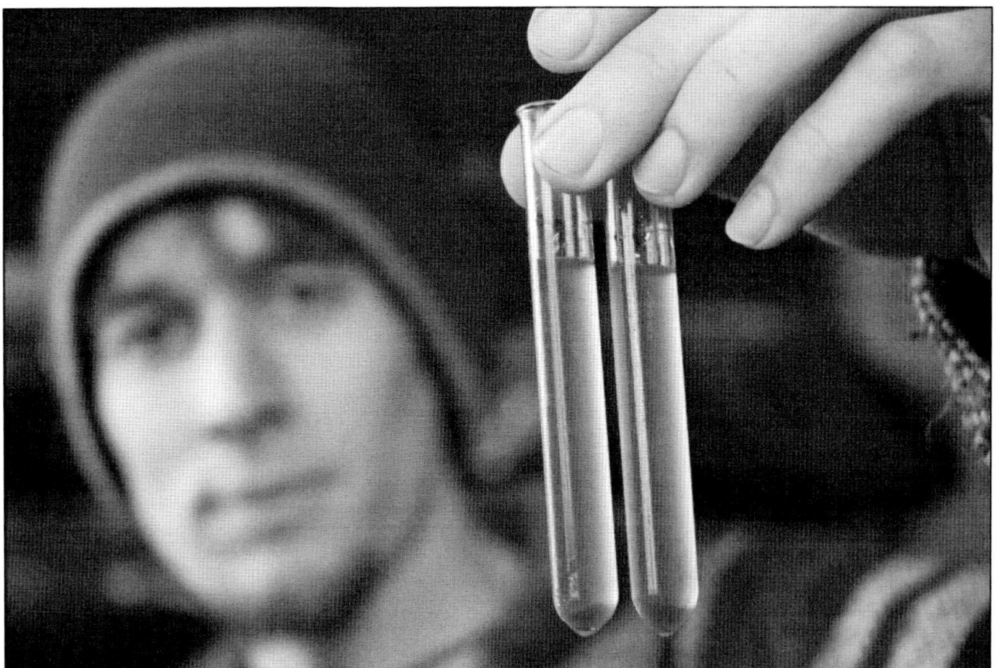

BIO-FUEL. The bottom floor of the Phil Mechanic Building holds a manufacturing facility for bio-diesel, which is made from discarded cooking oil collected from restaurants. Roadside pumps are located throughout the county. (Courtesy Jolene Mechanic.)

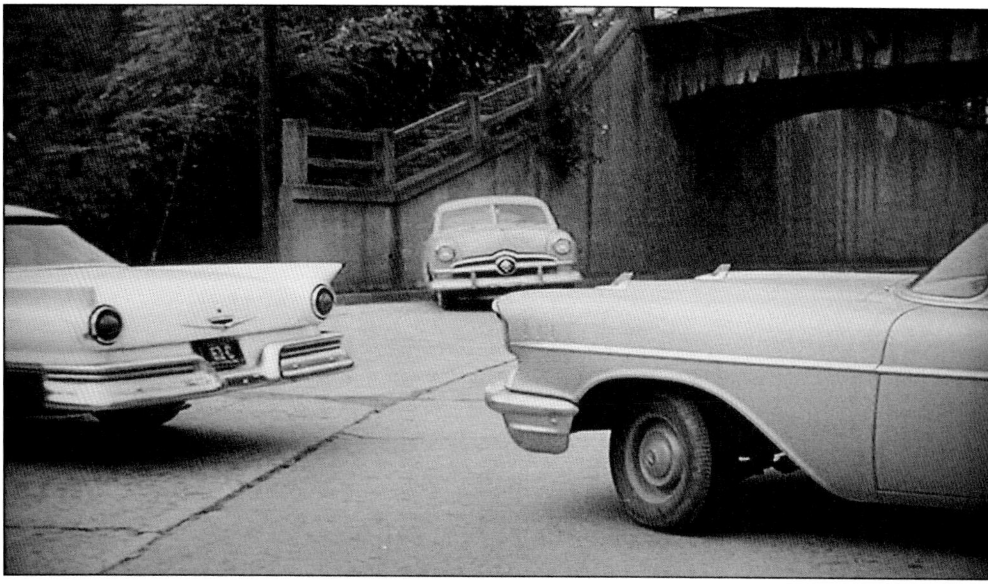

PARK STREET BRIDGE—THEN. In the film *Thunder Road*, Lucas Doolin is trapped by U.S. Treasury agents after coming through this bridge, which is located behind AVL Technologies and under Park Avenue south. Formerly, East Haywood Street used to run under Park Avenue. (Courtesy MGM.)

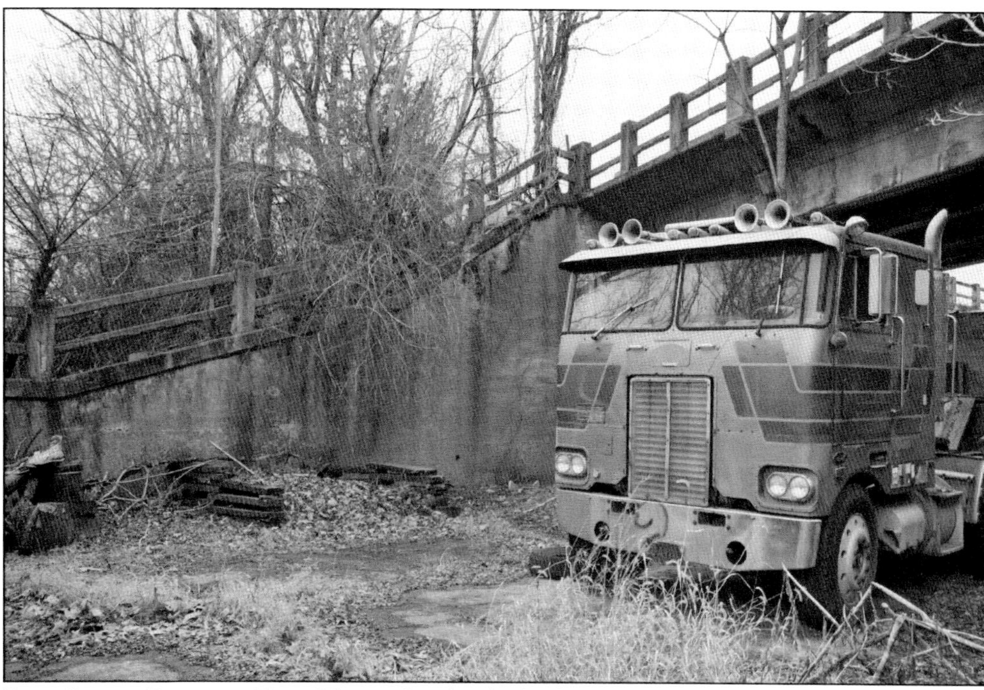

PARK STREET BRIDGE—NOW. The road under the bridge is blocked by an AVL technologies shed on one side and a truck lot's locked fence on the other. (Photograph by Henry Neufeld.)

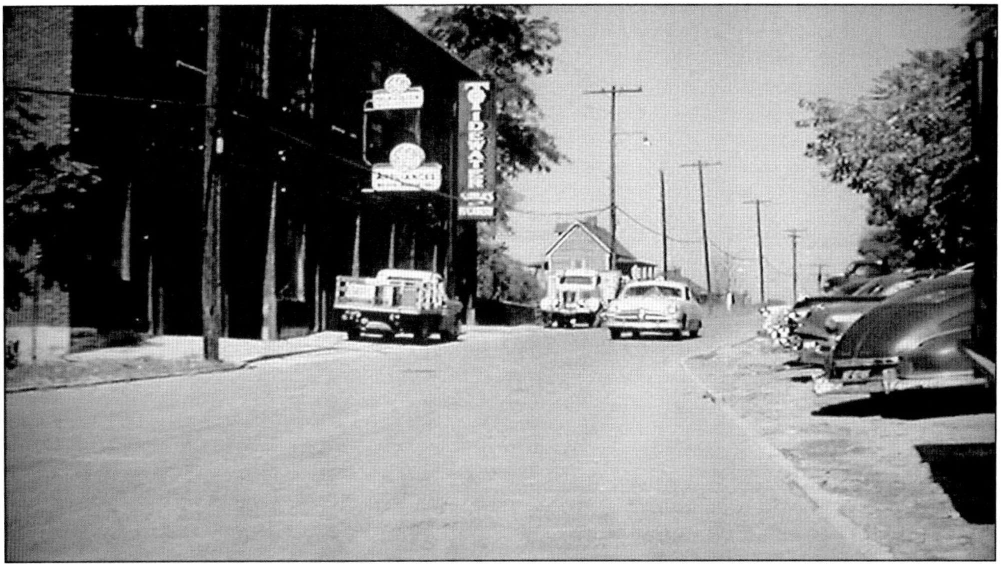

North Roberts Street—Then and Now. In the film *Thunder Road*, Lucas Doolin first came up Roberts Street before getting trapped at the East Haywood Street underpass. Roberts Street in this section has always been industrial. The buildings shown here are now partly boarded up. The Phil Mechanic Building, formerly a construction company outfit, has thrived because of continued family ownership and bold new uses. (Above, courtesy MGM; below, photograph by Henry Neufeld.)

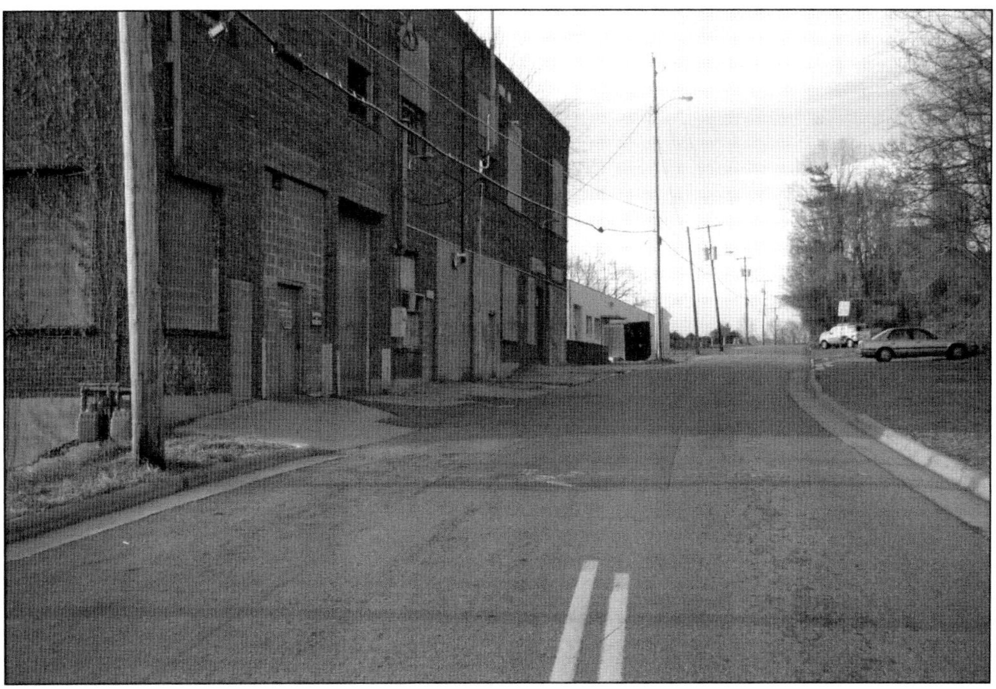

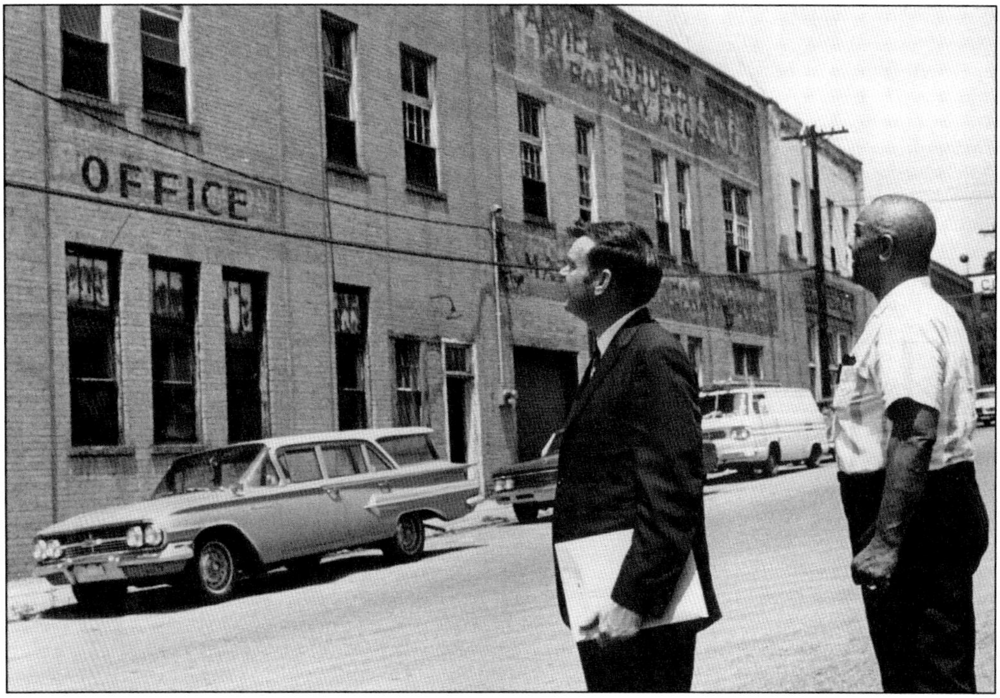

AFRAM, INC. In 1970, Dave Steel rented the former Farmers Federation Building on Roberts Street to Afram, Inc., a pioneer African American manufacturer that was started by community shareholders and other partners. (Courtesy North Carolina Collection, Pack Memorial Library.)

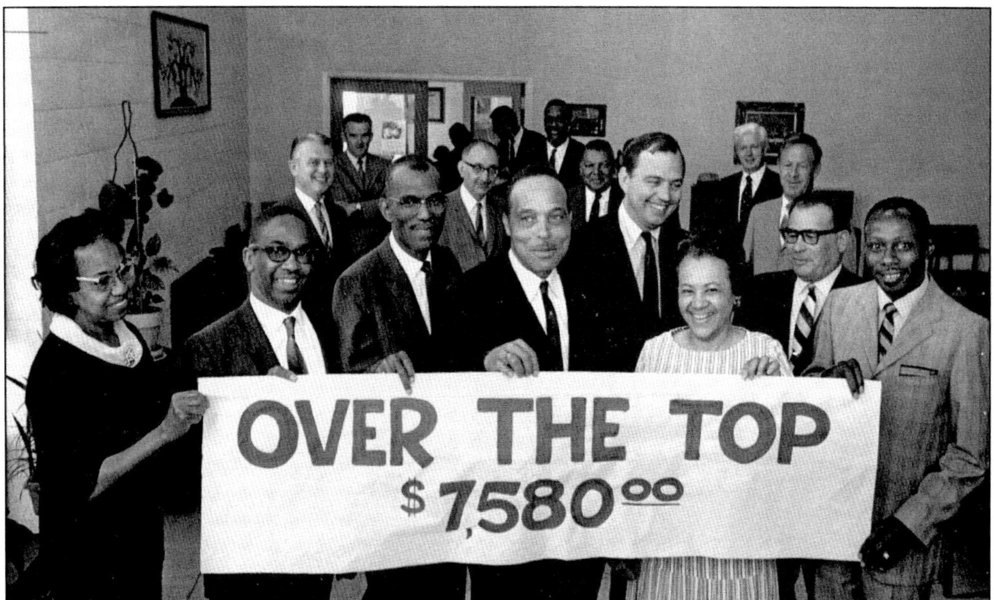

SHAREHOLDERS CELEBRATE. Afram pledge leaders raised $7,580, allowing Share Development Corporation to borrow another $15,000 from the Asheville Development Corporation (both chamber of commerce creations). These commitments then enabled an $180,000 loan from the Small Business Administration. (Courtesy North Carolina Collection, Pack Memorial Library.)

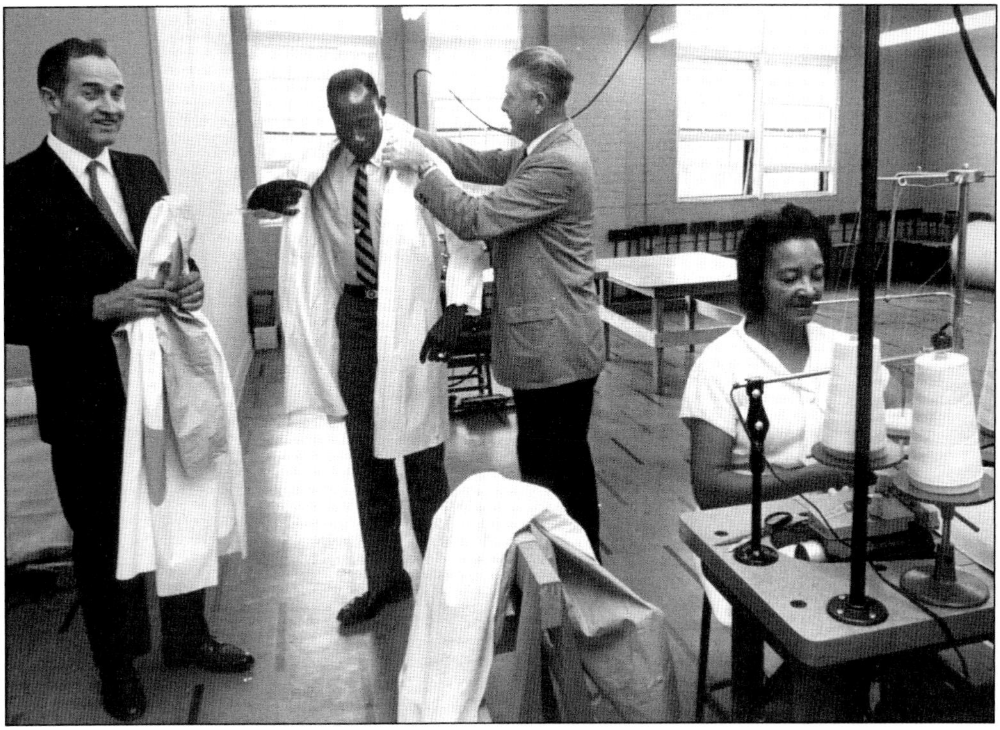

LAB COATS. Afram's first contract was with Kimberly-Clark, for which it made laboratory coats. Pictured from left to right are James Bergner; Matthew Bacoate Jr., general manager; George Tutale; and Bessie C. Owens. (Courtesy North Carolina Collection, Pack Memorial Library.)

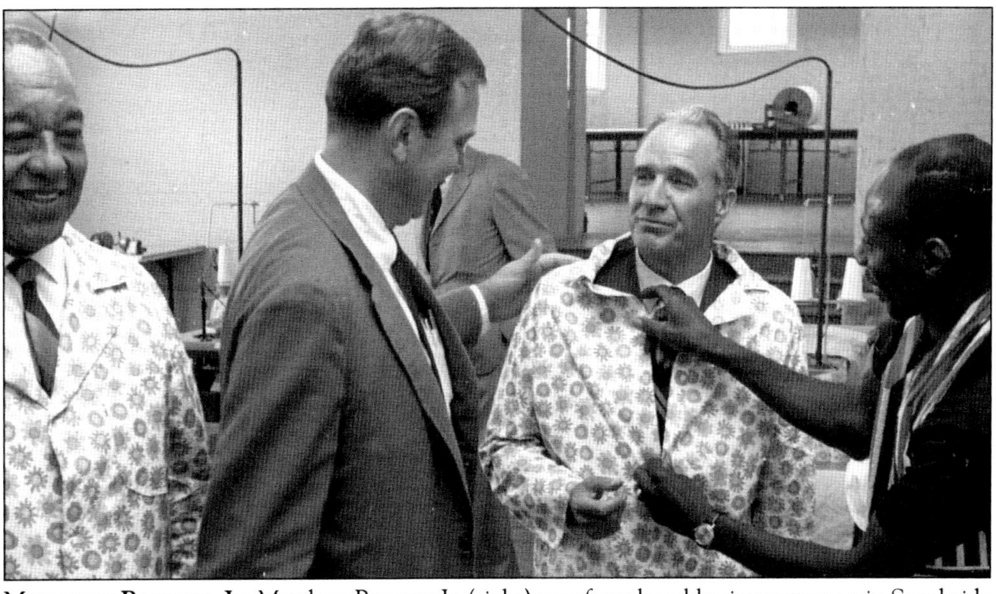

MATTHEW BACOATE JR. Matthew Bacoate Jr. (right) rose from humble circumstances in Southside to direct Afram, Inc. He had started off as a barrier-breaking black employee at the chamber of commerce, doing several jobs. Through a combination of skill, diplomacy, and insistence, he gained the chamber's appointment to head its employment project. (Courtesy North Carolina Collection, Pack Memorial Library.)

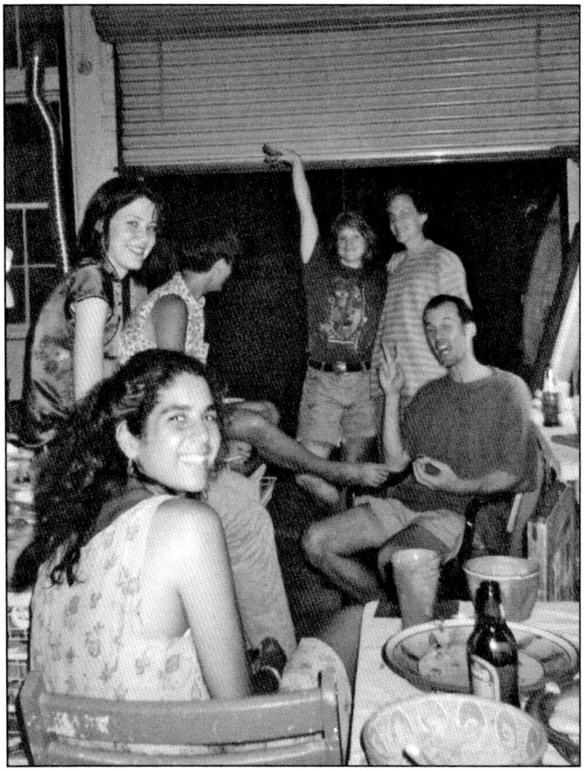

EARLY ROBERTS GROUP. When potter Marston Blow moved into 123 Roberts Street in 1996, she joined cotenants Future of Tradition, a group of street performers who worked out of the former typewriter ribbon factory after a year teaching capoeira and dance on Pack Square. "I'd be making pottery, and belly dancers would be like 'jing-a-jing-jingee'—'Hi, Marston!'—walking by" on their way to their entrance. Marston enjoyed the community that her cotenants brought. Parties and performances drew artists from other parts of the country and fostered Asheville's large "exotic" population. (Courtesy Marston Blow.)

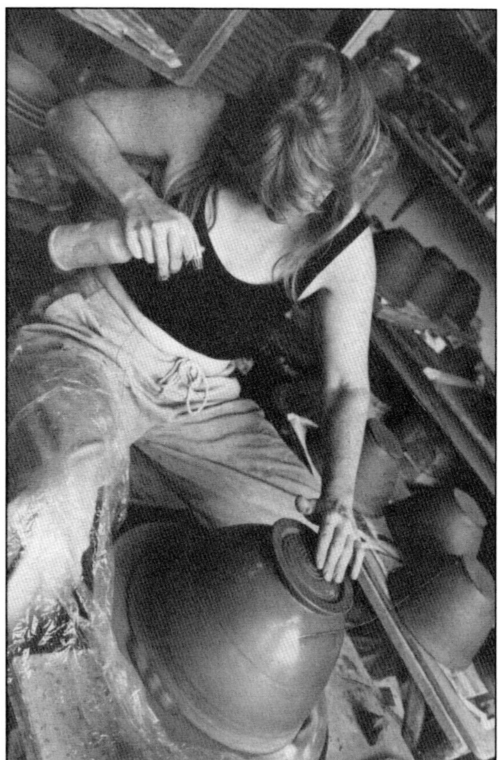

SINGING BOWLS. Marston Blow came to Asheville after leaving Cirque du Soleil, for which she had set up lighting. She took a class at Highwater Clays and developed a mastery of making bowls. Blow made the transition from the exotics era to the era of prosperity through singing bowls. Once, while experimenting with different clays and beset with an over-hot kiln, she produced a new type of bowl. She said, "When I moved them around, bong!—this long, bell-like tone expanded from them. One night," she continued, "I was in here playing with some friends, playing the bowls, being silly, and I wondered if they would sing like the Tibetan bowls." (Courtesy Marston Blow.)

CLAYSPACE CO-OP. Josh Copus is one of several young potters who work at Clayspace Co-op in the Wedge building. The building is owned by John Payne, a celebrated sculptor who has a shop on the lower level where he fabricates dynamic dinosaurs. The Clayspace potters dig their clay from local fields. (Photograph by Henry Neufeld.)

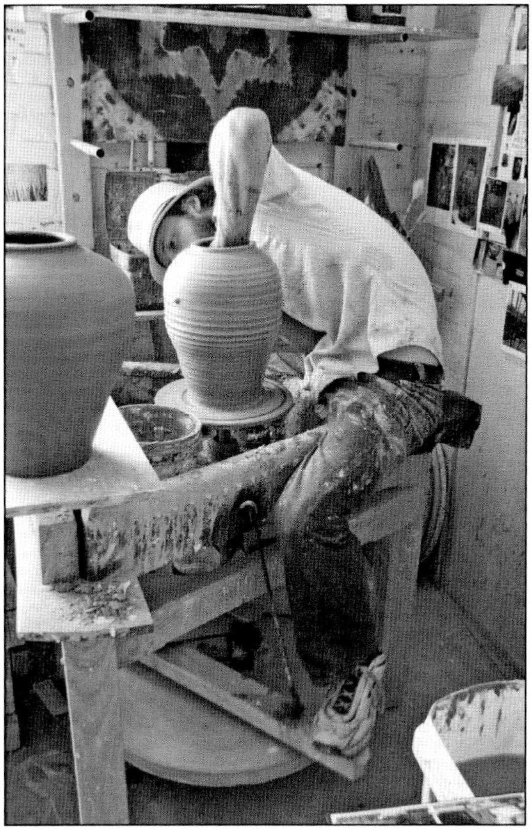

CRAFT TRADITION. The River Arts District potters and Highwater Clays draw on a long potting tradition in Western North Carolina, starting with the Cherokees and continuing through to the Southern Highlands Craft Guild and HandMade in America. The Allanstand Shop (below) was started by Frances Goodrich as a way of encouraging cottage industries in 1908. It came under the aegis of the craft guild in 1931 and is now part of the Folk Art Center on the Blue Ridge Parkway. (Courtesy North Carolina Collection, Pack Memorial Library.)

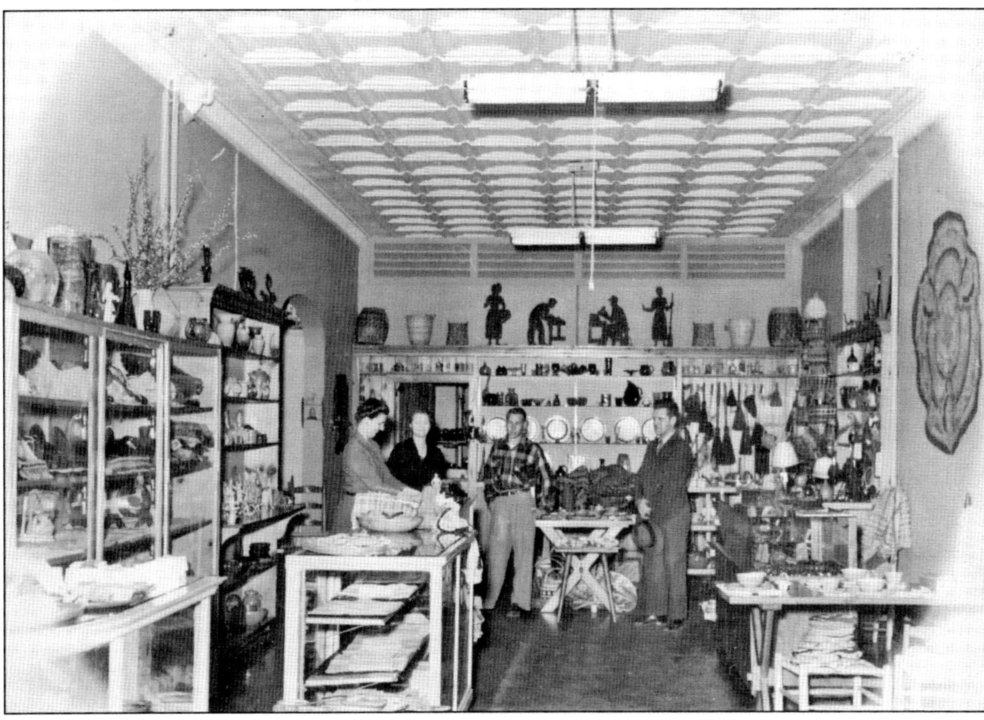

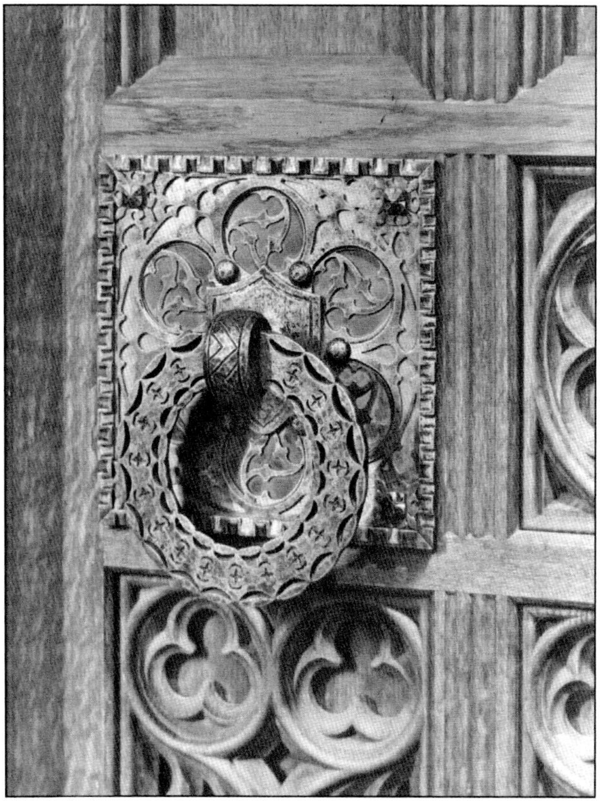

Wrought Iron. Asheville also has a wrought iron tradition, as exemplified by this door pull, which was created in 1933 by Asheville architect, painter, and blacksmith Anthony Lord. (Courtesy Chan and Miegan Gordon.)

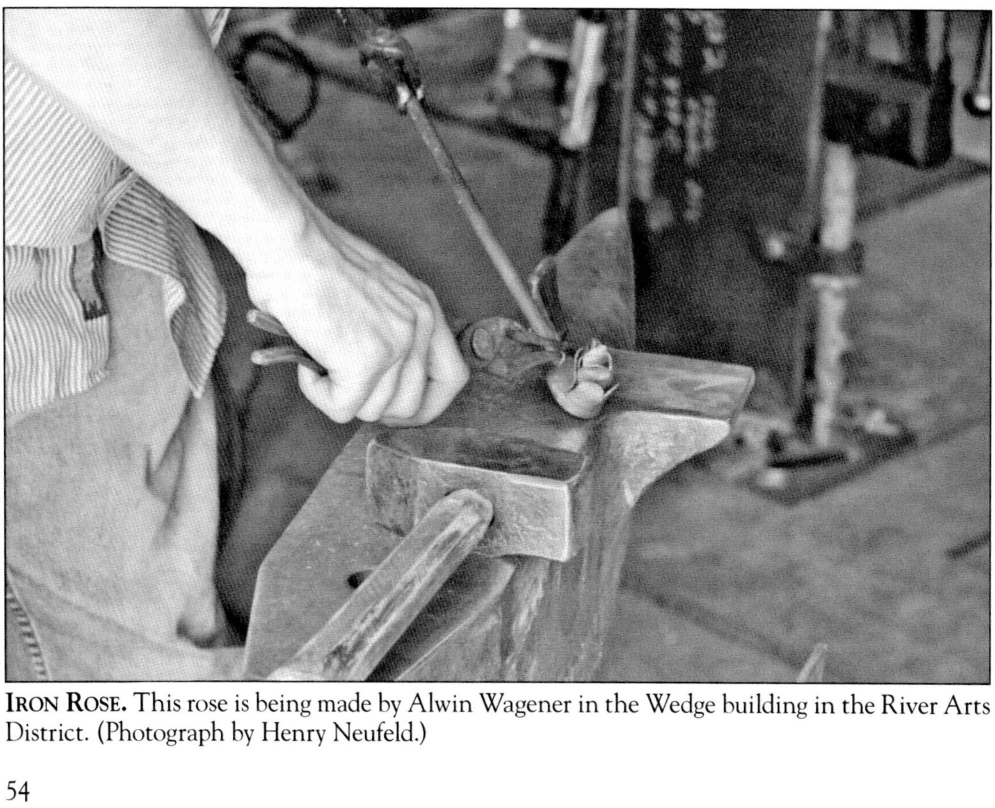

Iron Rose. This rose is being made by Alwin Wagener in the Wedge building in the River Arts District. (Photograph by Henry Neufeld.)

Four

THE CLINGMAN TRIANGLE

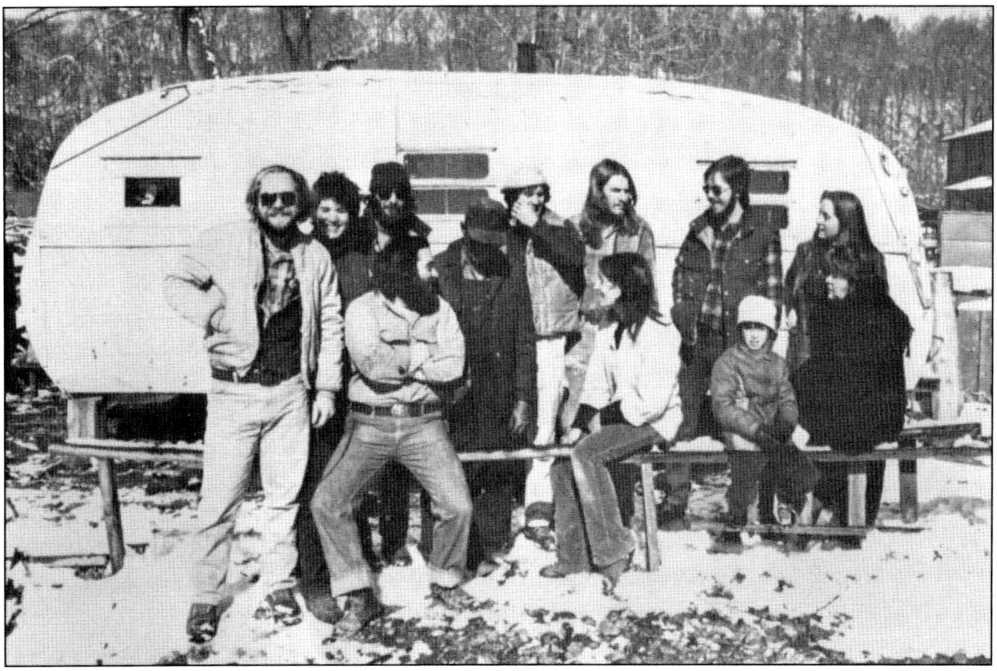

POTTERS' START. When the McCarthys first arrived in Asheville early in August 1979 from Texas, their first home was a tent. They registered their two children in the local school system, and Brian McCarthy, a potter, secured a workspace in the Highwater Center (later Flood Zone Studios) at 75 Thompson Street. Here, working with Highwater Clays, McCarthy, a former cost engineer, discovered his true calling—providing high-quality clays, potters' supplies, and sound advice. The Highwater Center group was a cooperative, many of whose members (above) went on to establish themselves elsewhere in the region. Their purpose was to provide workshops for artists at the lowest possible cost, create an environment in which artists in various media could share ideas and skills, and offer programs of instruction to the general public. From left to right are (first row) Tony Bradley (a key early player in the river district renaissance with Asheville Working Press); Brian McCarthy; Sarah Struby; Jonathan St. Onge (the McCarthys' son); and Hazel Robinson (founder of the Montford Park Players); (second row) Starr Wiginton; Robert Gurshay; unidentified; Larry Bradshaw (owner of the original Highwater Clays); Bo Ball; Michael Porter; and Michele Renner. (Courtesy Gail McCarthy.)

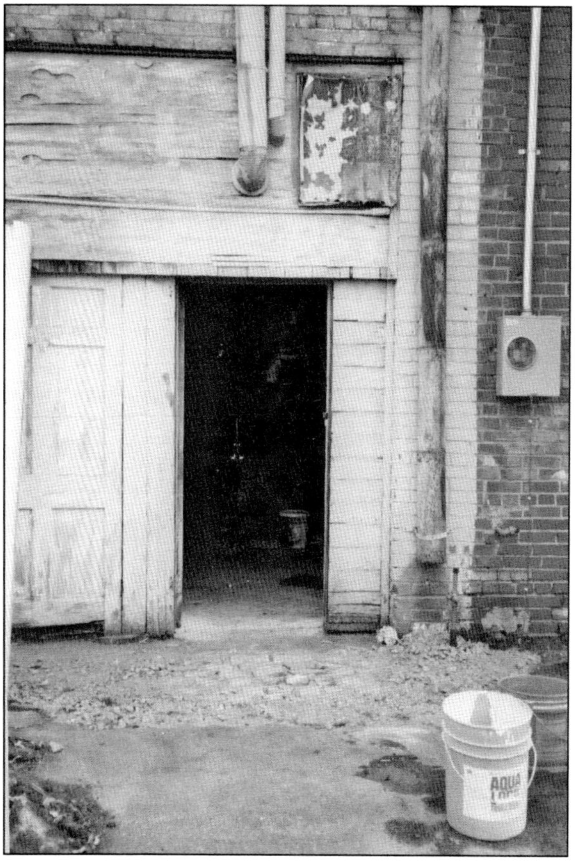

CLINGMAN CAFÉ—THEN AND NOW. When Gail and Brian McCarthy moved Highwater Clays, the rapidly growing pottery supply business they bought from Larry Bradshaw, to Roberts Street in 1994, there were only a few addresses in the district at which artists were working. Now there are a couple dozen. The 236 through 244 spaces they bought from Dave Steel were in bad shape, but one of them cried out, "I am a school," a dream the McCarthys had. The corner building, formerly Cecil's Lounge, became Clingman Café, one of the popular new eateries in the district and a meeting place for community groups. (Left, courtesy Gail McCarthy; below, photograph by Henry Neufeld.)

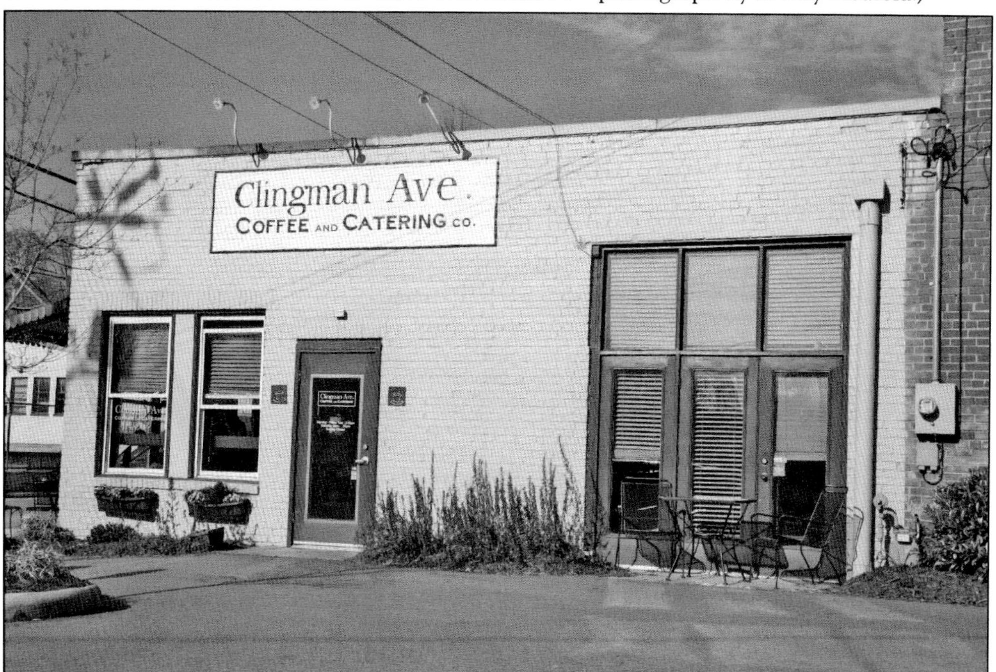

DOUGH MIXER. Gail and Brian McCarthy used this dough mixer in their first seven years of clay making in Asheville while working with Larry Bradshaw, the original owner of Highwater Clays on Thompson Street. When Bradshaw joined the Peace Corps, the McCarthys bought his business. With subsequent upgrades to mixers, they went from preparing 250 pounds in one hour to a ton in 20 minutes. They donated the dough mixer to Potters for Peace in Nicaragua, where it is used to make clay cholera filters. (Courtesy Gail McCarthy.)

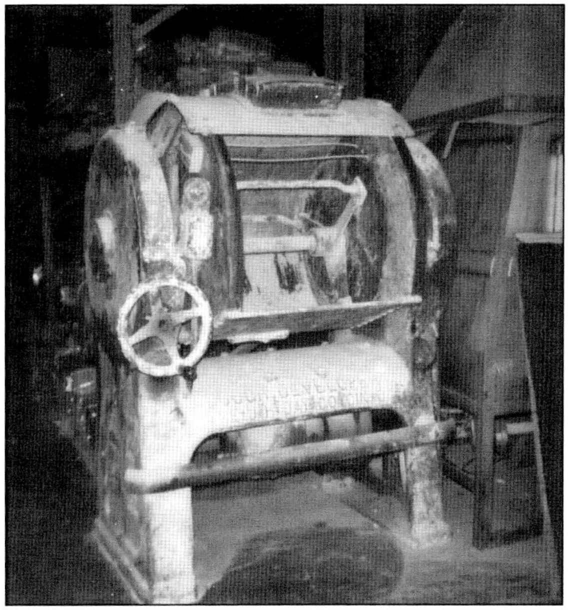

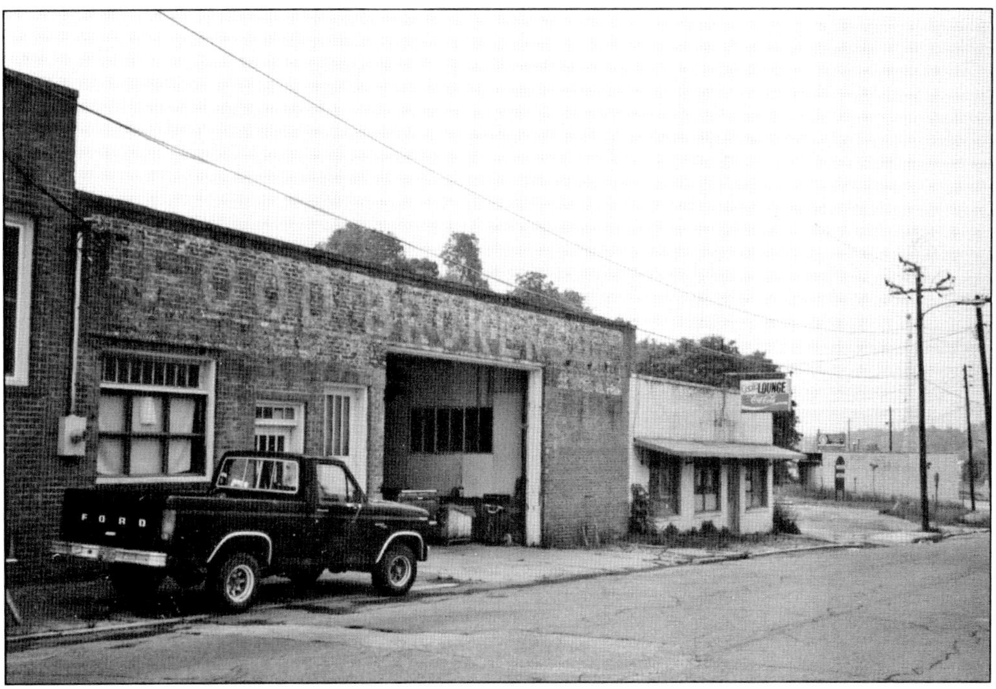

240 CLINGMAN. Clingman Avenue at the point of the Wedge now houses Clingman Café and the studio of Jonas Gerard, a nationally recognized abstract expressionist painter. This is what the buildings looked like in 1994 before their transformation. (Courtesy Highwater Clays.)

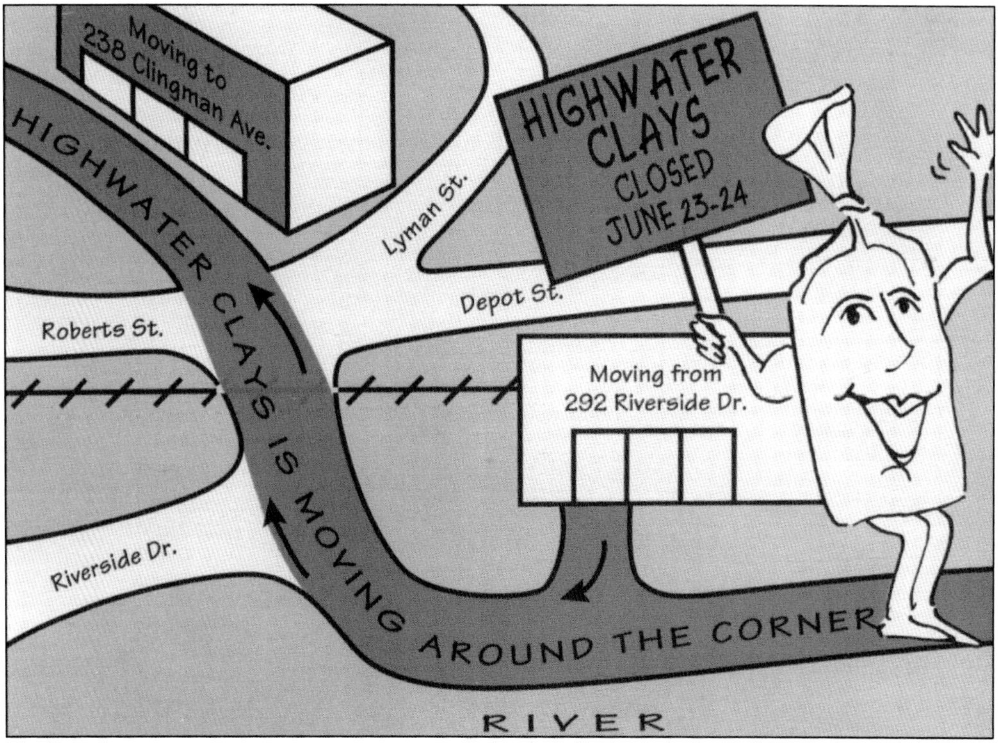

ODYSSEY CENTER FOR CERAMIC ARTS. In 2004, while continuing to expand, Highwater Clays moved its clay and potters' supply business to 600 Riverside Drive. The Clingman Avenue spaces, acquired in a previous move, were devoted to the Odyssey Center, which included offices, classrooms, and studio spaces for resident artists such as Joey Sheehan, pictured at right. In 1998, the McCarthys' son and daughter-in-law, Jonathan and Fei-Wen St. Onge, joined the firm as business and system managers. Forty-four-thousand-pound loads of clay go out on trucks to sites throughout the east. Highwater provides dozens of clay bodies, including several signature clays such as Loafer's Glory, the type that Eileen Black uses at Cotton Mill Studios (see Chapter 1). (Photograph by Henry Neufeld.)

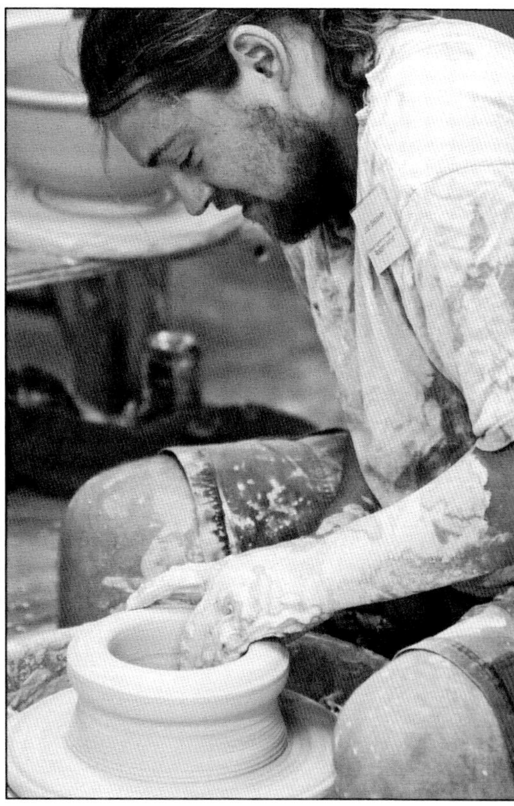

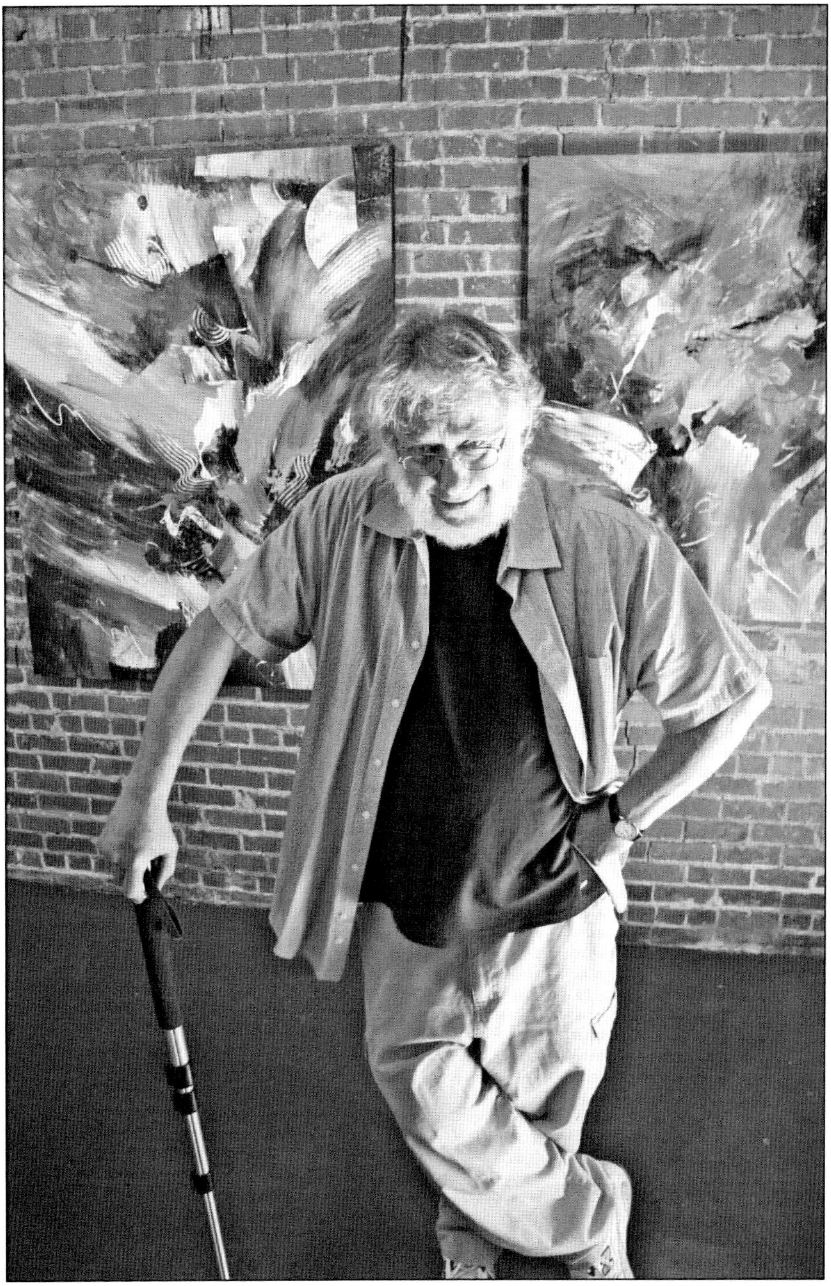

JONAS GERARD. After 40 years in Miami, Jonas Gerard, a nationally known abstract painter, opened a studio at 240 Clingman Avenue on June 9, 2007. He has appeared on ABC's *20/20*, and his work is in such collections as the Pres. Gerald Ford family and the Smithsonian Institute. He is known for his use of acrylic paints, performance painting, large expressionist canvases, colorful landscapes, and tiles. "My work," Gerard stated, "is derived from a creative process that I have been practicing for over 15 years, where the unknown and the intuitive are allowed to manifest without judgment or interpretation." Historically, Gerard represents the interest that outside established artists now have in the district, a contrast to the area's bohemian genesis only a dozen years ago. (Photograph by Henry Neufeld.)

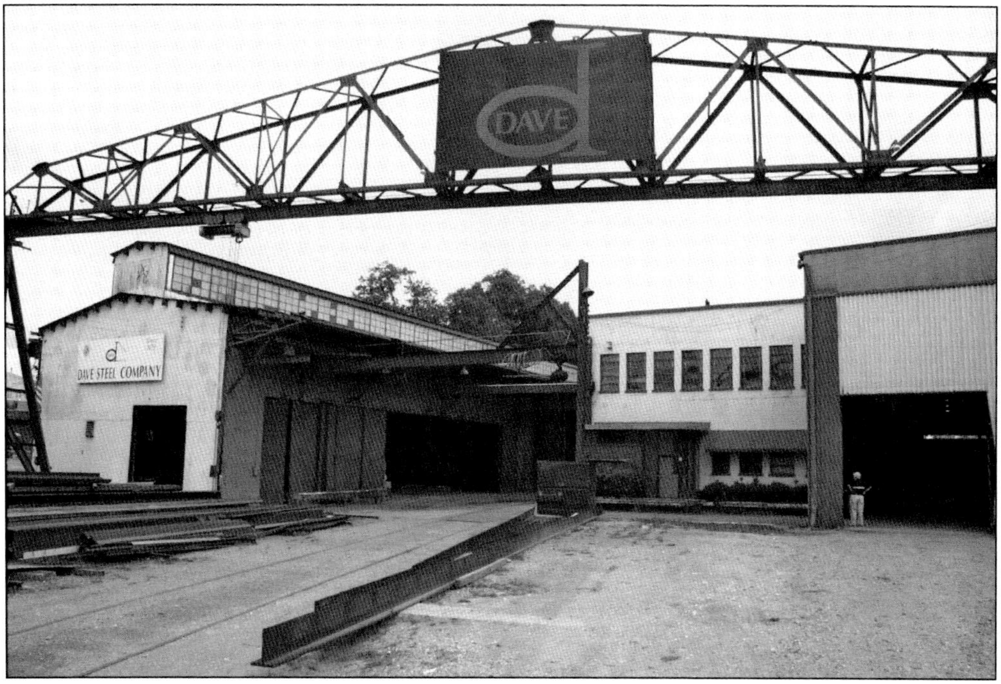

DAVE STEEL—NOW. Dave Steel, a steel manufacturer, commands a large wedge of land between Roberts and Clingman Streets, the last surviving major industry in the River Arts District. Blasting and painting of steel beams take place here before they are shipped to the fabrication plant located 1.25 miles away on Meadow Road. (Photograph by Henry Neufeld.)

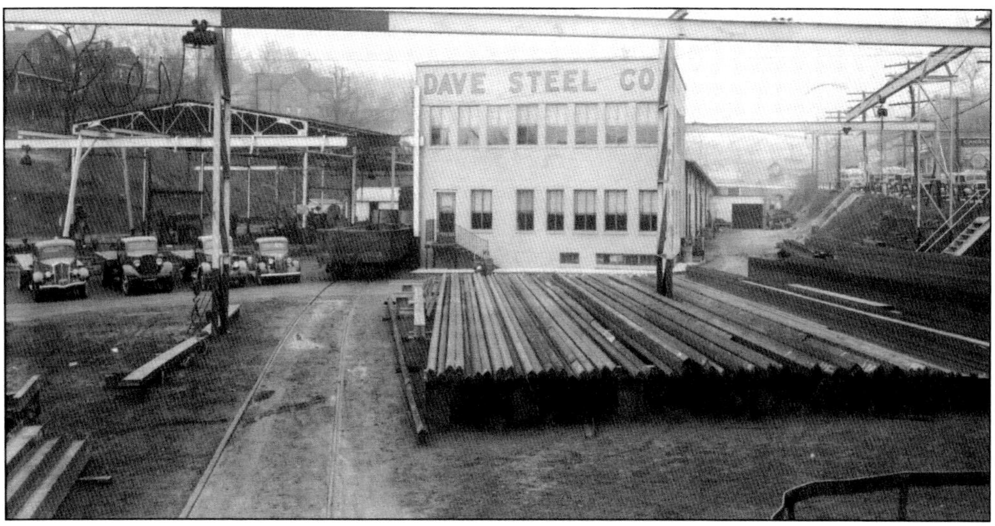

DAVE STEEL—C. 1935. Joseph Dave established his steel fabrication firm in 1929, doing many small jobs at first and running the business like a family. The company helped build the region's new factories and provided the navy with metal plates for its medium-sized landing ships during World War II. (Courtesy Jerry Dave.)

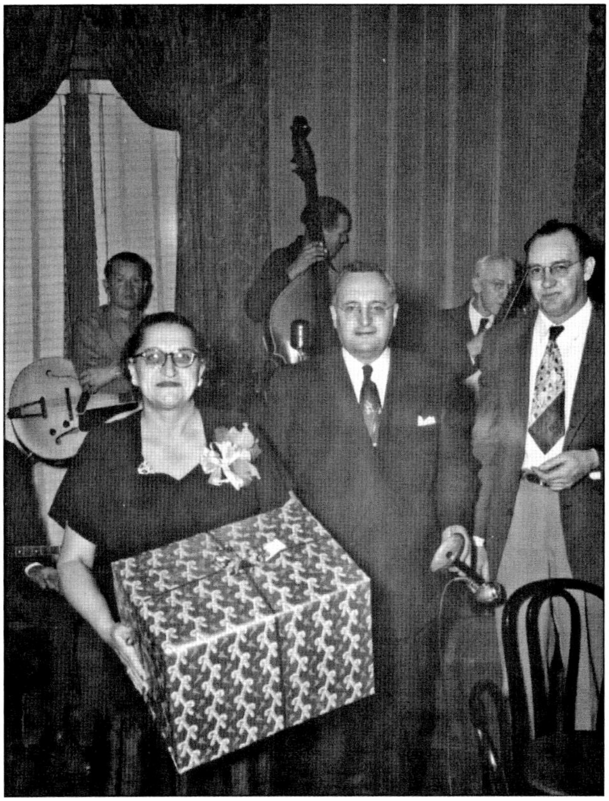

DAVE FAMILY ROOTS. Joseph Dave was born in Lithuania, where his father, Lipe Teivo, had been sent for Russian military training. The Teivos immigrated to the United States in 1905 when Joseph was a child. At Ellis Island, the family name was changed to Dave, and the Daves settled in Durham, North Carolina. In 1923, Joseph, an engineering graduate with a Southern upbringing, landed a job with Southern Steel and Cement in Asheville. It served as his stepping stone. He is pictured with his wife, Ann, at their 50th anniversary. Joseph Dave was an active member of the Jewish community as well as the community at large. (Courtesy Jerry Dave.)

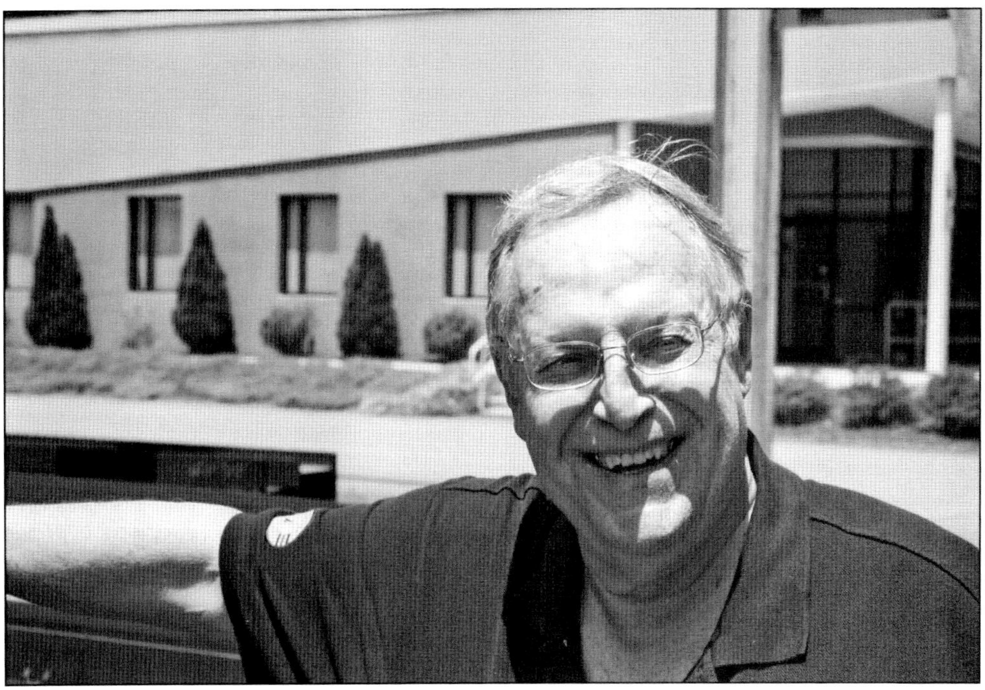

JERRY DAVE. Joseph's son, Jerry, automated the factory and built a new plant. He poses in front of the office at his Meadow Road location. (Photograph by Henry Neufeld.)

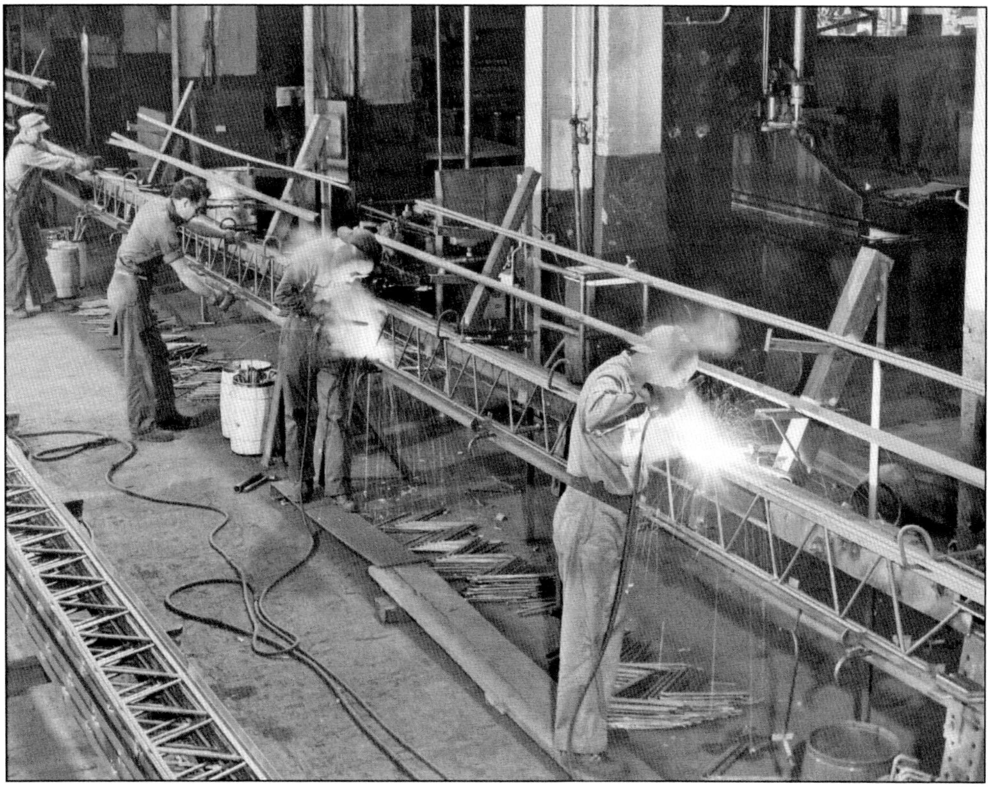

FABRICATORS FOR DAVE. In the old factory, it had taken six men to lay out the steel, cut it, and punch it. In the new one, it took one with a computer. Welding is still done by hand, however. Throughout Dave Steel's history, its special niche has been its ability to do custom jobs and respond to clients' last-minute changes. (Courtesy Jerry Dave.)

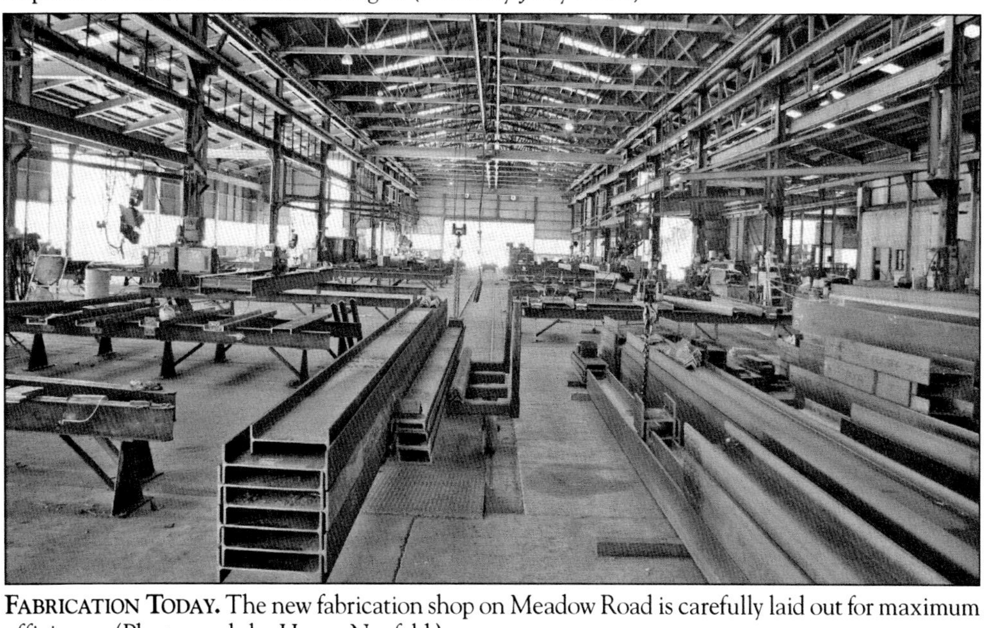

FABRICATION TODAY. The new fabrication shop on Meadow Road is carefully laid out for maximum efficiency. (Photograph by Henry Neufeld.)

Five

The Warehouse Area

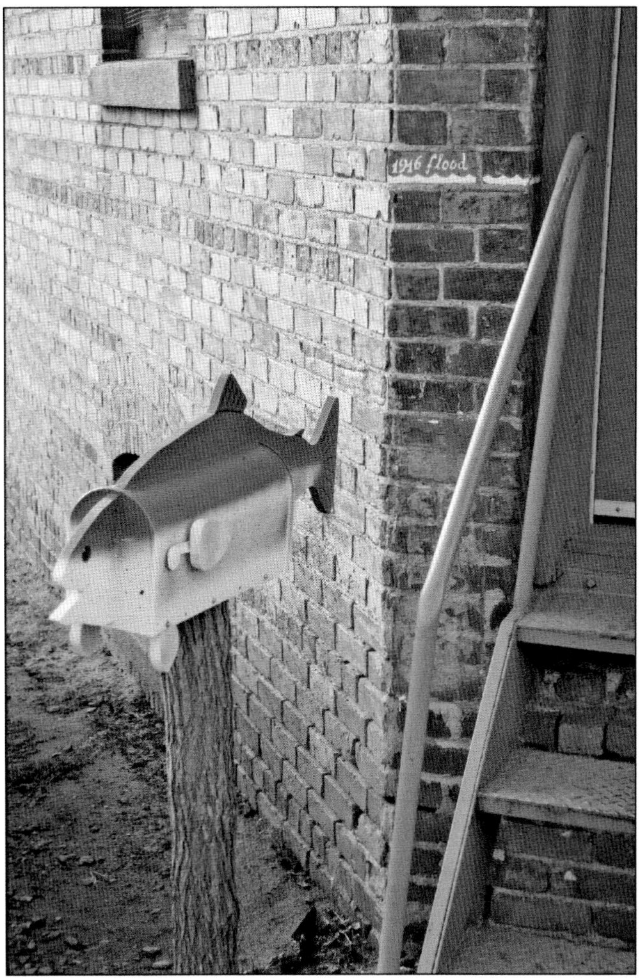

Warehouse Studios. The former building for Williams Feed Store at 170 Lyman Street, positioned between the railroad and Riverside Drive, is a landmark. In 1989, RiverLink acquired it to open its offices and establish Warehouse Studios, a home to several artists. It was the first adaptive reuse of a former industrial building for artists' studios in the river district. A wavy white line on the brick near the entrance indicates the height of the 1916 flood. Further toward the river is 12 Bones, a popular lunchtime barbecue restaurant that has occupied the former Country Kitchen restaurant, which was damaged by the flood of 2004. The restaurant serves pulled pork with a variety of sauces. Owners Tom Montgomery and his wife, Sabra Kelley, vow to serve the neighborhood and keep prices down. Lyman Street continues along the river to Riverview Station, located in the former Hans Rees Tannery. (Photograph by Henry Neufeld.)

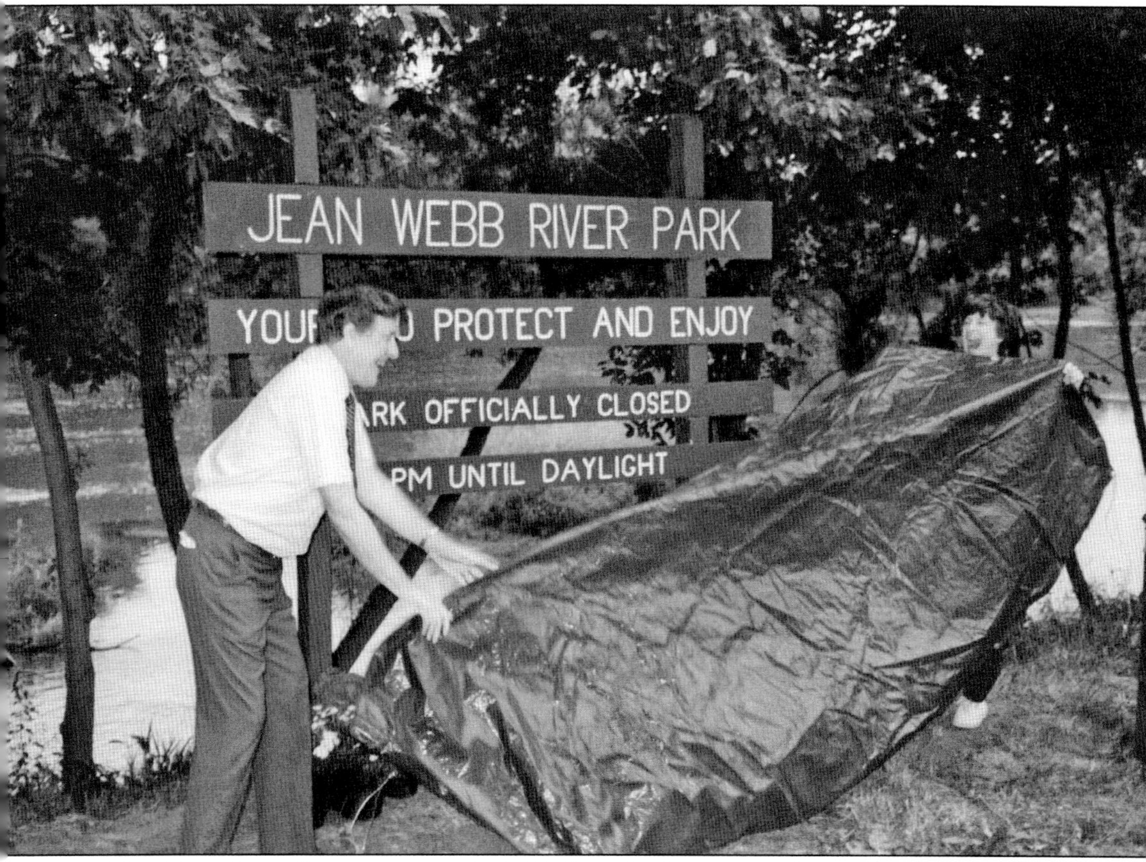

The RiverLink Phenomenon. In 1988, RiverLink, a nonprofit agency that grew out of a committee for Asheville's 2010 plan, helped open Jean Webb Park near the West Asheville Bridge. R. Curtis Ratcliff, Buncombe County chair of commissioners, and Jean Webb, RiverLink board member, unveil the sign. RiverLink's mission was "to address water quality concerns throughout the French Broad River basin, expand public opportunities for access and recreation, and spearhead the economic revitalization of Asheville's dilapidated riverfront district." On October 1, 1992, RiverLink purchased what is now Warehouse Studios with a $36,000 grant from the Janirve Foundation and $64,000 from Public Interest Projects, North Carolina. The date is a major turning point in river district history. RiverLink established its offices in the building and became an early progenitor of the arts community in the district. During the decades before 1987, riverside property had been the location of industries, garbage dumps, and slaughterhouses, each of which polluted the river. In 1923, the J. A. Baker Packing Company erected a plant to kill 500 hogs a day and 250 head of cattle a week on Riverside Drive between the Southern Freight Depot and the French Broad River. Baker, the company president, chose Asheville over Greenville because of its proximity to a stock-raising district and the financial and moral support it received from Asheville businessmen. (Courtesy RiverLink.)

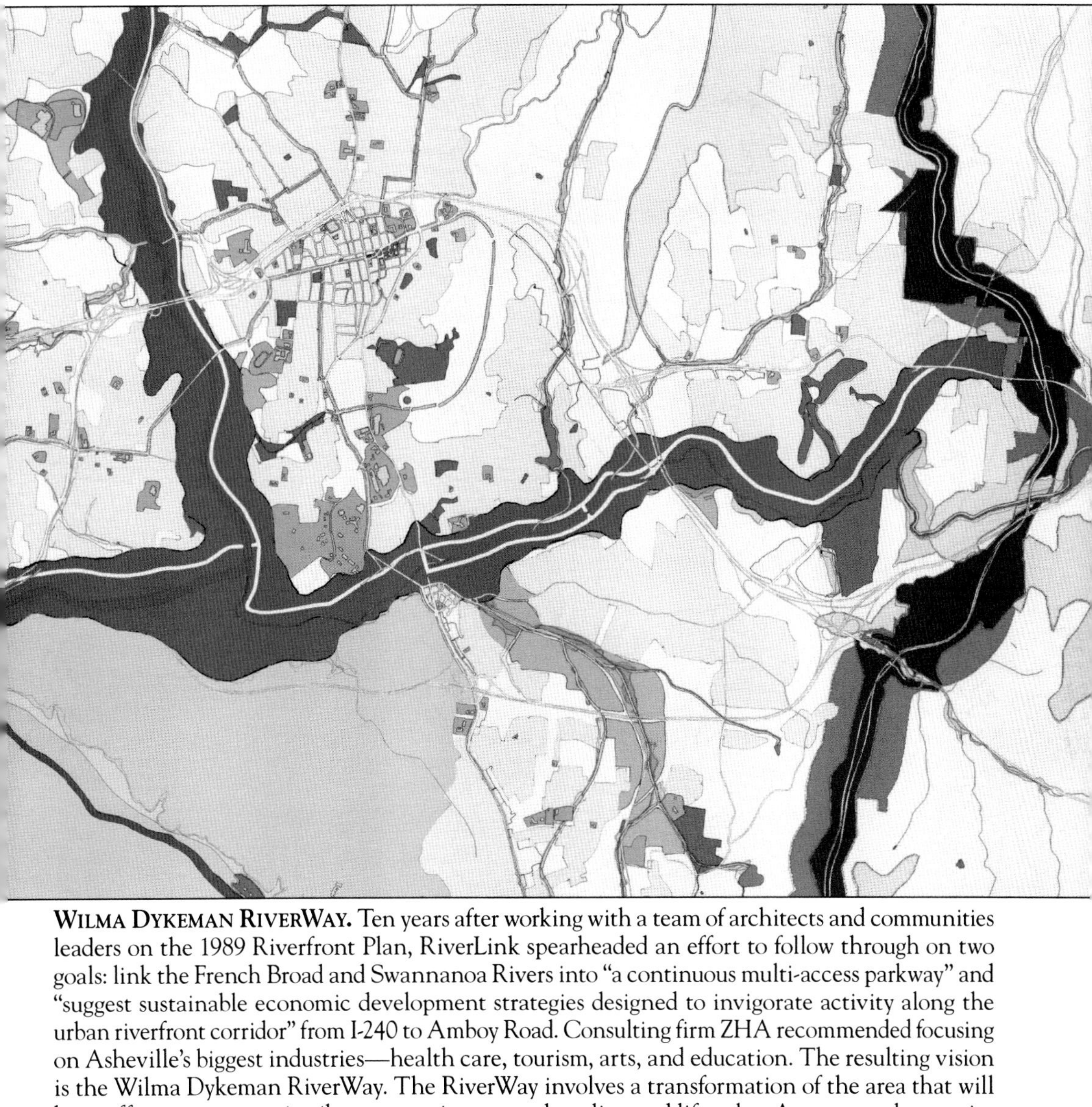

Wilma Dykeman RiverWay. Ten years after working with a team of architects and communities leaders on the 1989 Riverfront Plan, RiverLink spearheaded an effort to follow through on two goals: link the French Broad and Swannanoa Rivers into "a continuous multi-access parkway" and "suggest sustainable economic development strategies designed to invigorate activity along the urban riverfront corridor" from I-240 to Amboy Road. Consulting firm ZHA recommended focusing on Asheville's biggest industries—health care, tourism, arts, and education. The resulting vision is the Wilma Dykeman RiverWay. The RiverWay involves a transformation of the area that will have effects on economic vibrancy, environmental quality, and lifestyles. A concern about noise pollution and eyesores has inadvertently led to clashes with class-sensitive people about certain projects—such as the removal of the Asheville Speedway for Carrier Park (see Chapter 10); the current effort to silence the train whistle as trains pass through; and the interest in redeveloping the lot on which Tommy Tuten's and Johnny Penland's Auction House sits at 155 Craven Street. RiverLink is also actively involved in recreation and education. The executive director has hired a full-time riverkeeper and education coordinator. (Courtesy RiverLink.)

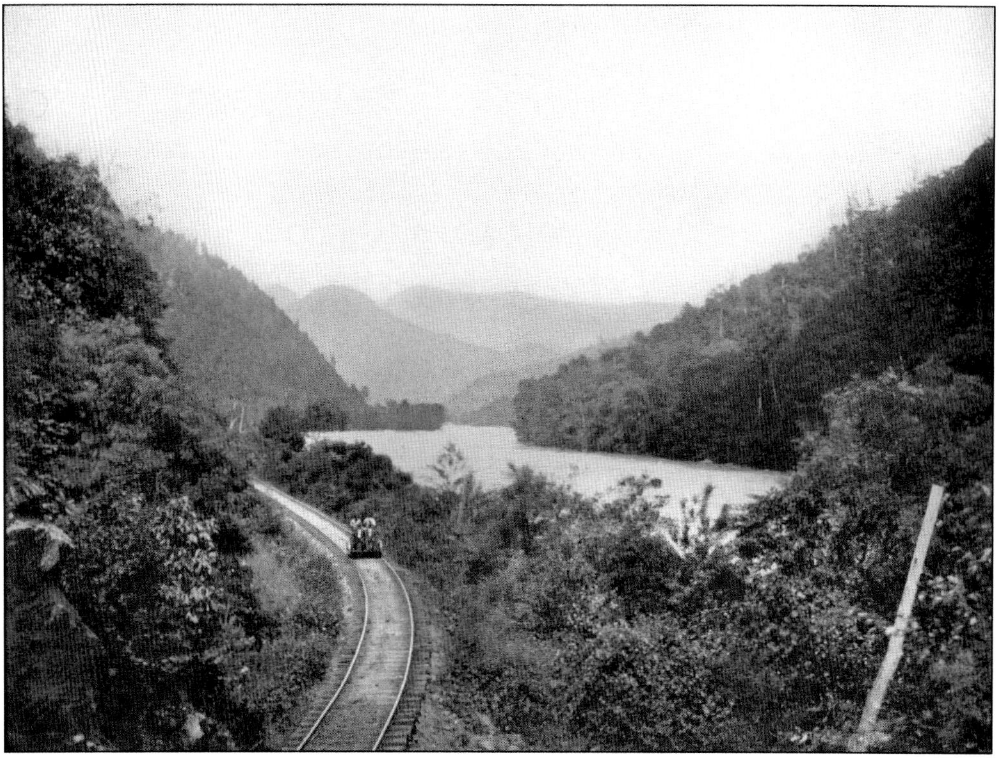

Scenic Views. Early-20th-century booklets promoted the beauty of the river—above, "The Southern Railway Skirting the French Broad River" from "With Pen & Camera thro' the 'Land of the Sky'" (1900); below, "Junction of the Swannanoa and French Broad" from "Rogers' Asheville" (1899).

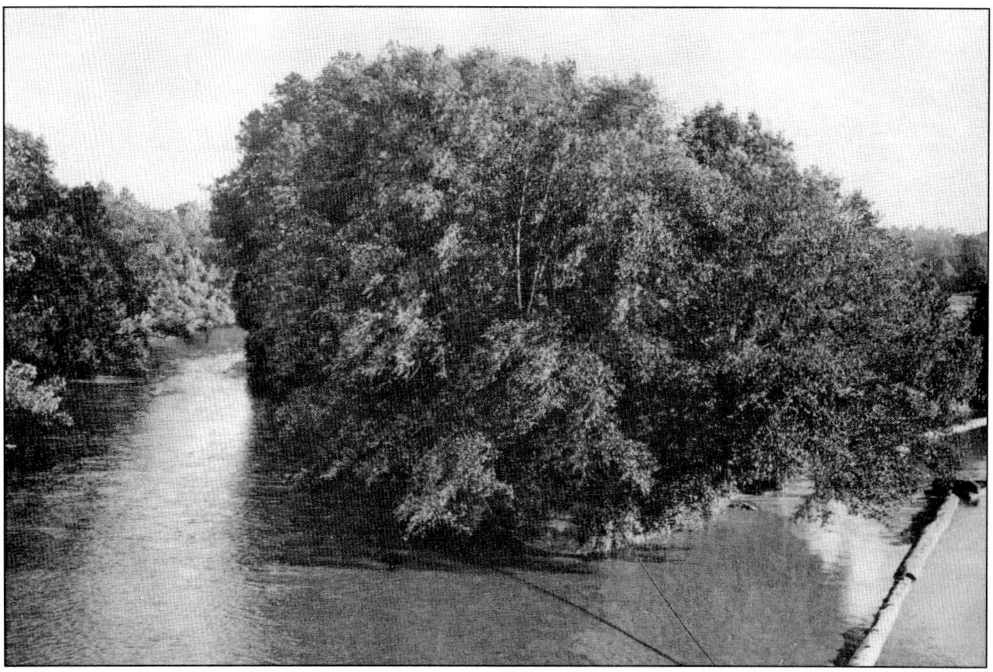

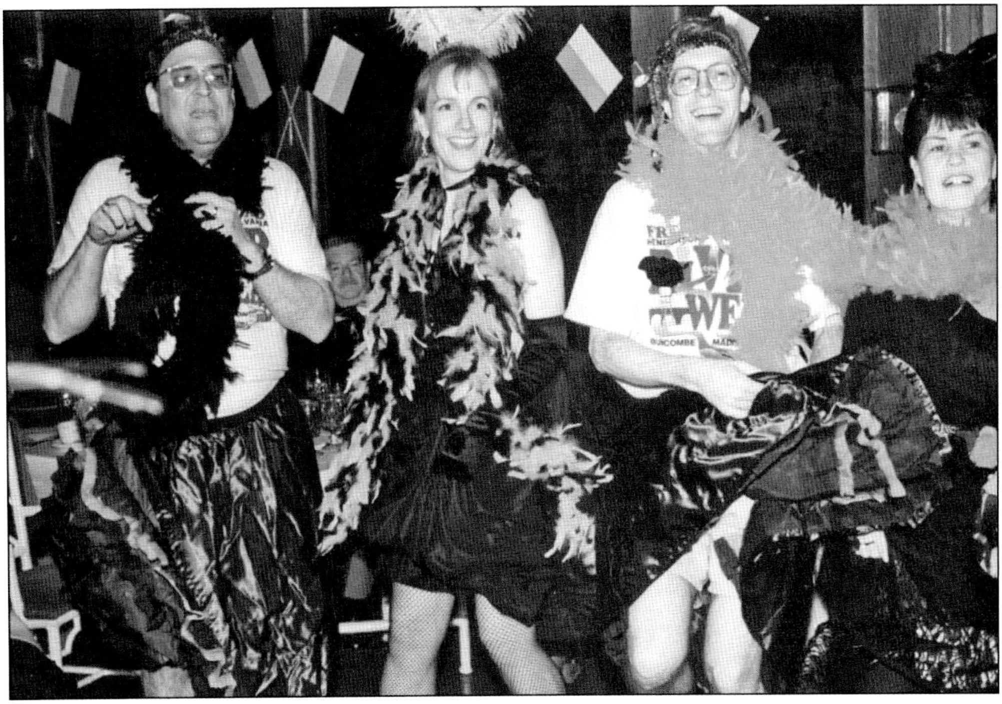

FRENCH BROADS. RiverLink made use of the fun associated with the river's name at the 1997 fund-raiser entitled "Fall in Love with the French Broad Cabaret." Bedecked partygoers of both sexes and a soft sculpture (right) paid homage. The river's name had derived from traders who had pushed past the Broad River to a similarly wide one in what had been French territory. (Courtesy RiverLink.)

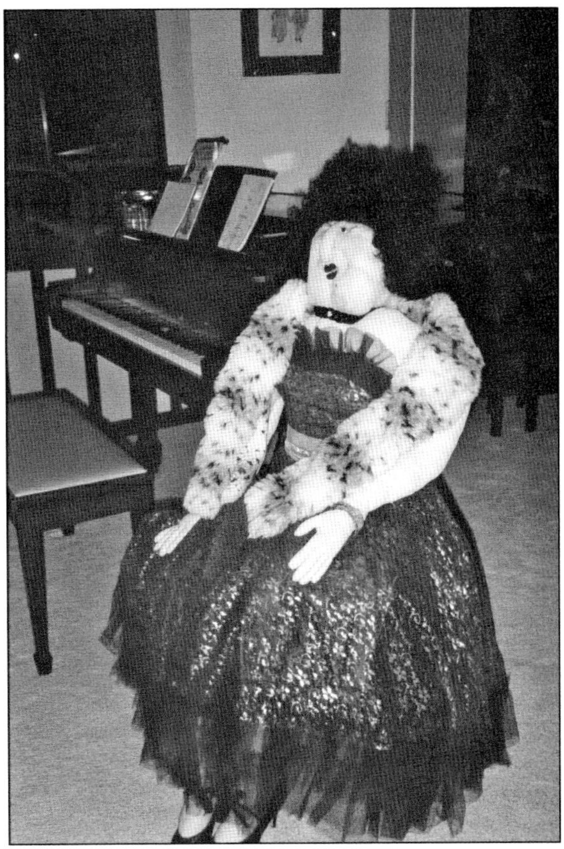

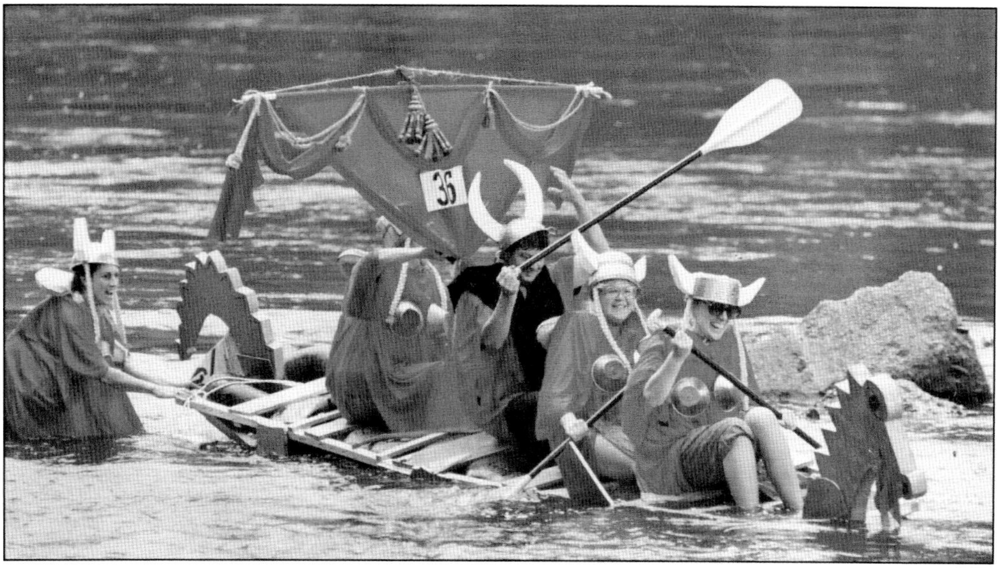

VIKING CREW. The Asheville Community Theatre technical crew took on water when they got stuck on the rocks during RiverLink's "Anything that Floats" race in September 1992. From left to right are Sara LeDonne, Maggie Hagen, Glenn Somers, Barb Schweizer, and Susan Maley. (Courtesy Asheville *Citizen-Times*.)

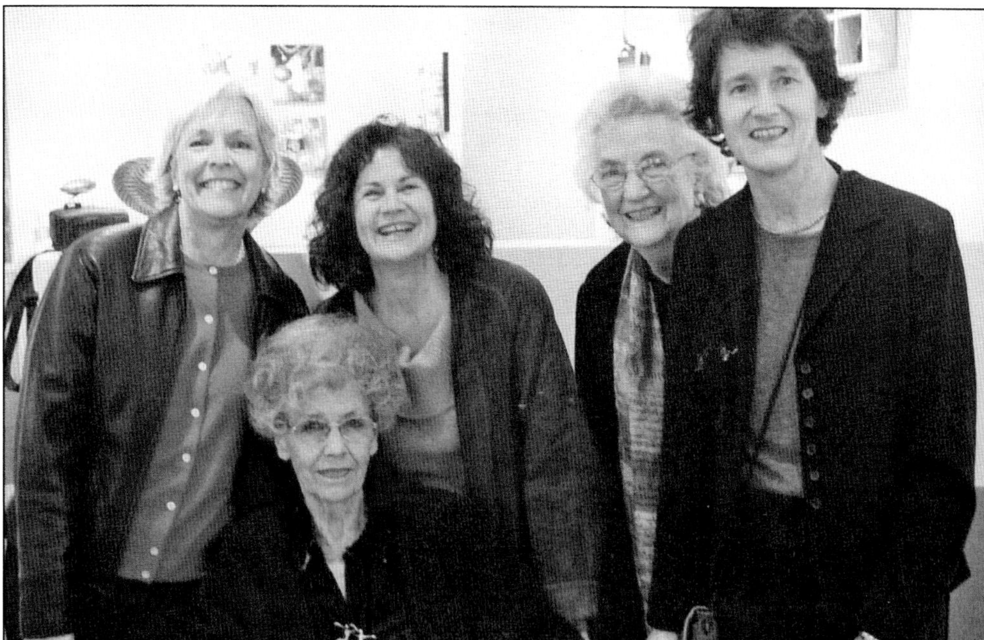

THE WAREHOUSE FIVE. Painter Barbara Fisher (right) displays this photograph on the wall of her studio as a reminder of the community formed with some of the early artists in Warehouse Studios. The other four are, from left to right, Monika Teal, Marie Hudson, Betty Clark, and Charlie Griffin. Fisher came to the district to have uninterrupted creative time as well as interactions with other artists. The current growing tourist traffic increases a certain kind of sales. Fisher also does some business through galleries. She participates in the River District Artists' now semi-annual Studio Stroll, paying a percentage to the group, of which she is a member. (Courtesy Barbara Fisher.)

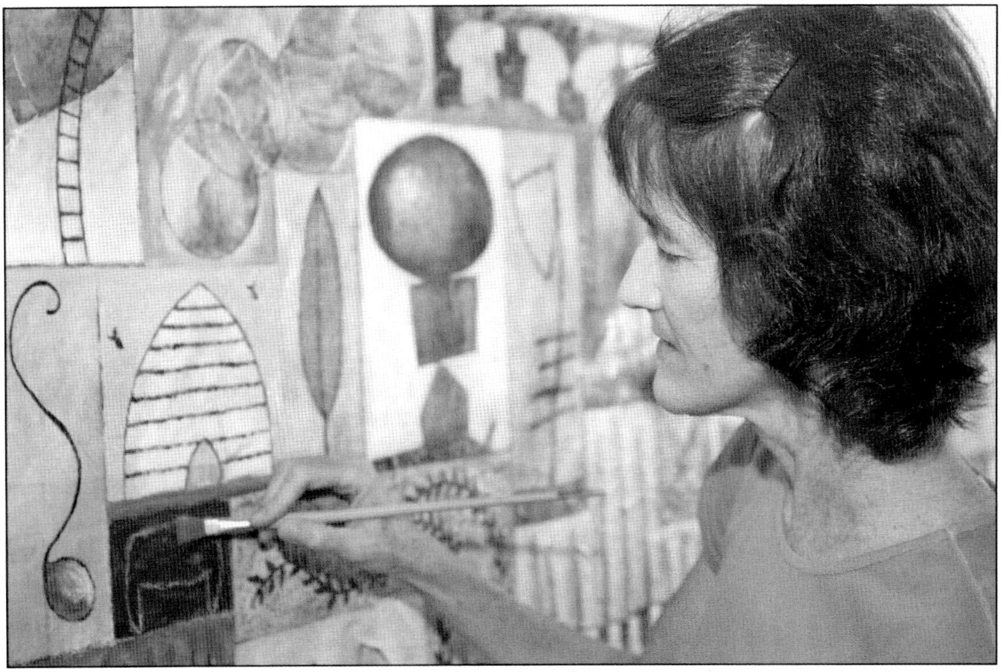

ICONIC PAINTING. Barbara Fisher found that when she came to the river district, her palette brightened and she began incorporating local iconic imagery. *Train of Thought* is the title of the recent oil by Fisher below. (Courtesy Barbara Fisher.)

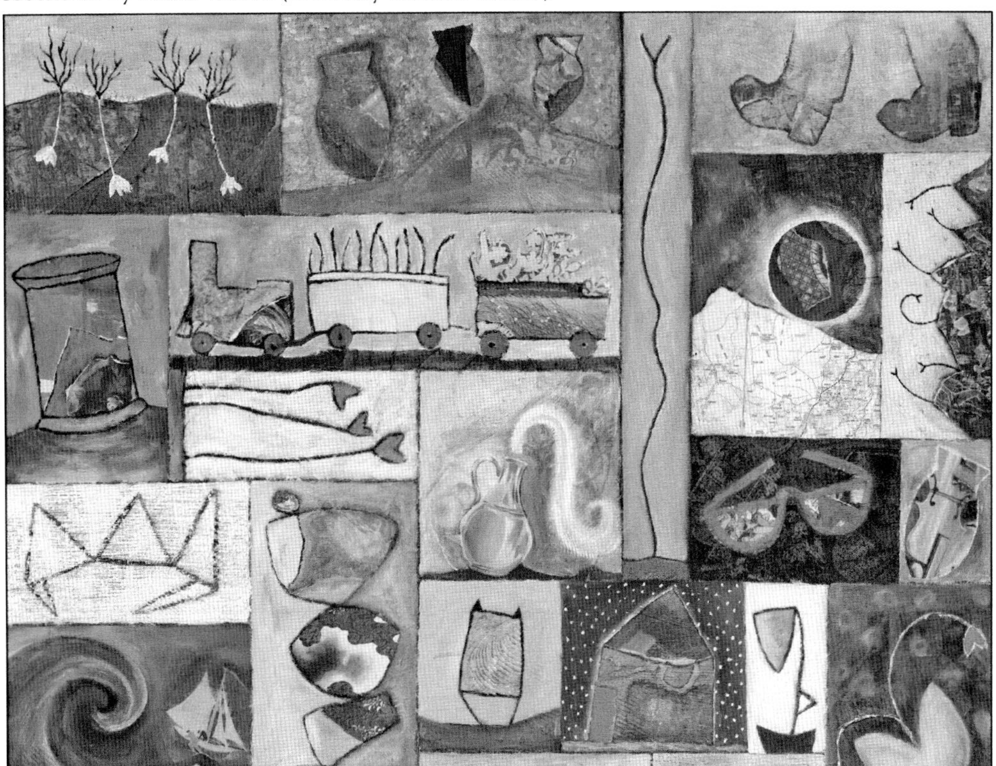

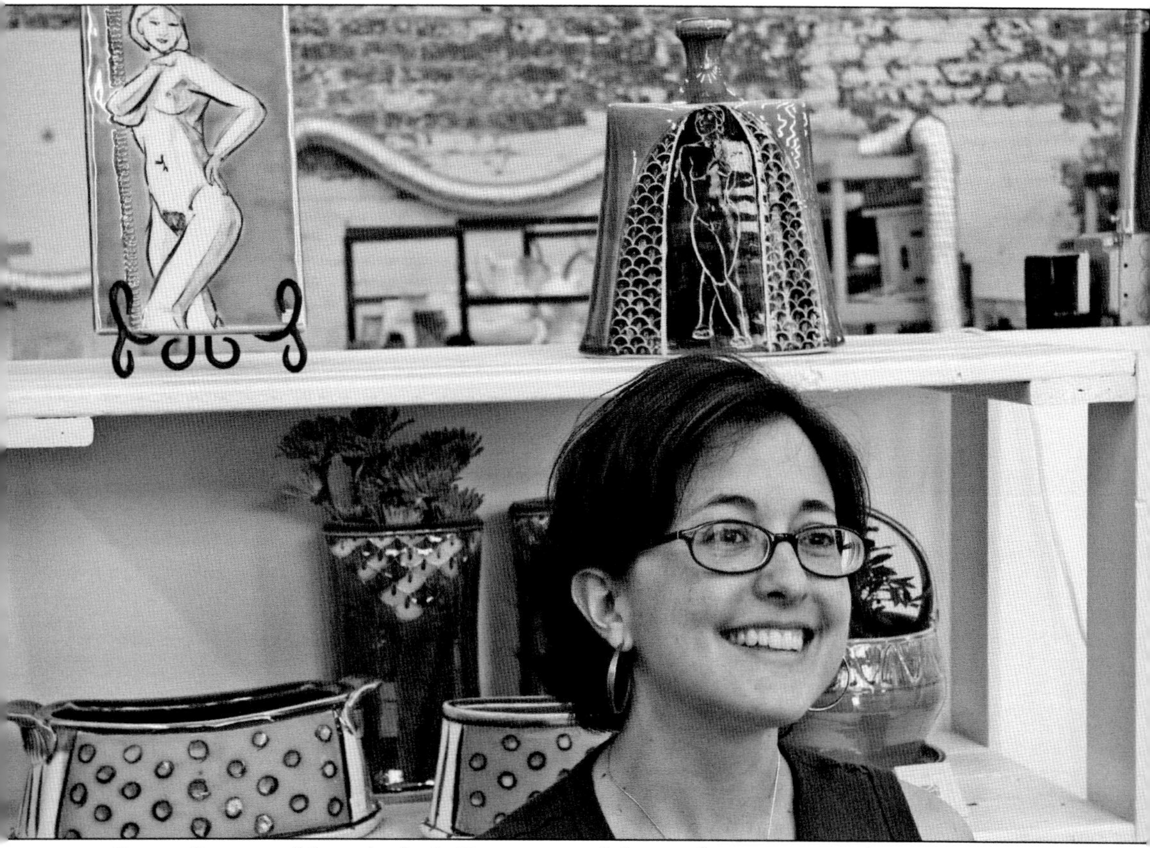

CURVE STUDIOS. Maria Andrade Troya is one of about a dozen artists working in Curve Studios. Troya graduated from UNC–Asheville with a bachelor's degree in fine arts, was a teaching assistant at the Odyssey Center for the Ceramic Arts, and served as secretary for River District Artists in 2006. In her work, she is inspired by the human figure and combines her printmaking skills with her pottery. (Photograph by Henry Neufeld.)

Six

The Tannery Area

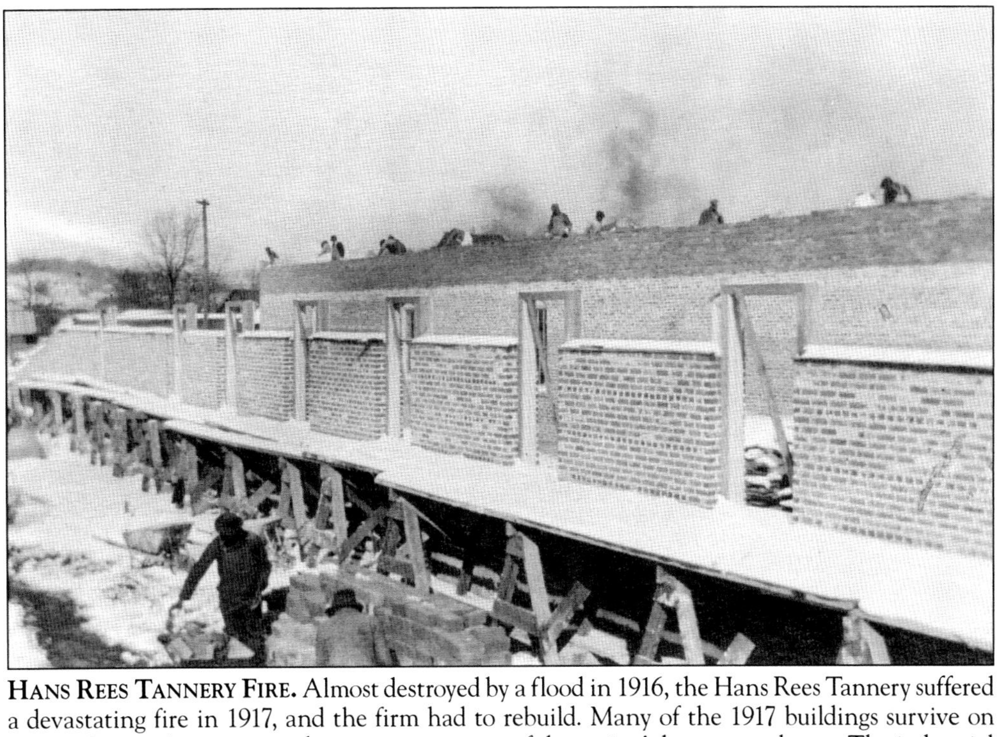

Hans Rees Tannery Fire. Almost destroyed by a flood in 1916, the Hans Rees Tannery suffered a devastating fire in 1917, and the firm had to rebuild. Many of the 1917 buildings survive on Lyman Street. At one time, the tannery was one of the region's largest employers. The industrial revolution in America hinged on leather belting, the largest manufacturer of which set up shop in Asheville in 1898. Having invented the process by which cowhides could be cured, tanned, and finished to turn high-powered transmissions, Hans Rees and Sons sought browner pastures—namely the chestnut oak stands of Western North Carolina. The company built 30 buildings on 22 acres between the French Broad River and the Southern Railway, and came to take in 30,000 pounds of cattle hide each day. "There is surrounding Asheville an almost inexhaustible supply of bark," a 1912 promotion stated, "and the water is of the purest, two things necessary to the production of the best leather." (Courtesy North Carolina Collection, Pack Memorial Library.)

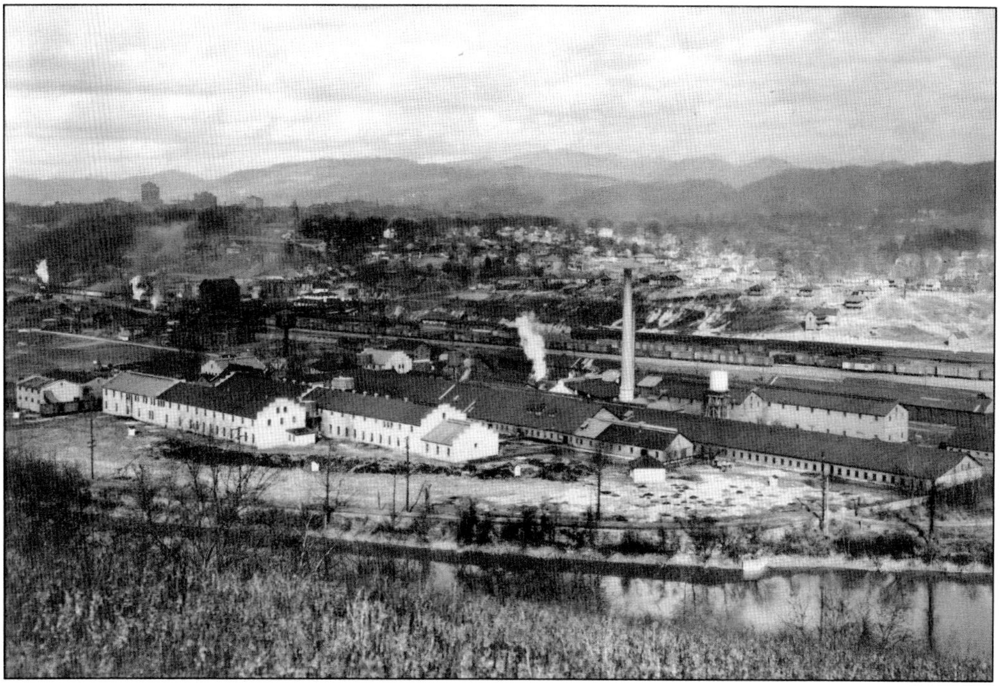

THE TANNERY—THEN AND NOW. Charles Waddell documented the region's industries in his 1929 publication *Asheville Industrial Data*, in which the above photograph appeared. The city has grown up, and the tannery had declined. Despite the industry's focus on soles and saddles in the late 1940s, the introduction of composition belting spelled the end, and the tannery buildings, recognizable by their saw-tooth roofs, have found different uses. (Below, photograph by Henry Neufeld.)

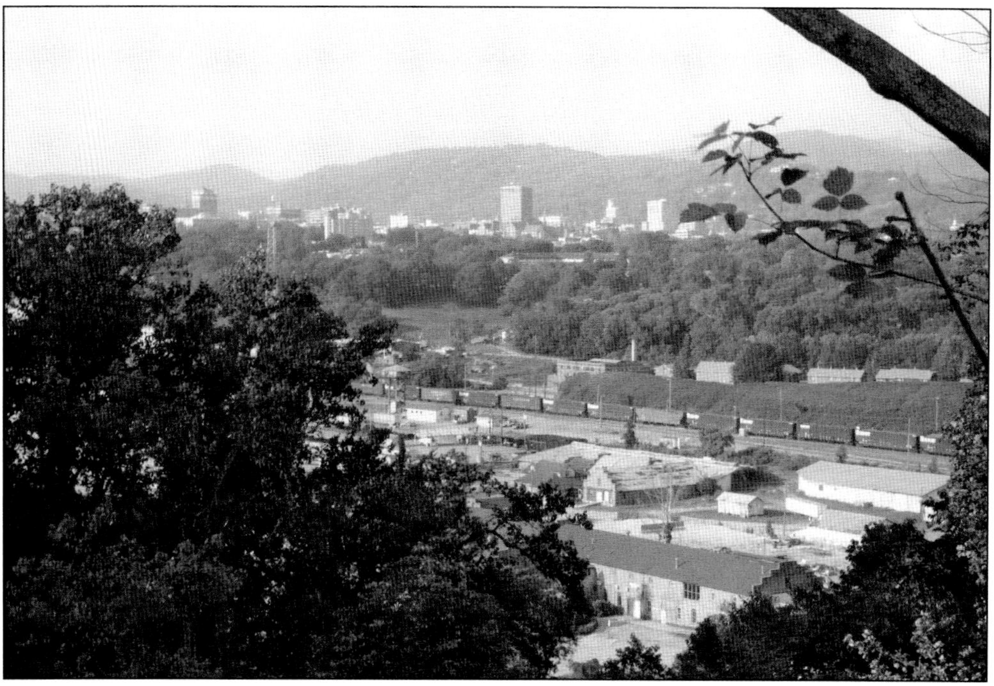

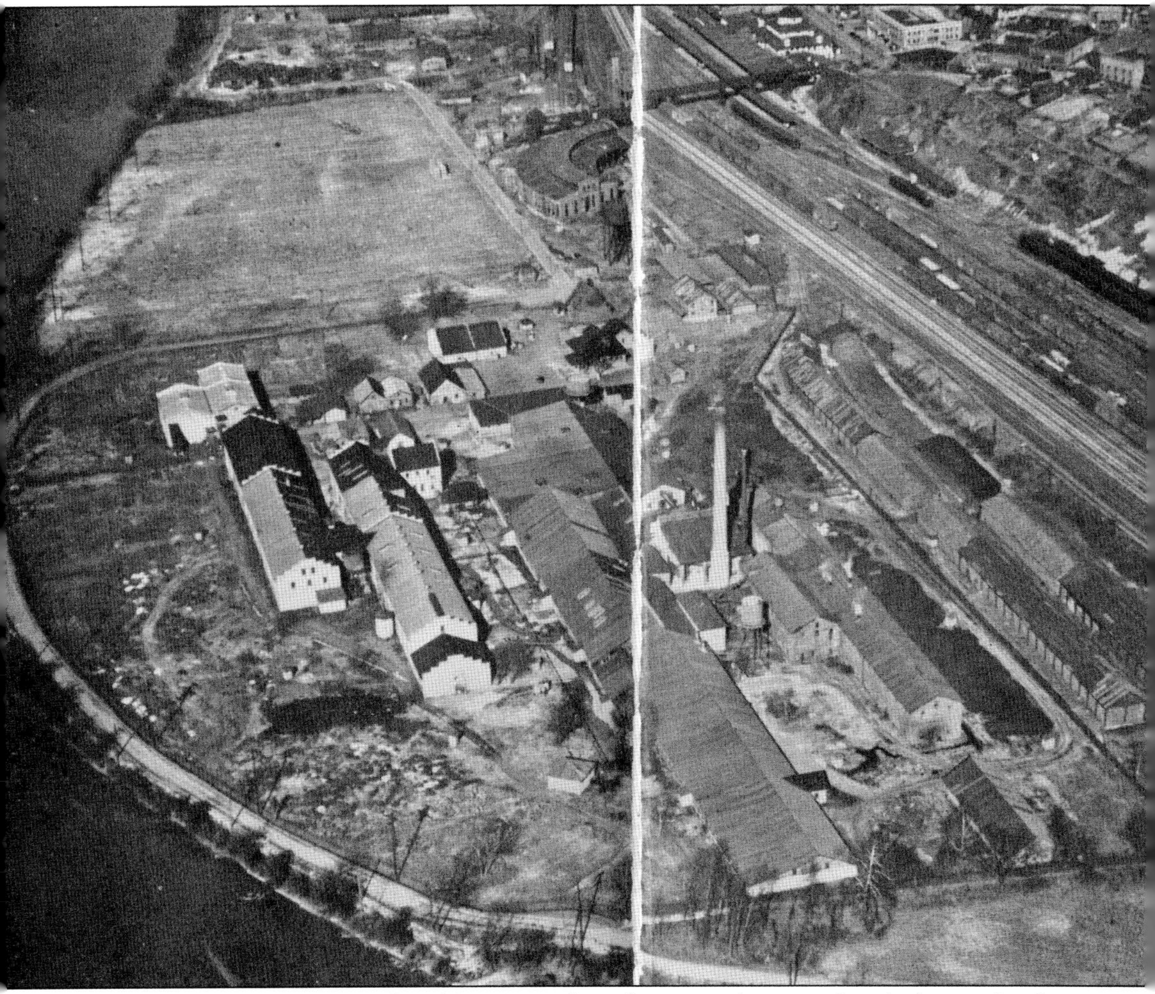

TANNERY HISTORY. Hans Rees hired 3,000 people and supported many others by buying local chestnut oak bark and chestnut wood (the Biltmore Estate was one of the suppliers, and George Vanderbilt was a friend of Hans's son, Arthur). Tanning was neither a pretty nor an easy job. First a tanner had to get the flesh, hair, and outer skin off hides with limewater and a knife. Then the hides were put into a succession of vats (Hans Rees had 300) filled with ooze of increasing levels of tannic acidity. Chestnut oak bark provided the liquor through an extraction of its tannin. Removed from the vats after two weeks, the hides were placed between layers of bark for several months. A currier finished the job by softening, shaving, scouring, lubricating, drying, blacking, rubbing, and dyeing the hides. The hides came mostly from Chicago, but there was at least one local supplier, Sigfred Sternberg, owner of Consolidated Hide and Metal Company on Depot Street. Later Sigfred passed his business to his son, Joseph. (Photograph from *Leadership for a Century: The Story of Hans Rees' Sons, 1846–1946.*)

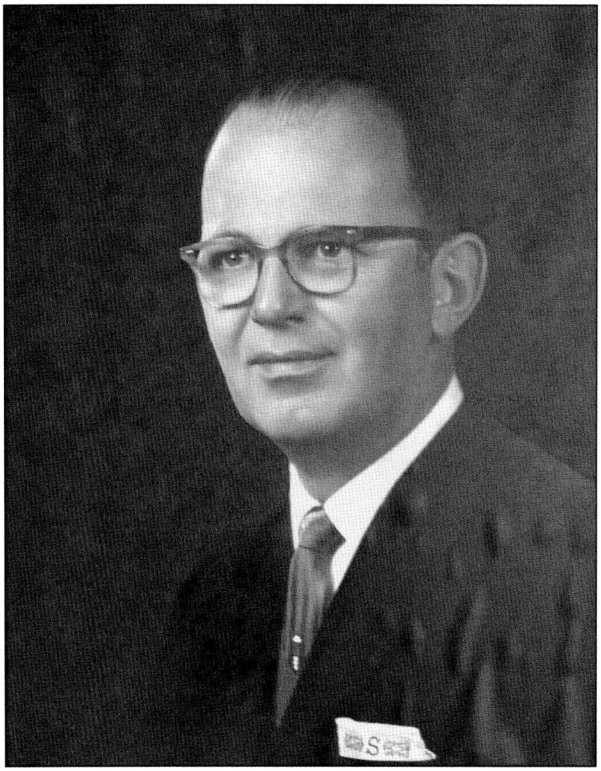

JOSEPH STERNBERG. "My dad," wrote Jerry Sternberg about his father, Joseph, in his *Mountain Xpress* column "The Gospel According to Jerry," "salted and cured the hides in brine in the basement of [his] Depot Street building. . . . After several weeks, they were shipped to the tanneries." Accompanying a deliveryman to Hans Rees Tannery one day, young Jerry once "made the mistake of wandering into one of the huge, forbidding tanning rooms. The hides were placed in big baskets and dipped in a tannic-acid solution under constant agitation," he said. "Much of the machinery was wooden, because the tannic acid corroded metal. The eerie screech of wood on wood, the chemical haze and the bizarre stench absolutely terrified me." (Courtesy Jerry Sternberg.)

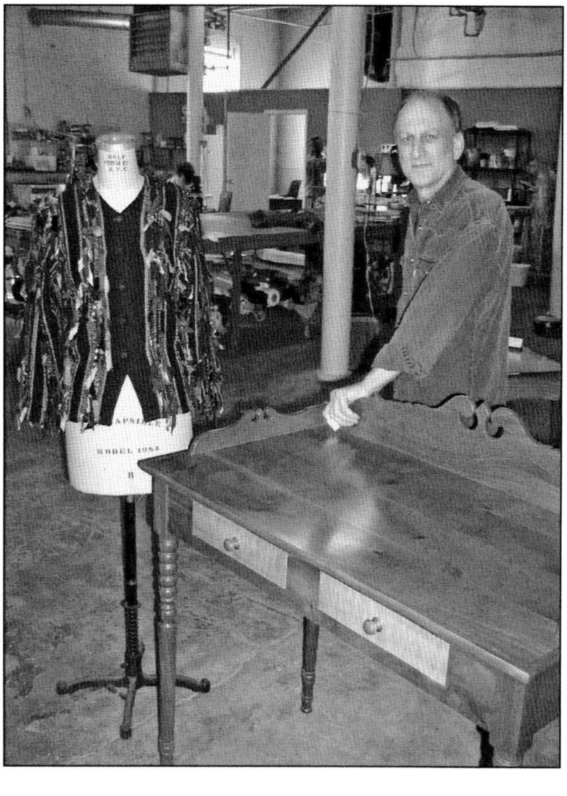

FINE CRAFTS. Helaine Greene purchased the tannery buildings in 1996 with the intention of "building a creative community of artistic people." The place is now called Riverview Station and is at the southern end of the river stroll. Between the large work spaces of fine woodworker and antique restorer Marc Mandon (pictured) and innovative tailor Mo is their gallery, Avaloo. Mo's jackets and separates—"fusions of new and reclaimed materials"—sell at John Cram's Bellagio in Biltmore. (Photograph by Rob Neufeld.)

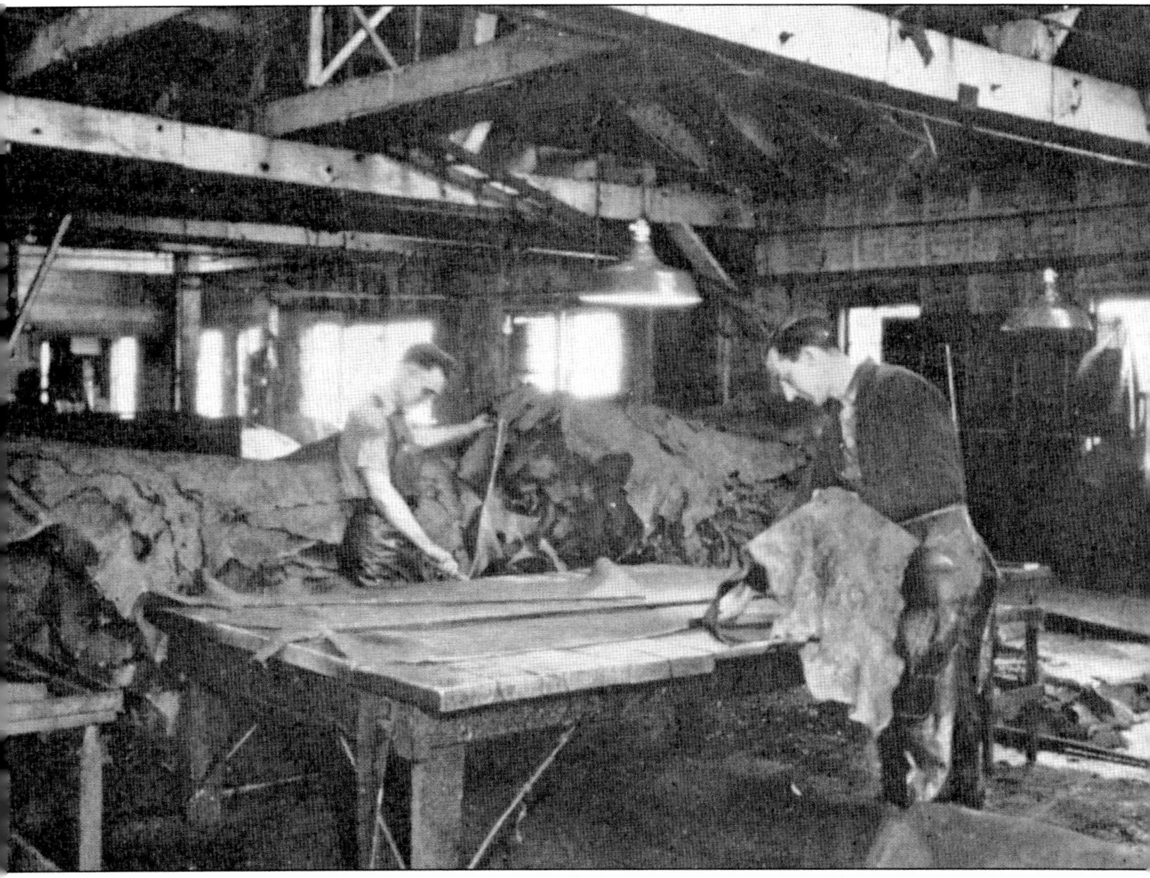

A TANNERY LOVE STORY. A WPA interview tells how tannery worker Glenn Dayton eloped with Elizabeth Bruce, his high school sweetheart. Elizabeth was an orphan, according to her daughter, Irma Dayton Rudisill of Candler. When Elizabeth was three, a train hit her father, Elvin, a driver for the Southern Coal Company, as it passed the Asheville Cotton Mill. When she was nine, her mother, Emma Farlow Bruce, died of pneumonia. Elizabeth went to live with her grandfather Nathan, a cotton mill worker, and her grandmother Pallie Farlow, the unofficial watchwoman of the West End. "I can see her now with that little hair in a bun and her apron on and a sweater," Rudisall said. "I actually have in my bedroom the little green chair that she used to sit in and watch out the window at what went on up and down Hall Street." Hall Street used to exist where the pedestrian bridge crosses I-240 from West End to Hillcrest. Grandpa Farlow had the first car in the community and gave people rides. Glenn's father, barber John Dayton, was well off. Family members on both sides had lived in the neighborhood for at least a couple of generations, and when deaths set children adrift, there were a number of households ready to embrace them. Grandma Farlow had not allowed Elizabeth to date. To see Glenn, Elizabeth had to pretend to be going to the Haywood Street Methodist Church. When Glenn got a job in the tannery—leaving high school to make $9 an hour—he and Elizabeth hightailed it to Greenville, South Carolina, to get married on June 8, 1938. Factory jobs proved to be stepping-stones to better opportunities during the Depression. Glenn, who had a rheumatic heart, went on to work for 30 years for Pearlman's Furniture. He and Elizabeth moved with his parents to Rumbough Place in Malvern Hills, where Irma grew up. (Photograph from *Leadership for a Century: The Story of Hans Rees' Sons, 1846–1946*.)

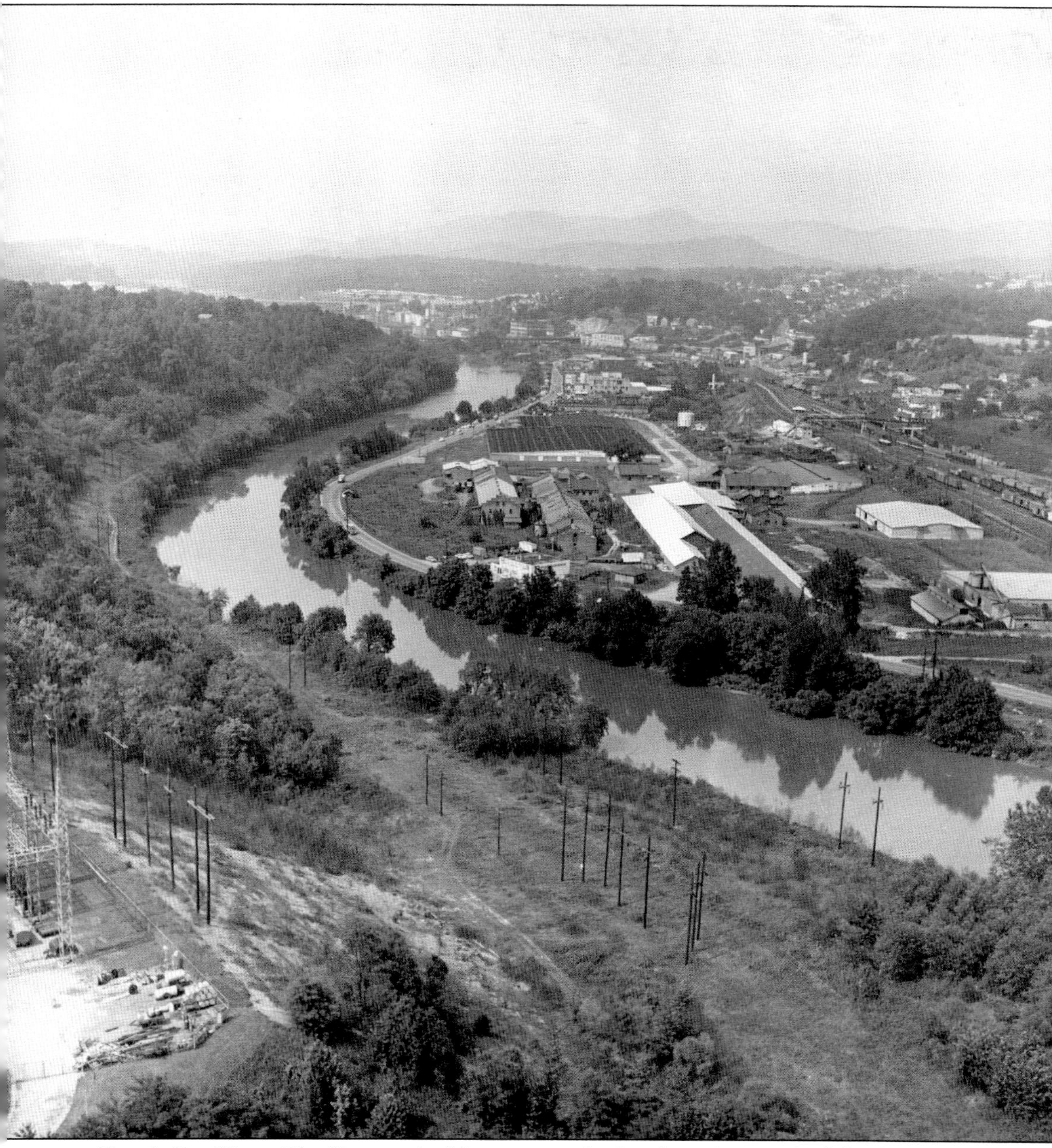

BIRD'S-EYE VIEW. The Tannery buildings are in the bend on the east (right) side. Just above it, cars were using the riverside to park. This picture makes clear the suitability of the site for agriculture. (Courtesy North Carolina Collection, Pack Memorial Library.)

Seven

THE DEPOT AREA

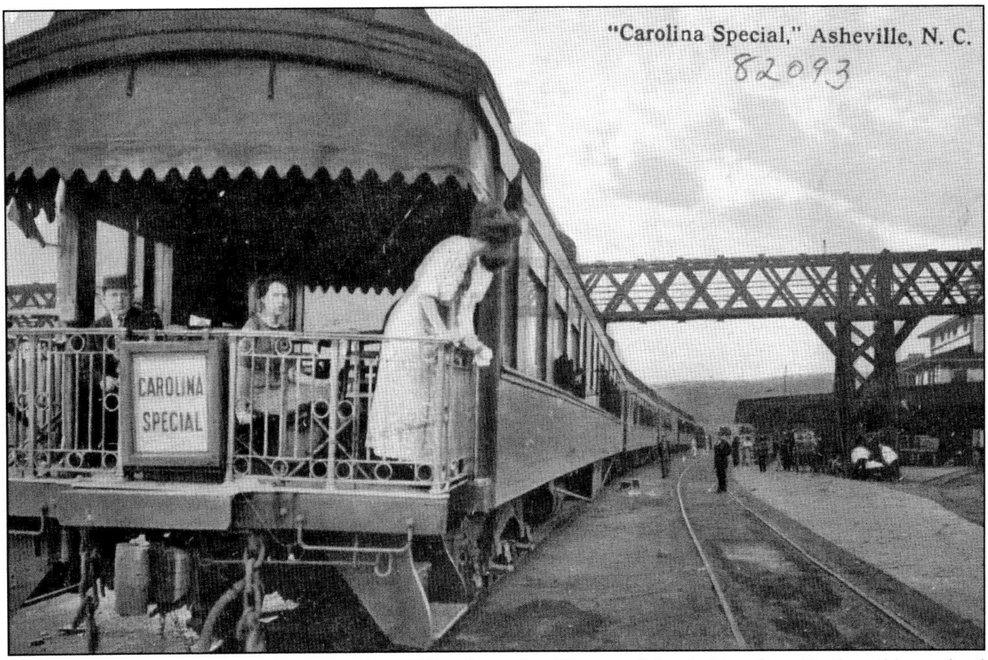

THE TRAIN COMES TO ASHEVILLE. In 1879, when the Western North Carolina Railroad breached the Blue Ridge Mountains in Black Mountain, it was long overdue. The Civil War, post-war corruption, and the monumentality of the task had stalled previous efforts. Convict labor, allowed by North Carolina for the first time, made the project more economically feasible, but still, there were cost overruns and many deaths. The railroad took the riverside route through Asheville following the path of the Buncombe County turnpike, along which stock drives had proceeded. The Southern Railroad Passenger Station became the center of activity, with hotels and nightclubs for workers and patrons separated by race cropping up. In 1894, the Southern Railway took over the railroad. There were routes to Spartanburg, Salisbury, Knoxville, and Murphy. The one that traveled from Knoxville through Paint Rock and along the French Broad River was called "The Carolina Special." Railroad work was a dangerous occupation. Local lore is full of stories of collisions, runaways, derailments, rock slides, injuries, and asphyxiation. Passenger service ended in the 1940s. In 1982, Southern merged with Norfolk and Western to form the Norfolk-Southern Railway. (Courtesy the author's collection.)

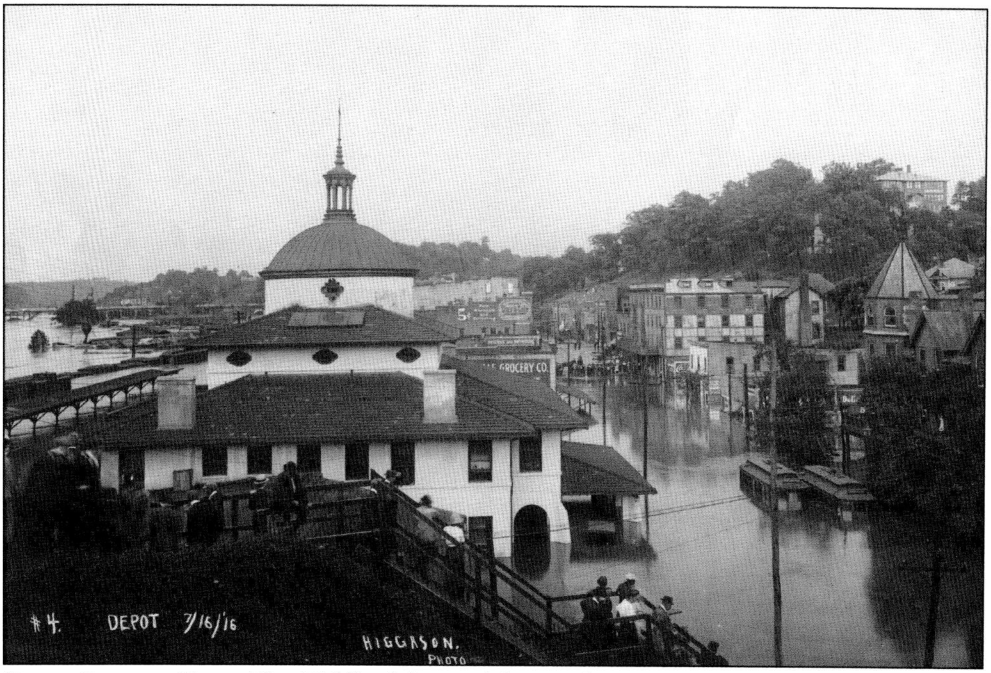

DEPOT STREET—THEN. The 1916 flood damaged the grand passenger station. Submerged streetcars are in the middle of the street, and the original Glen Rock Hotel is across the street. (Courtesy North Carolina Collection, Pack Memorial Library.)

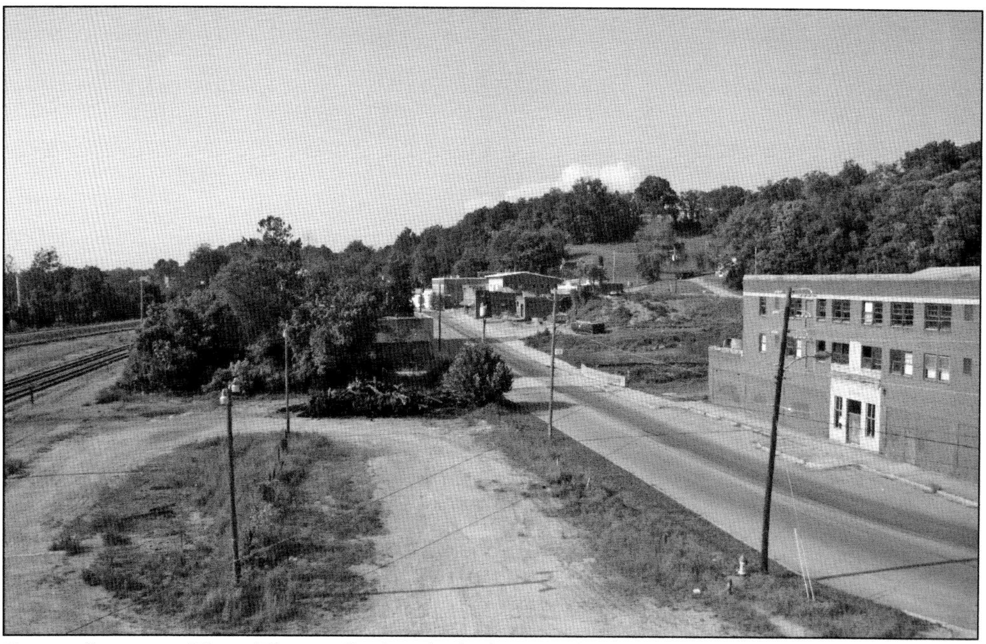

DEPOT STREET—NOW. The roadbed and telephone poles line up, but little else matches. The old Glen Rock Hotel gave way to another with the same name. Long abandoned, the new one is now the basis of a Mountain Housing Opportunities (MHO) multi-use project that will serve as an anchor in the River Arts District and a residential addition to nearby neighborhoods. (Photograph by Henry Neufeld.)

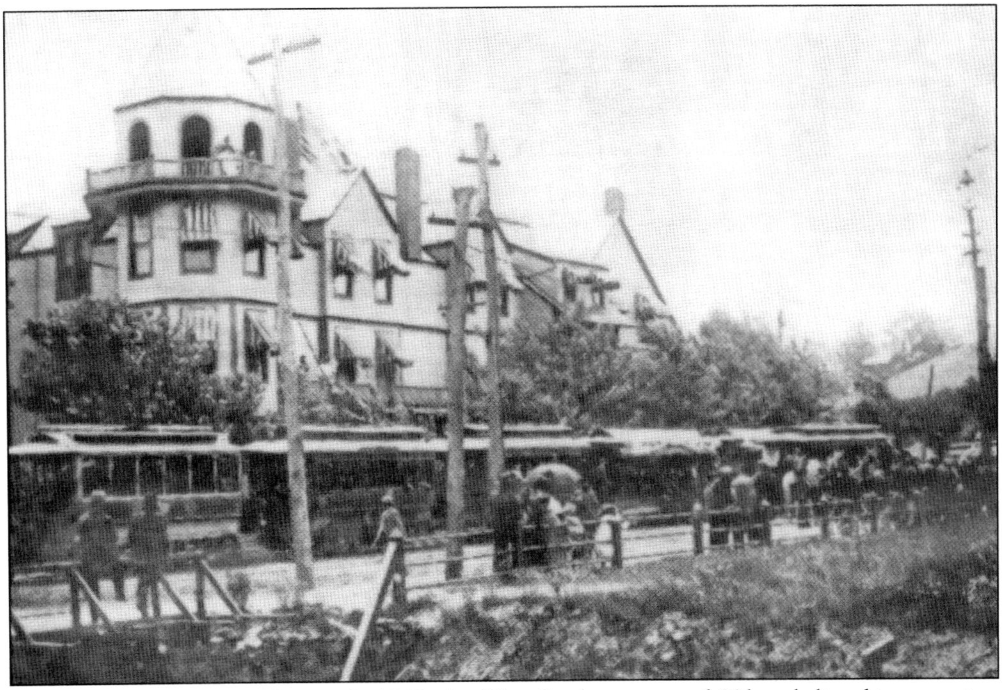

ORIGINAL GLEN ROCK HOTEL. In 1900, the Glen Rock was one of 66 hotels listed in a tourism guide published by the Southern Railway. It accommodated 125 guests at $2 per night, compared with $8 per night at Thomas Wolfe's mother's Old Kentucky Home, $5 per night at the Grove Park Inn, and $1 per night and up at the downtown Langren Hotel. (Courtesy North Carolina Collection, Pack Memorial Library.)

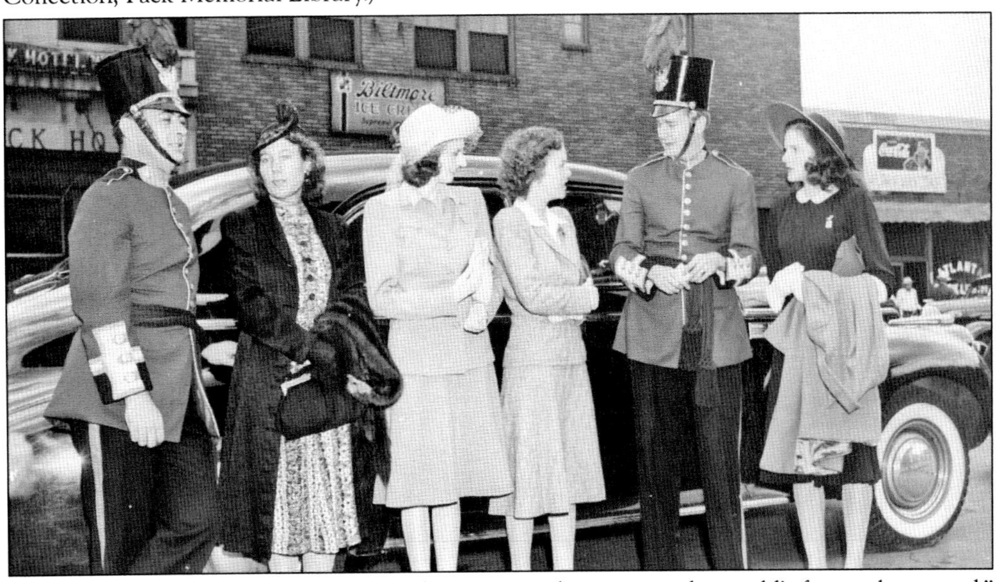

RHODODENDRON ROYALTY. "The South's greatest play-time in the world's finest playground," was the description given in full-page advertisements of Asheville's five-day-long Rhododendron Festival. The festival was a Mardi Gras that attracted hundreds of thousands of people from 1928 through 1941 and involved participants from 10 states. Here "royalty"—the queens of the ball—arrives at the Glen Rock Hotel. (Courtesy Mountain Housing Opportunities.)

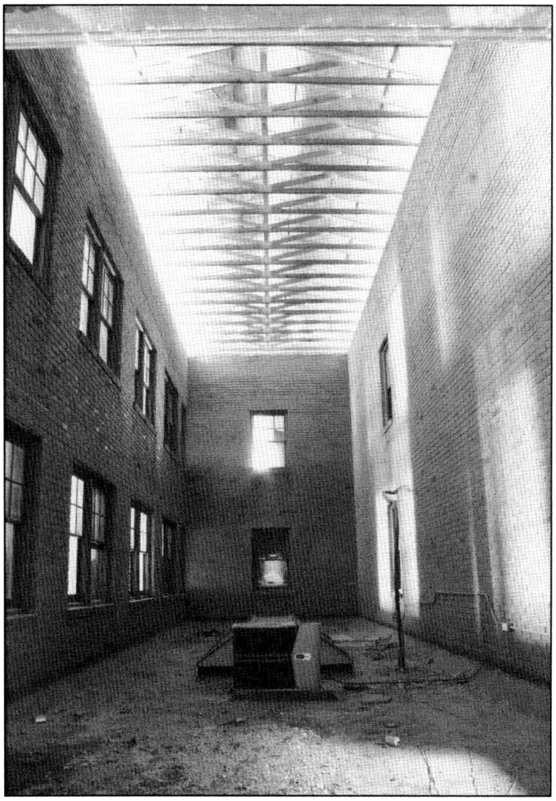

Hotel under Renovation. In its last years during the late 1950s, the Glen Rock Hotel was home to railroad workers and itinerants. MHO's renovation of it for office, retail, and green space, and affordable housing is only one of the functions that MHO has served since its inception in 1988. (Photograph by Henry Neufeld.)

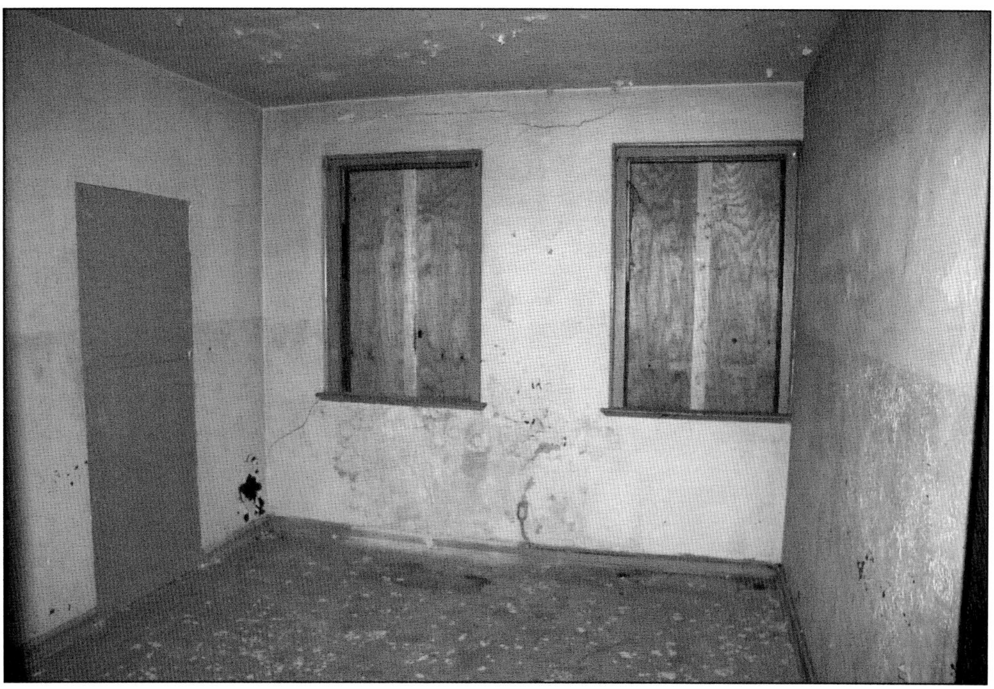

Blue Room. The rooms were spare, but one regular tenant painted the walls of this space turquoise. (Photograph by Henry Neufeld.)

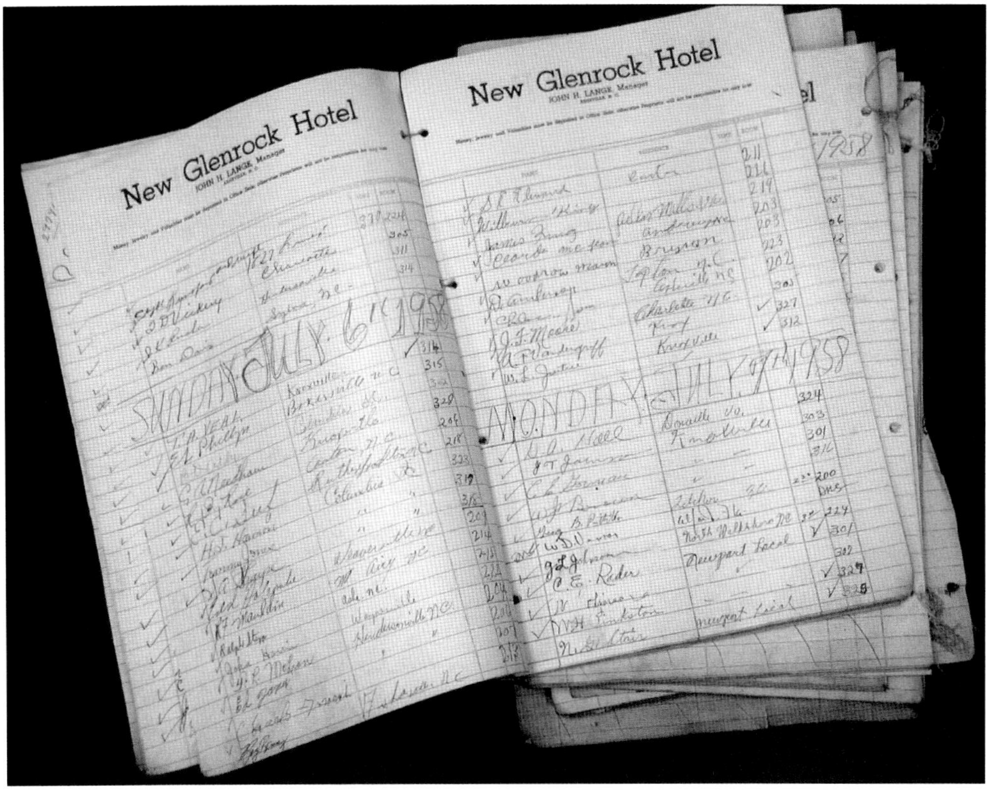

HOUSING OLD AND NEW. MHO retains the last registers of the "new" Glen Rock Hotel as homage to those whose incomes made housing difficult in the past. The current project includes restoration of the hotel as office space and the construction of a new, 80,000-square-foot, mixed-use building. The key to the ambitious plan was a new city zoning category, the "urban place district," which is meant to encourage higher-density development. It was created in 2005, and the Glen Rock project was the first to receive the designation. The Chesterfield Mill was later assigned the same designation. (Above, photograph by Rob Neufeld; below, model by Reinhardt Architecture for MHO.)

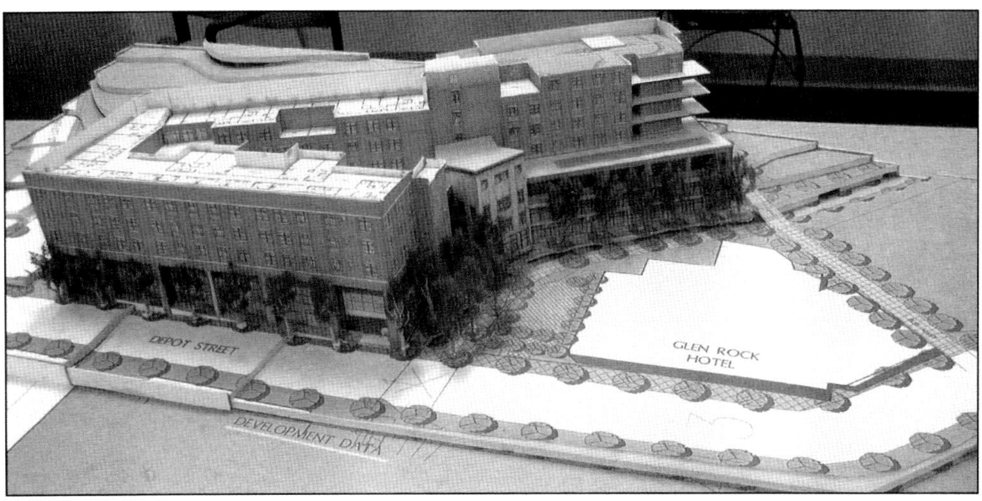

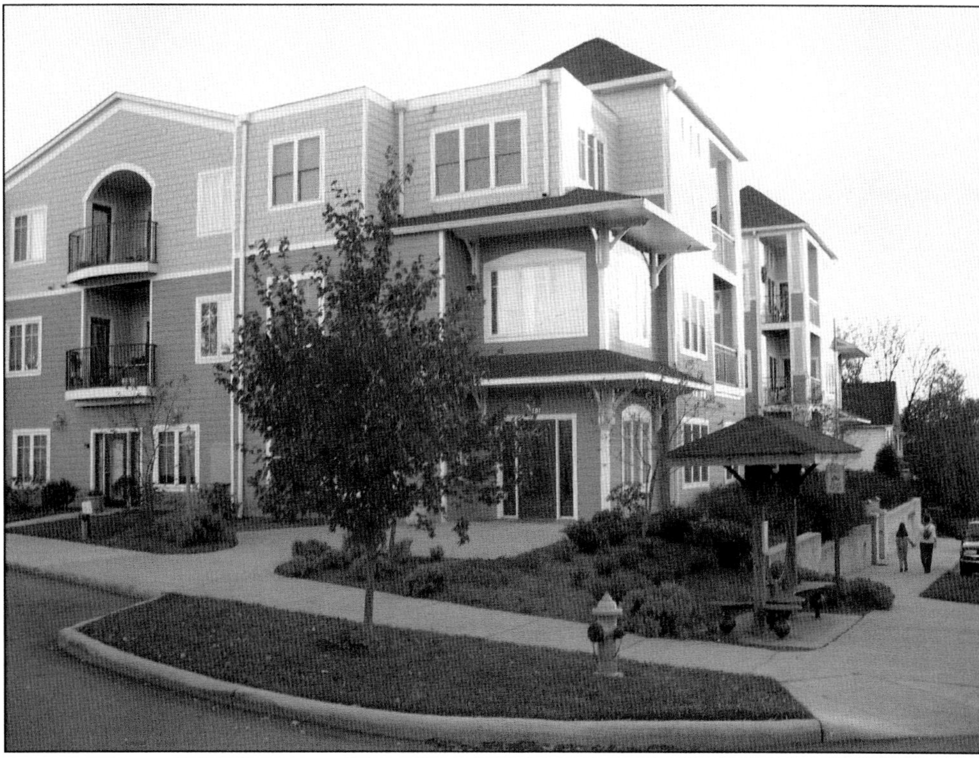

MERRITT PARK. This complex of three-story buildings located on Clingman Avenue just past Hilliard Avenue (see Chapter 4) features MHO's foray into affordable condominium apartments. It is also the home of MHO's offices. Across the street is Prospect Terrace, a rehabilitated neighborhood with a new park, Owens Bell. Up the ridge to the west is West End. (Courtesy MHO.)

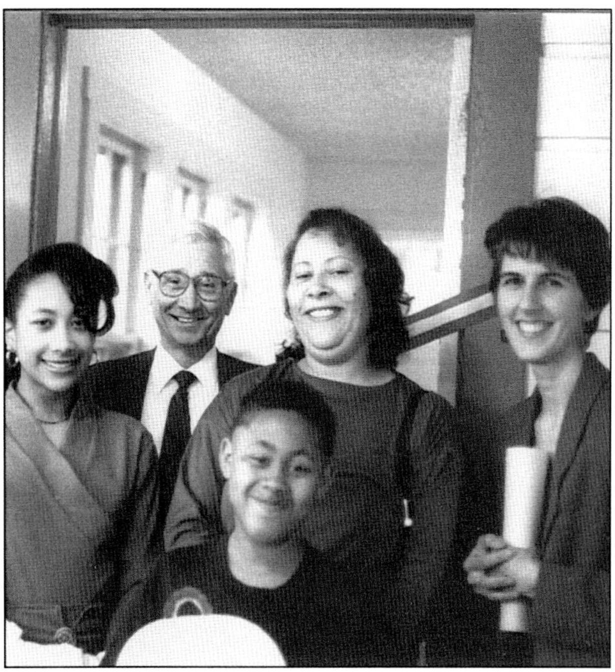

FIRST HOUSE PROVIDED. Following an affordable housing conference in Asheville in February 1988, leaders saw the need for a nonprofit organization to address the housing rehabilitation and development needs of the area. Soon MHO was locating substandard houses to purchase at low cost, renovate, sell at an affordable price, and arrange mortgages with low down payments. The Mercer Green home, dedicated on April 4, 1991, on Wellington Street in West Asheville (a few blocks from Riverview Drive—see Chapter 10), was the first one transformed from vacancy to occupancy through MHO's affordable housing program. (Courtesy MHO.)

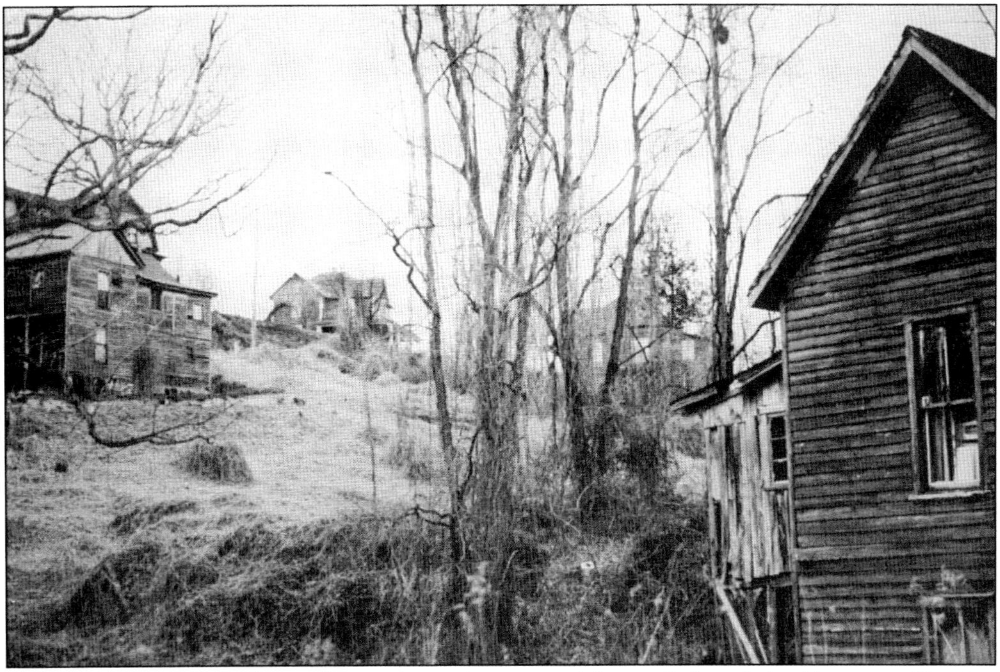

PROSPECT TERRACE—THEN. Across from what is now Merritt Park and the Mountain Housing Opportunities offices had been a neighborhood in serious decline—a prime target for MHO's affordable housing initiative. (Photograph by Scott Dedman, courtesy of MHO.)

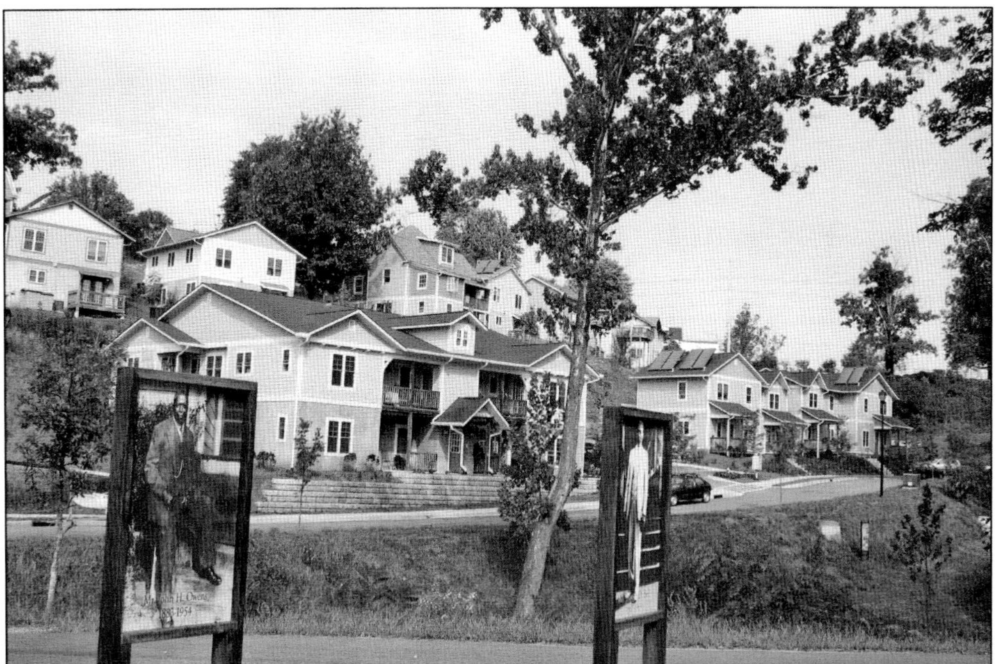

PROSPECT TERRACE—NOW. Prospect Terrace, a development of 17 condominiums and houses completed by MHO in 2007, utilizes building techniques, systems, and materials that reduce energy use and the impact on natural resources. In other words, they are "green." (Courtesy MHO.)

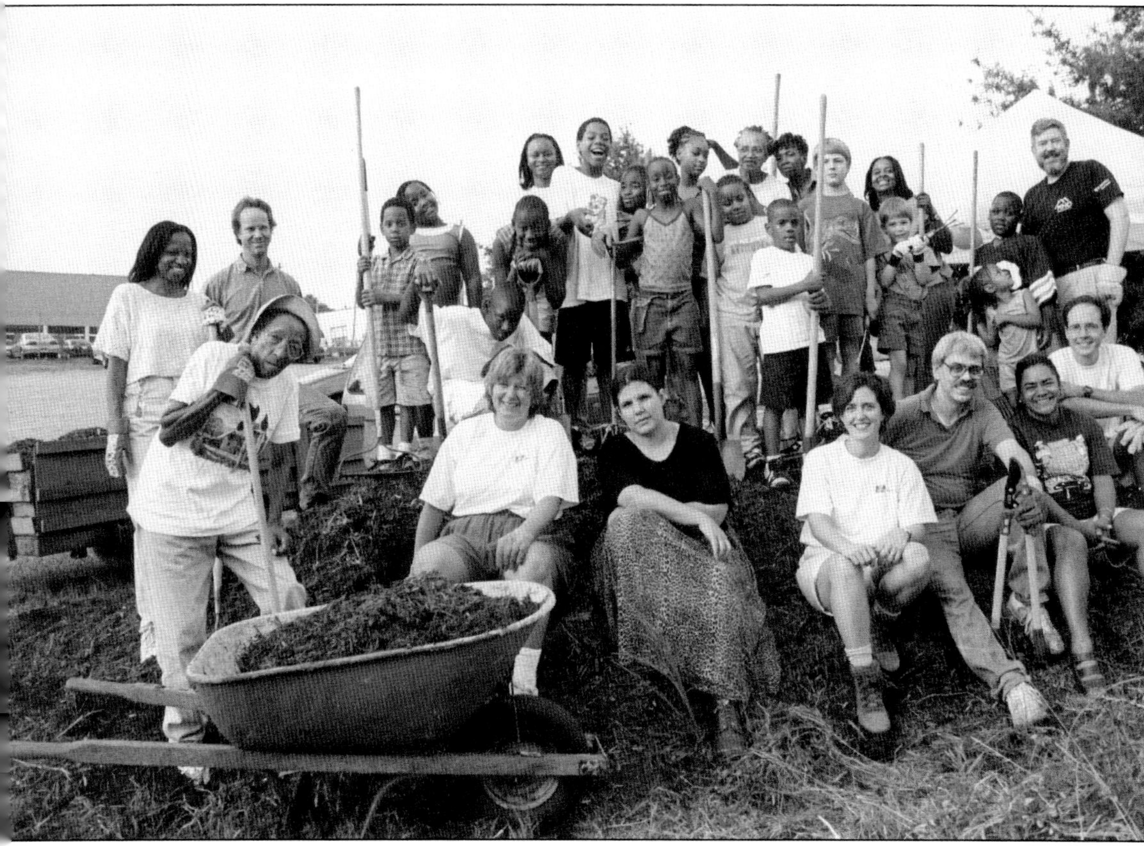

NEIGHBORHOOD TRANSFORMATION. MHO has initiated programs for home repairs, rural housing rehabilitation, the building of rental units, furnace replacement, and the improvement of neighborhoods. In 1997, MHO worked with the West End/Clingman Avenue neighborhood (WECAN) to renovate homes that had become dilapidated (see Chapter 9). Here WECAN neighbors, MHO staff, and other volunteers help establish a garden in the neighborhood. (Photograph by Evie Sandlin White, courtesy MHO.)

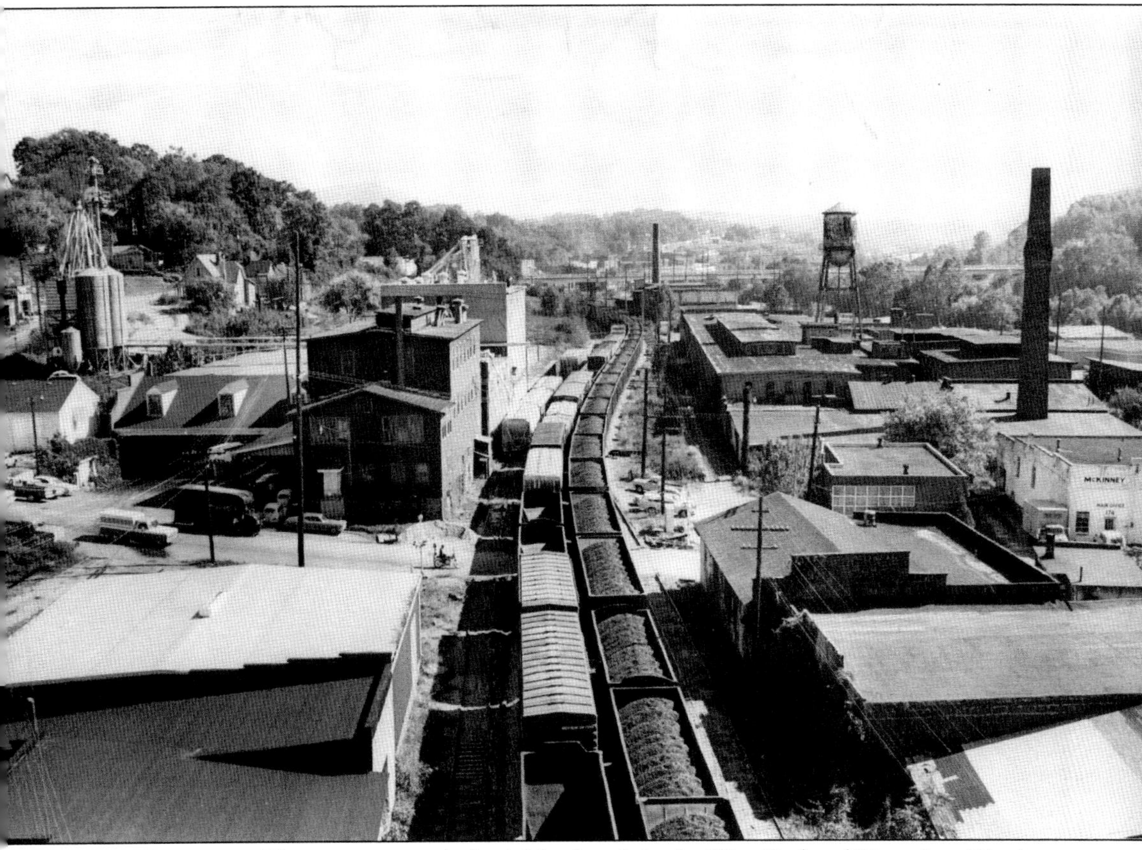

TRAIN WATCHING. The recent revival of neighborhoods in the West End and River Arts District follows decades of the area reeling from industrial failure, urban renewal, and neighborhood decline. As late as 1977, the railroad—as pictured here—continued to play an important role in supplying wood chips, coal, and building materials to industries. Train watching is a telling pastime at crossings. The district represents the times in its search for economic health. (Photograph by Bill Sanders, courtesy of Asheville *Citizen-Times*.)

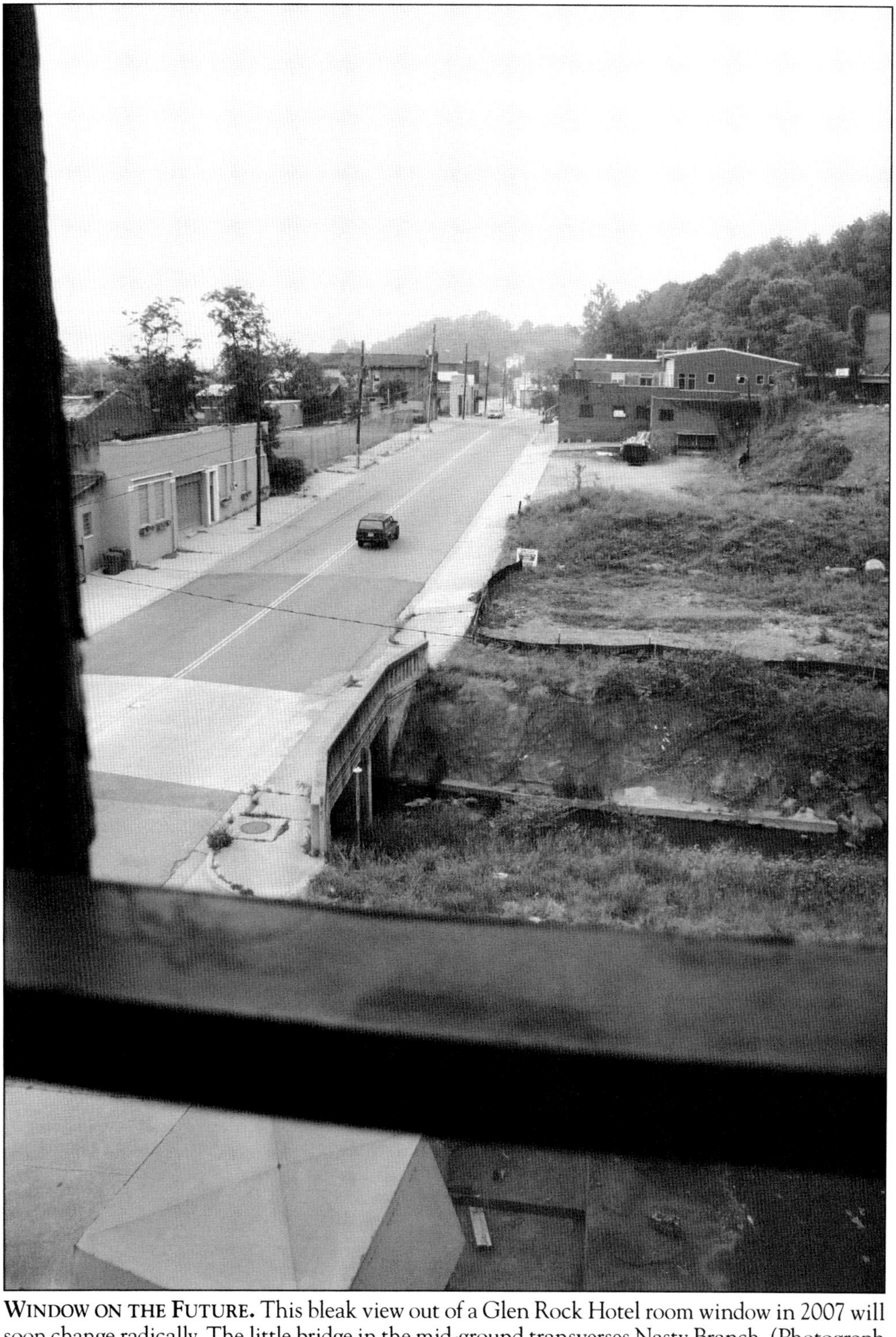

WINDOW ON THE FUTURE. This bleak view out of a Glen Rock Hotel room window in 2007 will soon change radically. The little bridge in the mid-ground transverses Nasty Branch. (Photograph by Henry Neufeld.)

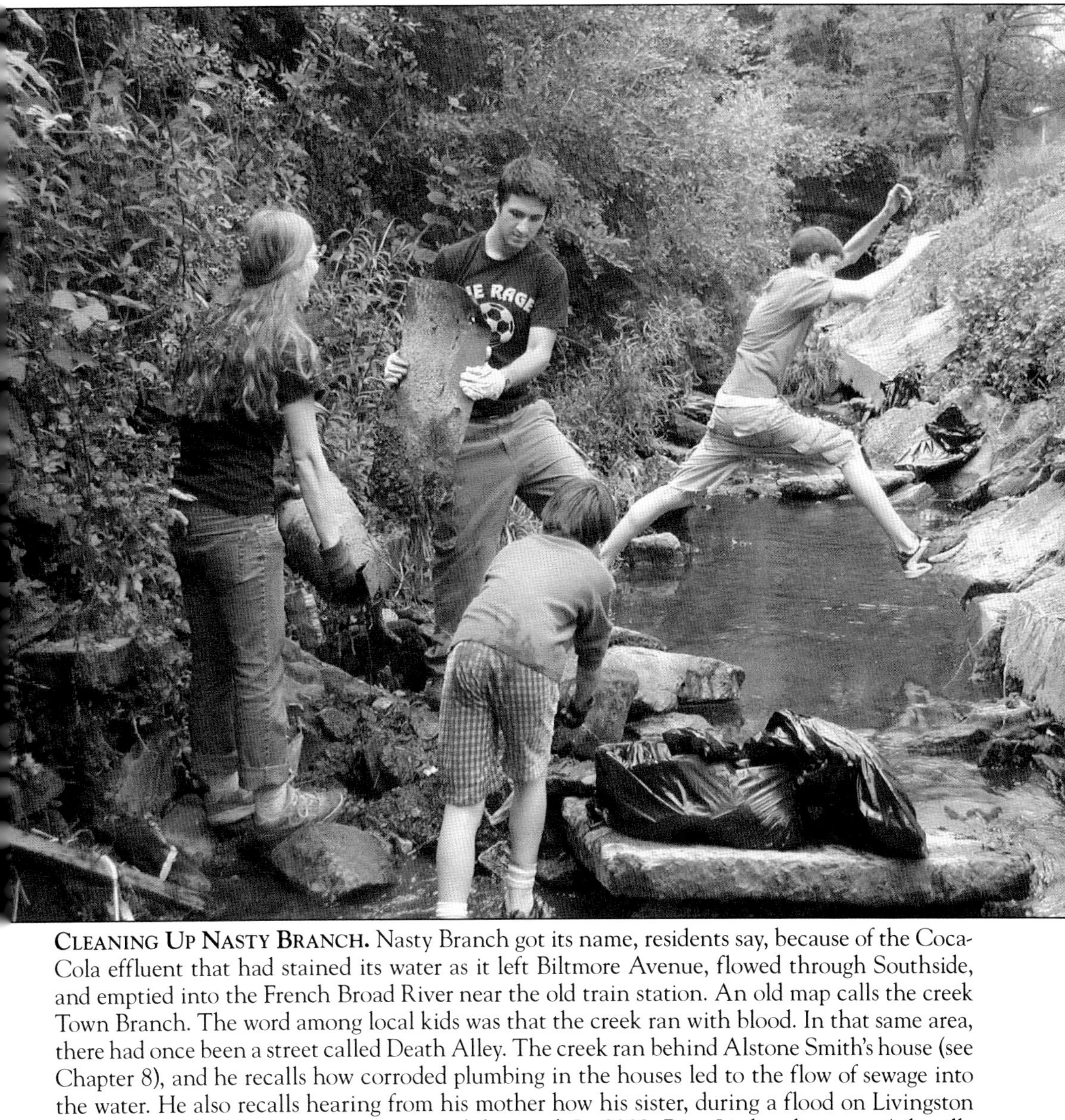

CLEANING UP NASTY BRANCH. Nasty Branch got its name, residents say, because of the Coca-Cola effluent that had stained its water as it left Biltmore Avenue, flowed through Southside, and emptied into the French Broad River near the old train station. An old map calls the creek Town Branch. The word among local kids was that the creek ran with blood. In that same area, there had once been a street called Death Alley. The creek ran behind Alstone Smith's house (see Chapter 8), and he recalls how corroded plumbing in the houses led to the flow of sewage into the water. He also recalls hearing from his mother how his sister, during a flood on Livingston Street, got sucked into an open sewer and drowned. In 2002, RiverLink volunteers, Asheville High School's Ecology Club, and participants in Together We Read's reading of *The French Broad* by Wilma Dykeman cleaned the stream (pictured above). (Photograph by Rob Neufeld.)

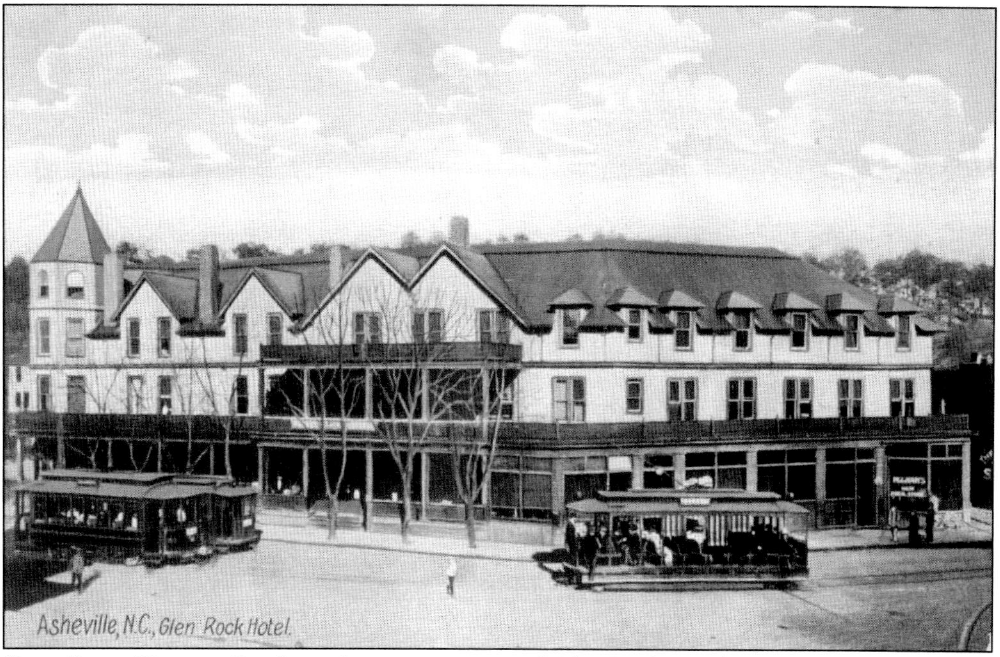

GLEN ROCK HEYDAY. Reaching the train station and Glen Rock Hotel in 1900 was an adventure because the train had to pass through seven tunnels. Horse-drawn wagons waited to transport vacationers and their trunks. Streetcars traveled to area resorts. The Glen Rock Hotel—and the Florence Hotel two blocks up—accommodated many railroad workers. The room fee included meals. In 1906, the Glen Rock received a license to sell liquor. (Courtesy Scott Dedman.)

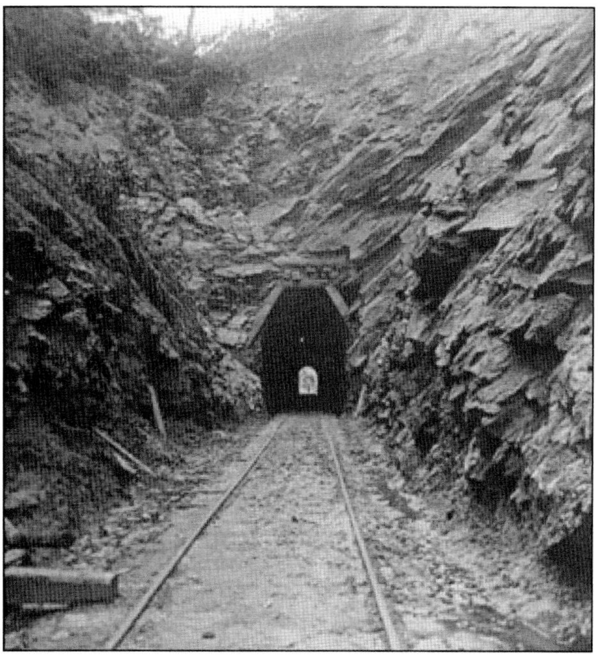

LICKLOG TUNNEL. This tunnel was one of seven that trains had to pass through to go from Old Fort to Asheville. (Courtesy North Carolina Collection, Pack Memorial Library.)

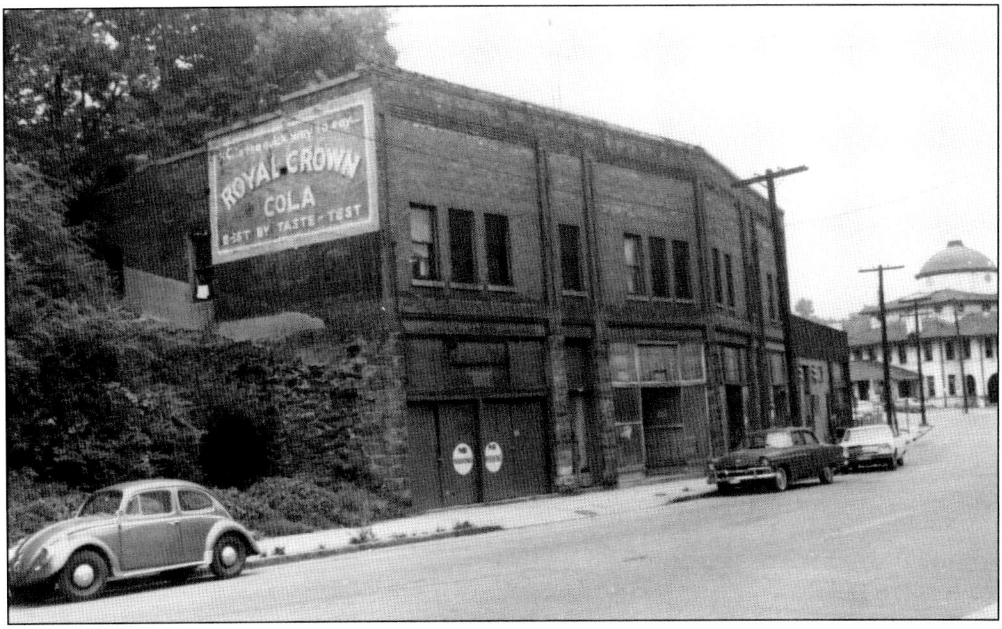

DEPOT STREET BUSINESSES. These buildings, now demolished—as is the depot in the background—once housed businesses patronized by the African American community. A shoe store occupied the central building. The building on the left was for Railway Express Agency (REA) storage. By 1966, the date of this photograph, the REA included trucks as well as railroad cars in its fleet. In 1975, the REA suspended operation. (Photograph by the City of Asheville in preparation for East Riverside urban renewal, recovered by Reid Fornoff, intern at MHO.)

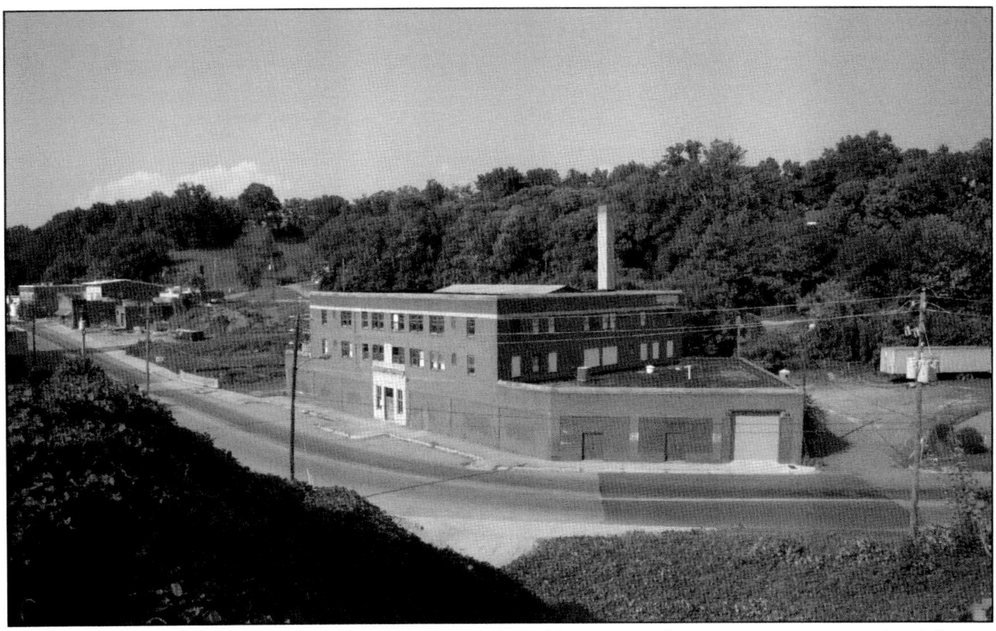

SITE OF DEPOT BUSINESSES. The Southern Railroad Passenger Station is gone, as is the African American business district that had existed on Depot Street in the right foreground. The Fine Arts League of the Carolinas, a nonprofit school, has moved into a building on the same block. (Photograph by Henry Neufeld.)

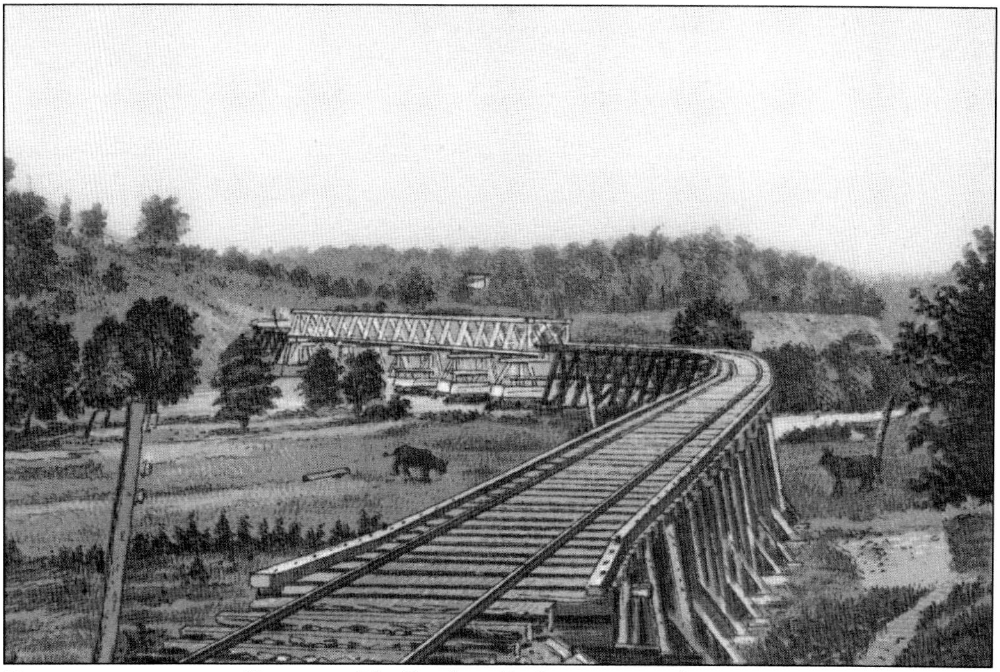

TRACKS THROUGH THE COUNTRY. The Southern Railway promoted its scenic approach to the river district with a book of etchings. (Courtesy Special Collections, North Carolina University.)

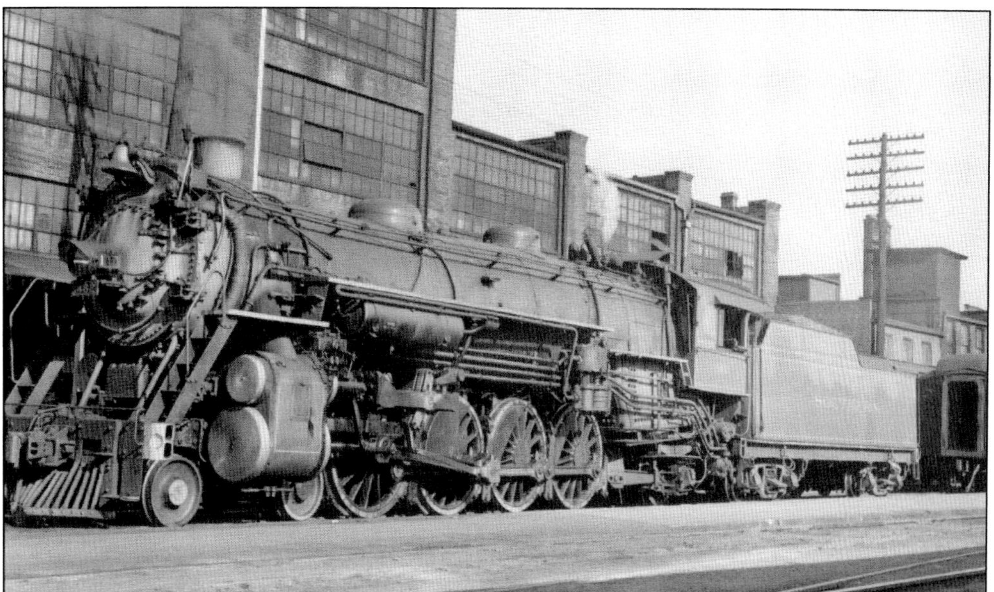

ASHEVILLE SOUTHERN LOCOMOTIVE, JUNE 1950. Passenger service through Asheville ended shortly after World War II, but freight trains have continued to serve the area. (Courtesy North Carolina Collection, Pack Memorial Library.)

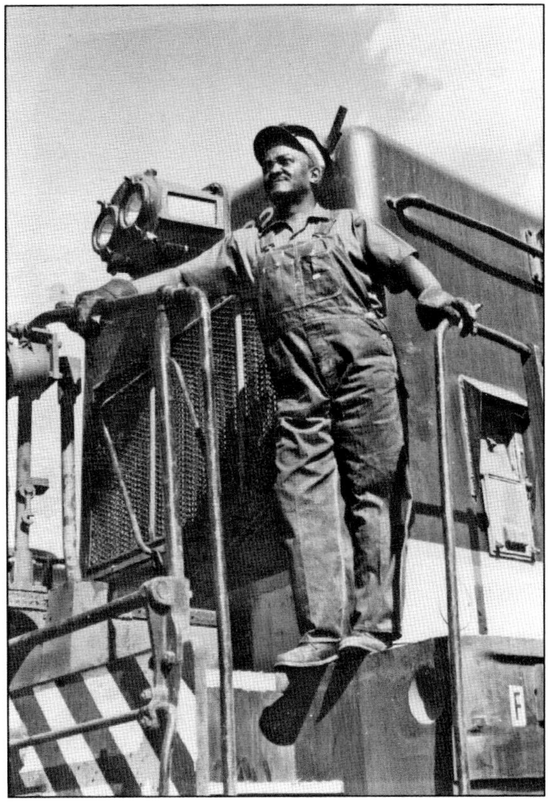

JAMES WATERS. Waters, a hostler (locomotive mover) at Southern Railroad's roundhouse, poses with one of the engines he maintained in the 1950s. When the Norfolk and Western Railway merged with the Southern Railroad in 1982, the era of old-fashioned railroading in Asheville ended, bringing changes as great as the demise of steam locomotives and the discontinuance of passenger service in earlier times. Jobs were cut, operations automated, safety requirements and pay were improved, and the nature of the work at Asheville's roundhouse was revolutionized. James's son, Ira, a 27-year engine maintenance veteran at the roundhouse, recalls, "When I first got there we had 200 people; now we're down to 30. Now, you can run a train for six days off diesel fuel. Back then, trains had to be serviced every day." He adds, "Blacks did the manual labor and whites were the foremen back then" and they mostly "stayed to themselves." (Courtesy of Ineetha Reeves Waters and the YMI Cultural Center.)

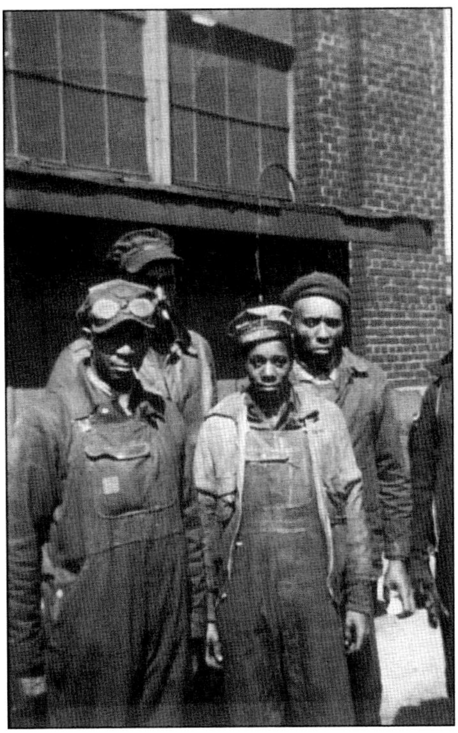

RAILROAD YARDMEN. Four African American railroad yardmen pose by the Asheville roundhouse in the 1960s. (Courtesy of YMI Cultural Center.)

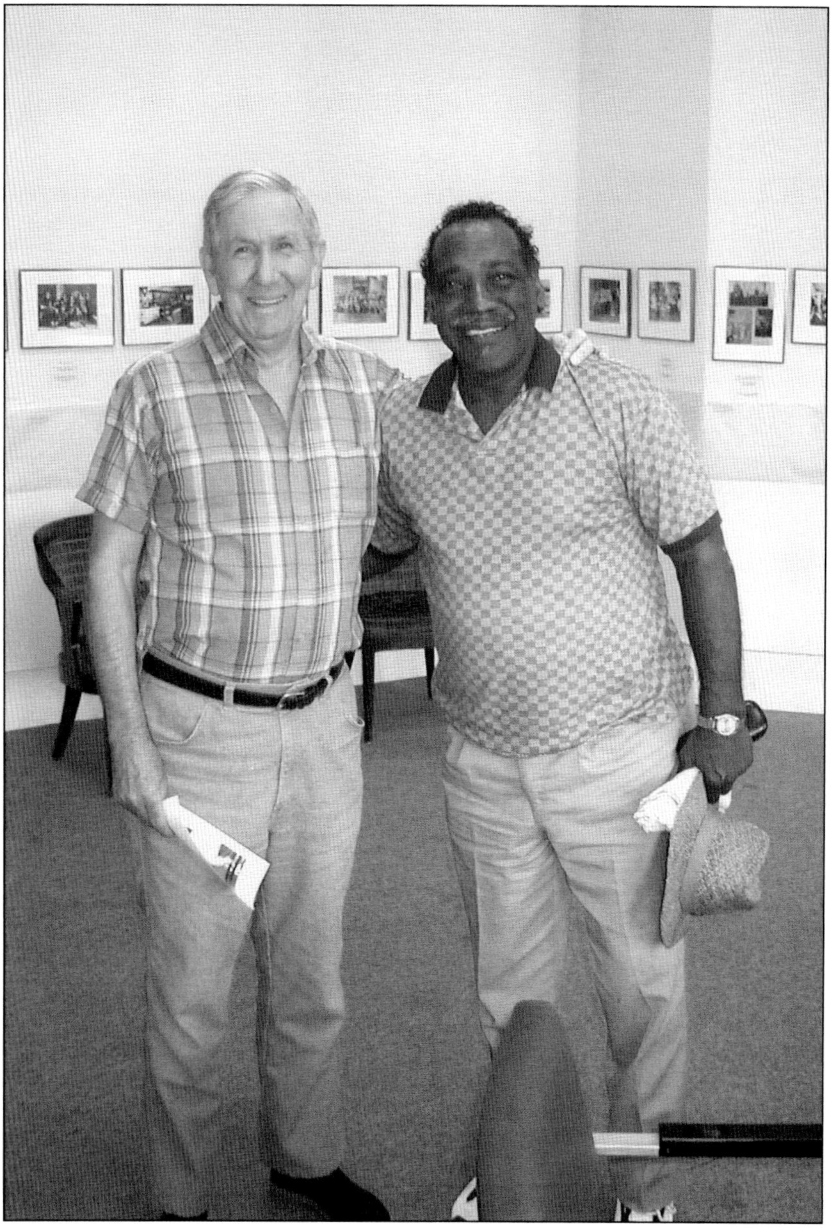

CONDUCTORS. James Harrison (right) of Asheville was one of the Jackie Robinsons of the Southern Railroad. In 1965, he and a few other African American railroad men broke the color line that existed between laborers and specialized trainmen, traveling to Atlanta for a six-week training course before eventually becoming a conductor. Back in Asheville, he faced another test—making decisions that required on-the-job experience. Eventually assigned the flagman position on the crew of conductor Paul Ross (left), he computed tonnage, determining if a given engine could make it up a mountain grade with its load of cars. Ross took Harrison under his wing, teaching him the intricacies involved in reducing cars, knowing that he would be a conductor one day. Kindnesses "like that count," Harrison said. Ross recalled, "James proved to me that he was going to do the work and not act like he wasn't going to do something because I was picking on him. That's when I became close to him." (Photograph by Rob Neufeld.)

Eight

SOUTHSIDE

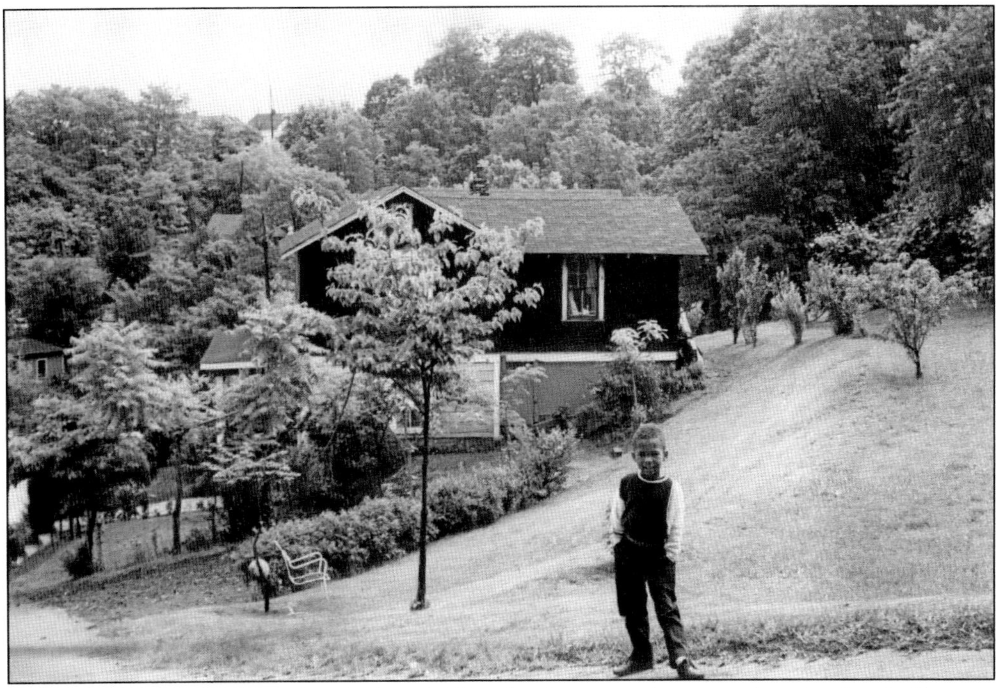

CHARLES STREET HOUSE. In the late 1960s, this house and many others in Southside—an African American community situated between the railroad depot and McDowell Street—were targeted by the city government for the federally funded East Riverside Development Project. The city took photographs of the houses to be demolished because of substandard conditions. A councilman stated that Southside "was going to be the nicest medium-income residential development anywhere, and that the area should be entitled to a branch library." Neither the medium-income homes nor the branch library came about. Along with the removal of substandard housing came the removal of the things that make up community. "In the East Riverside Area," said Rev. Wesley Grant, "we have lost more than eleven hundred homes, six beauty parlors, five barber shops, five filling stations, fourteen grocery stores, three Laundromats, eight apartments, seven churches, three shoe shops, two cabinet shops, two auto body shops, one hotel, five funeral homes, one hospital, and three doctor's offices." (Photograph from Asheville's East Riverside Project documentation.)

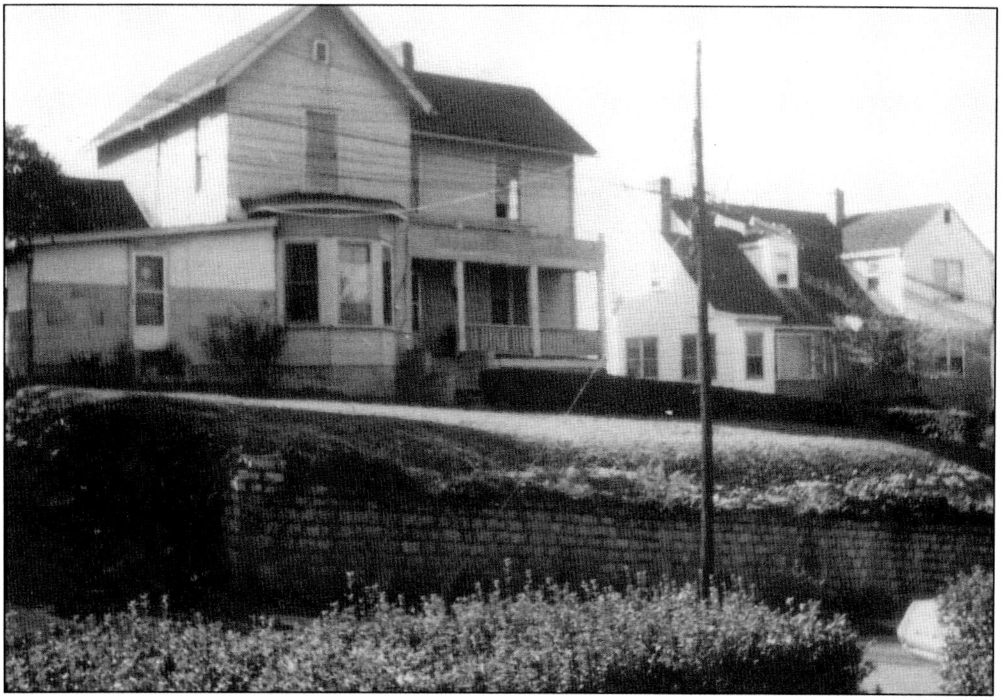

53–55 CONGRESS STREET—THEN. The late-1960s photograph of 55 Congress Street (left) meant that it was scheduled for demolition. (Photograph from Asheville's East Riverside Project documentation.)

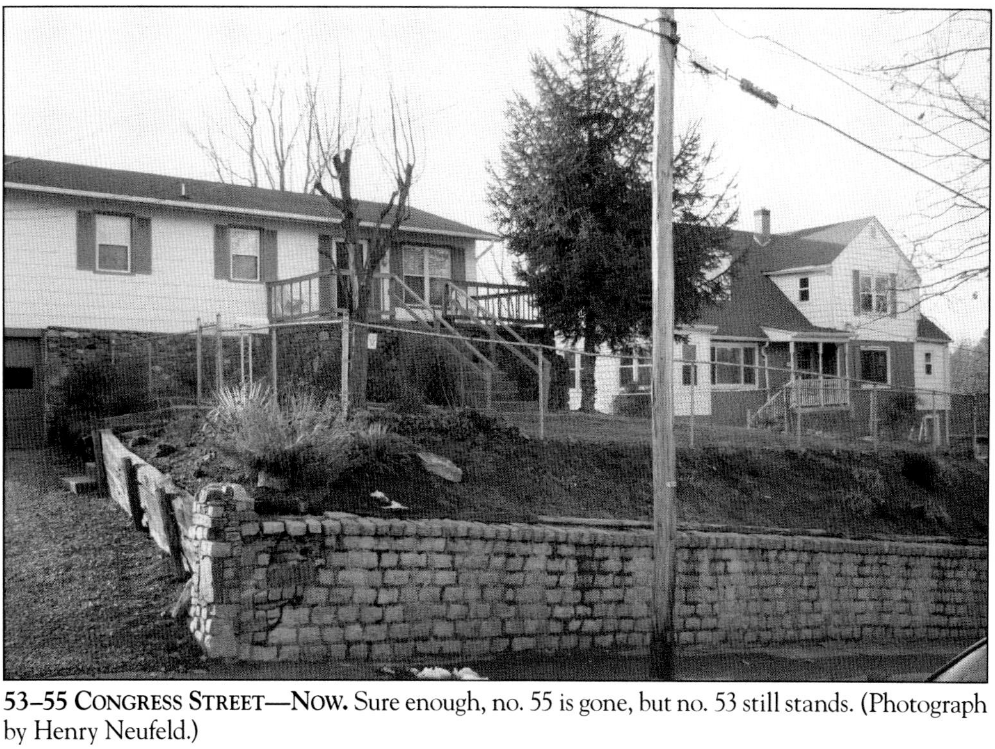

53–55 CONGRESS STREET—NOW. Sure enough, no. 55 is gone, but no. 53 still stands. (Photograph by Henry Neufeld.)

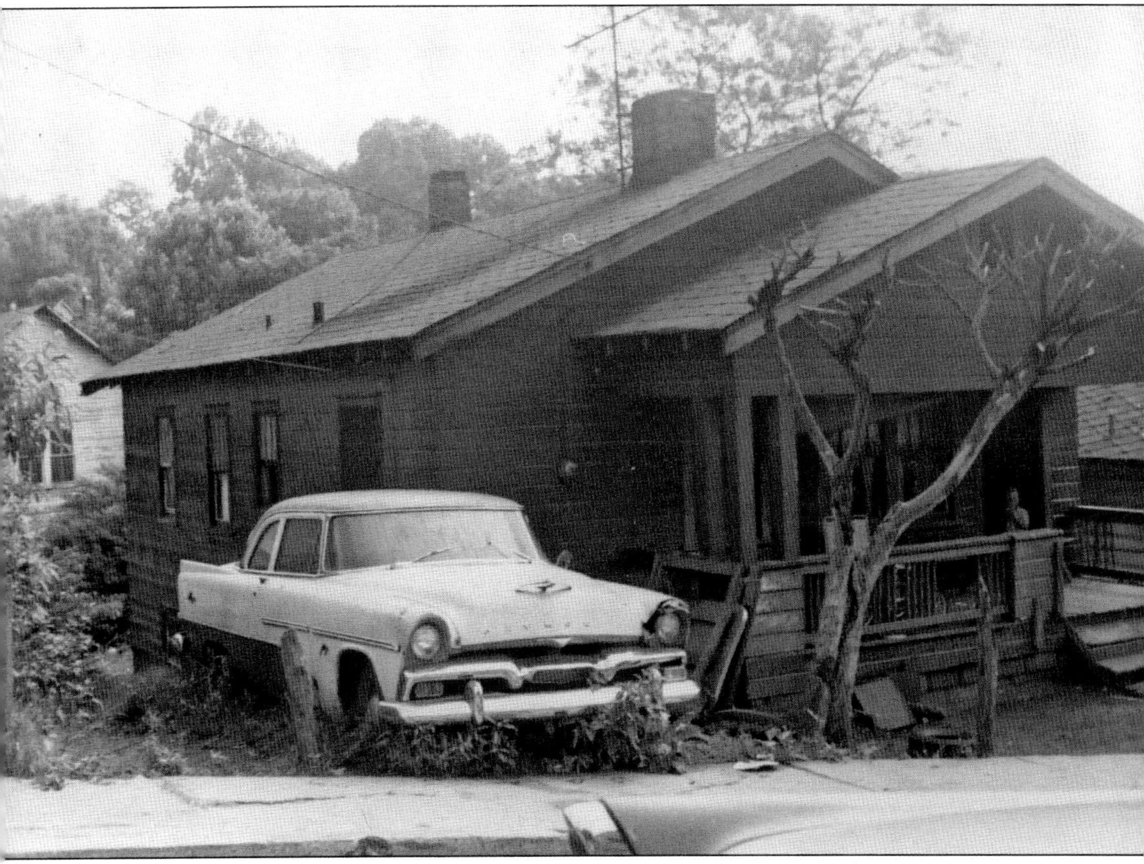

188 Livingston Street. Alstone Smith, a retired power company mechanic, grew up at 188 Livingston Street in what had once been the Beech Hill area in Southside. His family's house had been marked "deteriorating" on the project map. He acknowledges its condition. "We didn't have running water," Smith recalls. "We had to . . . get water from outside. Flushing the toilet, you had to take buckets of water in." The pipes that brought water to the house had corroded. "I've seen snow coming through the side of our walls," Smith added. "We'd stuff rags inside of the wall where the snow came in. No insulation, slat walls. I'm telling you, it was real." Nonetheless, Southside was like a big family, Smith revealed. There was a neighborhood school—Livingston Street School (now the Reid Center)—many black-owned businesses, and any number of grown-ups acting as parents. It had to be so. One's own parents often worked two jobs to get by. Smith's father worked morning to night at Carolina Tractor and at Ticar Chemical Company. He used to say, "Can't see when I leave, can't see when I come back." Nourished by the Southside environment, Smith and his buddies developed successful careers. "Always a-winnin', always a-grinnin', nobody like us," the boys used to chant. (Photograph from Asheville's East Riverside Project documentation.)

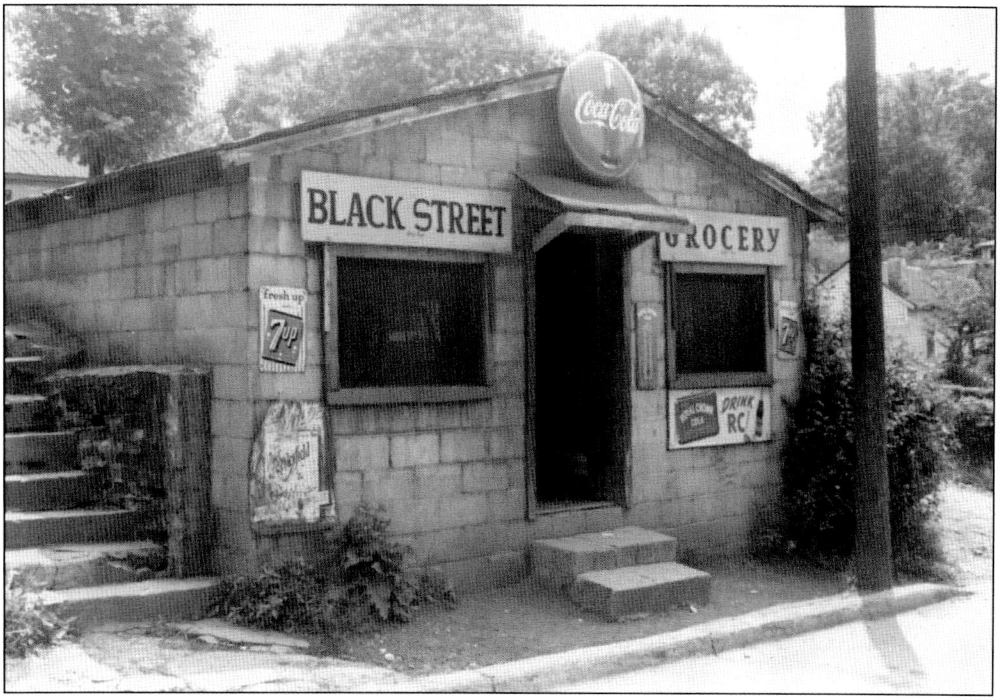

BLACK STREET GROCERY. Neighborhoods before the era of supermarkets featured several small grocery and specialty food stores serving people in easy walking distance. Pictured below is the Roland Hagen Produce Store. (Photographs from Asheville's East Riverside Project documentation.)

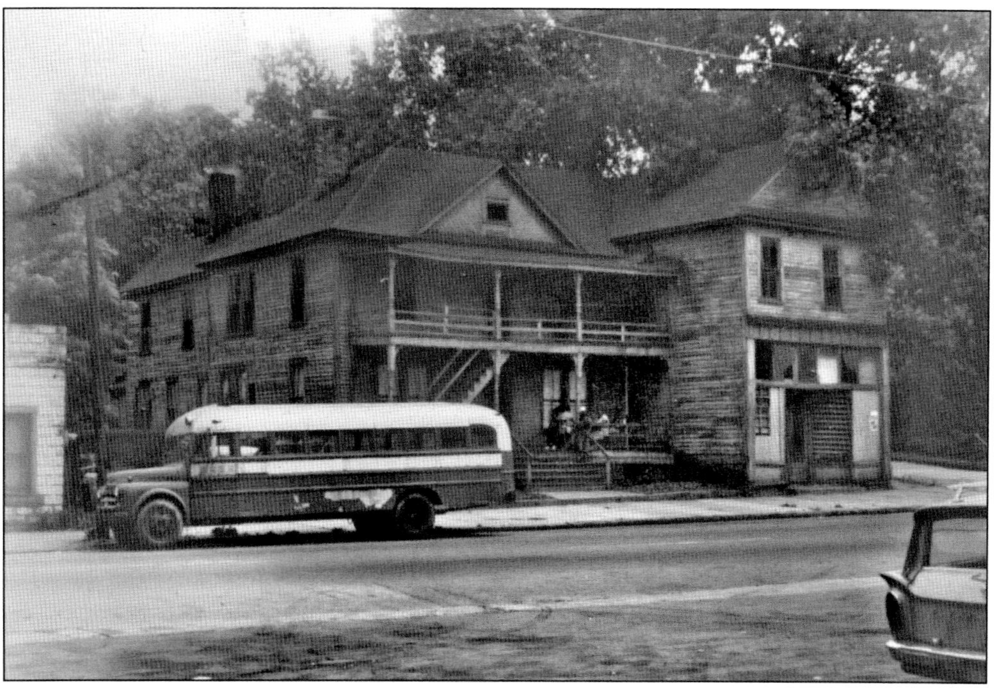

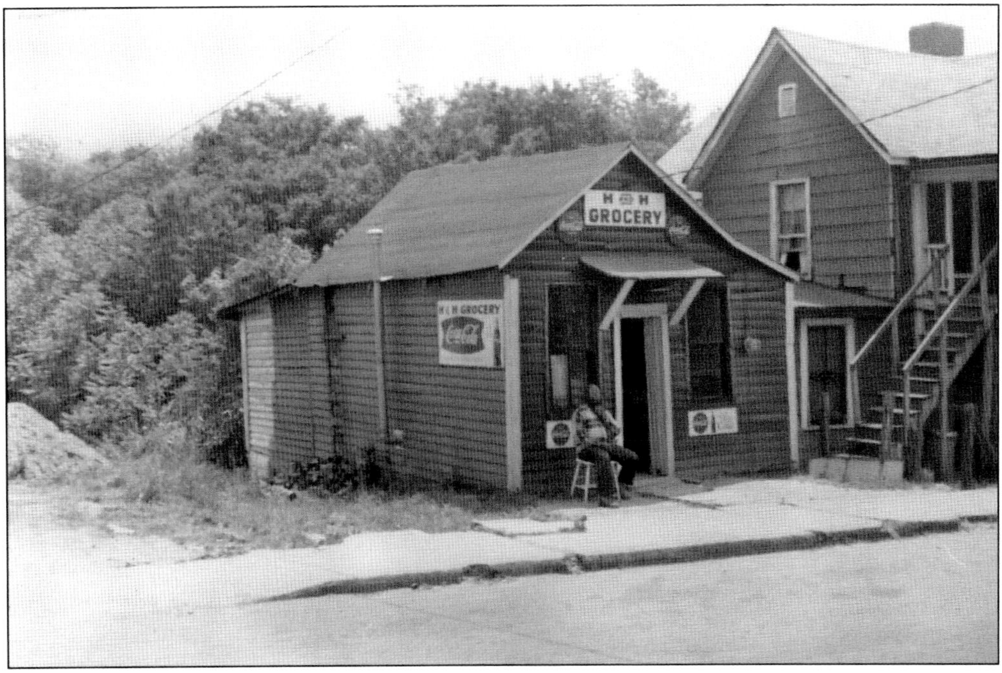

H&H Grocery. Many stores were connected to the owners' homes. (Photograph from Asheville's East Riverside Project documentation.)

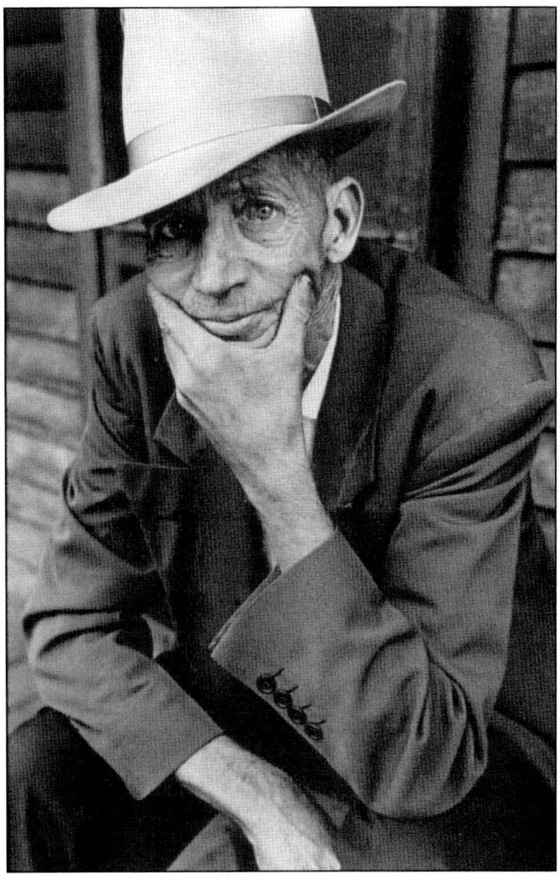

Man from Lyman Holler. The septuagenarian men who gather at James Green's mini-mart on Depot Street recall this Southside gentleman as "the man from Lyman Holler." The Southside community was large. The streets formed blocks, each of which included many homes whose backyards connected into a large open area. Each section of Southside had a colloquial name. The Livingston Street School (now the Reid Community Center), neighborhood churches, recreational areas, and family relationships bound the community together. (Photograph from Asheville's East Riverside Project documentation.)

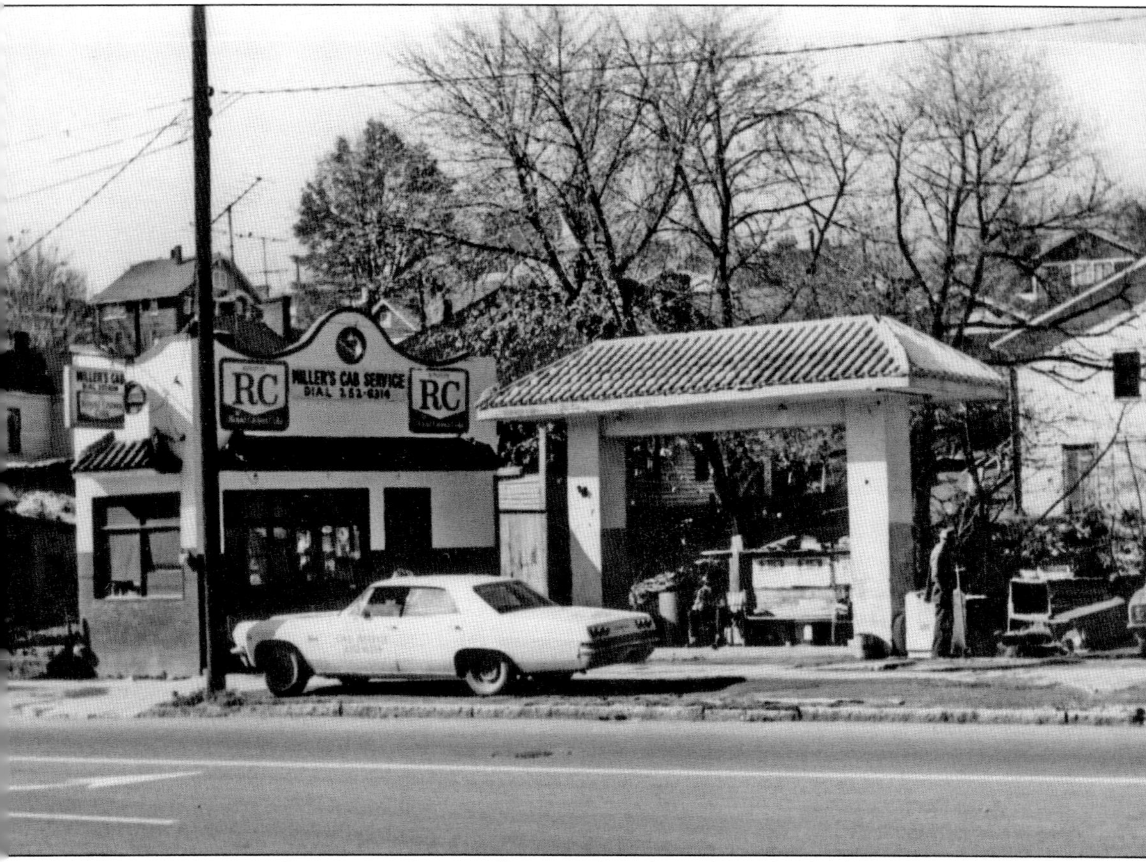

AMOS MILLER'S CABSTAND. Amos Miller owned a cabstand on what had been Southside Avenue. When Dianne Logan, whom he had often taken to the hospital for asthma attacks, became an orphan, he took her under his wing. Dianne's father had died of asthma when she was four, and her mother, on her way to buy her morning Goodie powder and coke chaser, was killed a few years later when an old man with a brakeless car dragged her through Death Alley. Dianne's grandmother Lela "Babe" Evans (who was born on Christmas Day) moved to Ralph Street from her home in West Asheville, giving up her prosperous bootlegging business to care for Dianne and her family. Miller later hired Dianne as a dispatcher. (Photograph from Asheville's East Riverside Project documentation.)

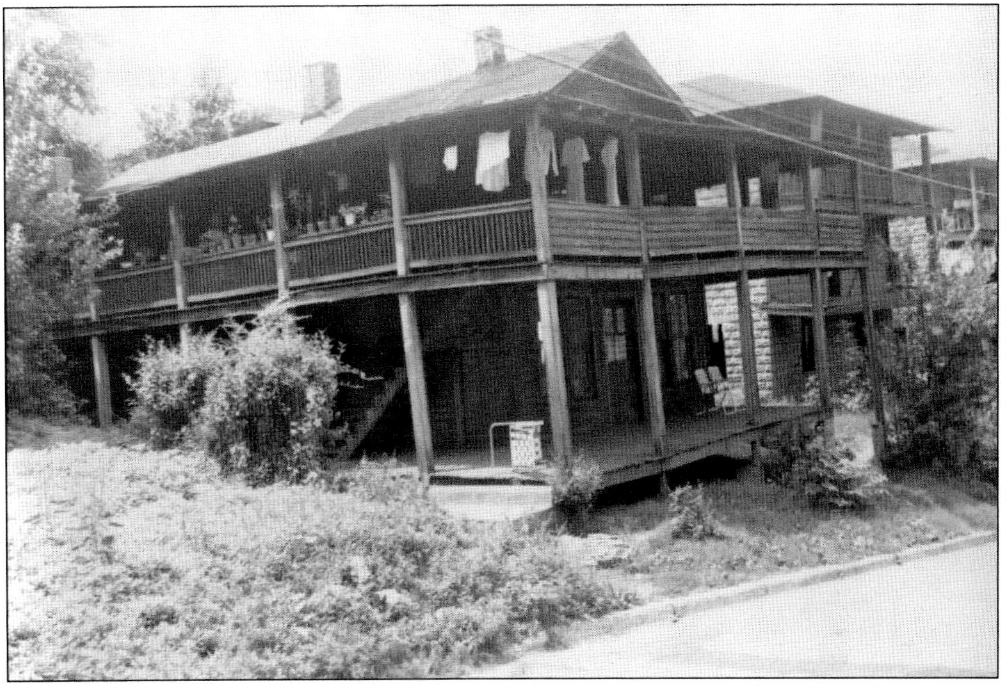

SOUTH FRENCH BROAD HOUSES. These homes with wraparound porches and balconies once stood near where the Bethel Seventh Day Adventist Church is now located. Behind the houses was an alley, and behind that were poorer homes with dirt floors and outhouses. (Photograph from Asheville's East Riverside Project documentation.)

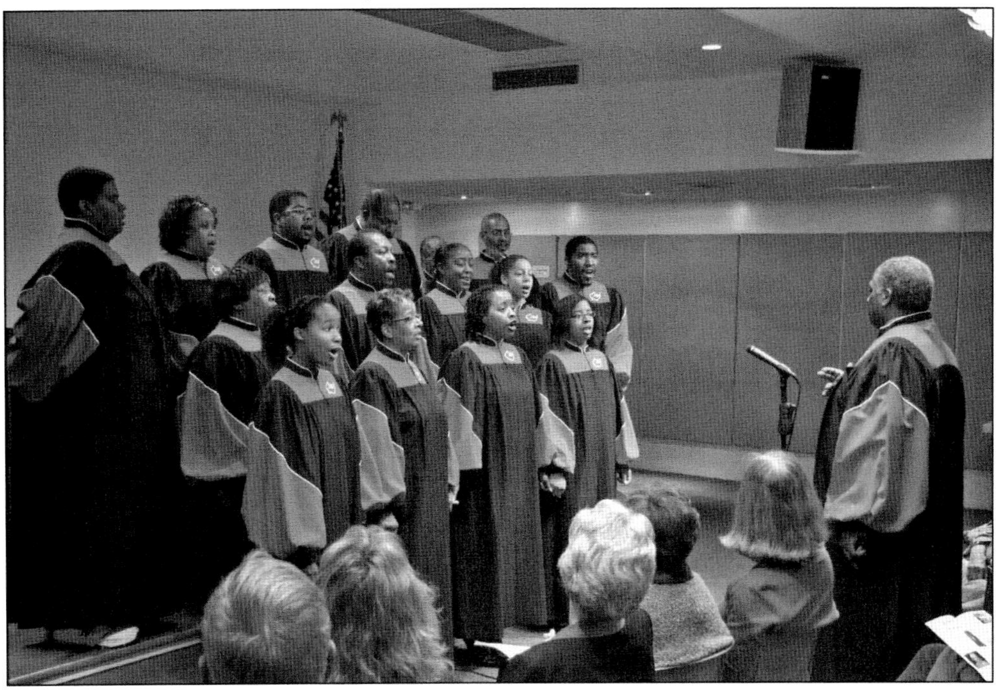

FAMOUS CHORALE. The acclaimed Bethel Seventh Day Adventist Choir, led by Calvin Carter, performs in many locations and produces audio CDs. (Photograph by Henry Neufeld.)

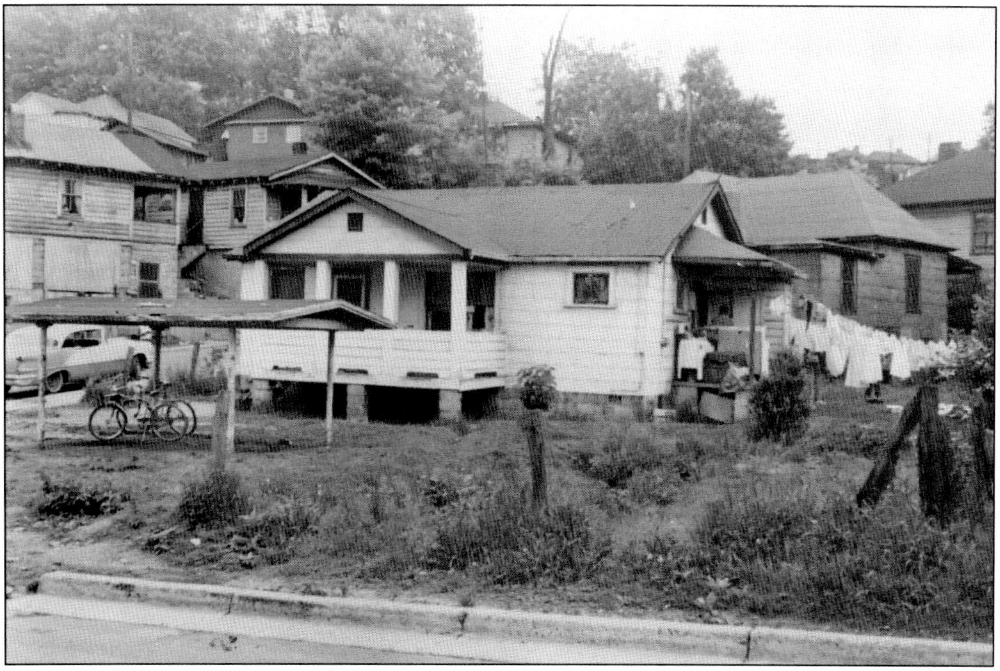

Targeted Neighborhood. Housing varied in Southside. Some homes were quite commodious, including a shed for bicycles, generous porches, and Colonial, two-story frames. (Photographs from Asheville's East Riverside Project documentation.)

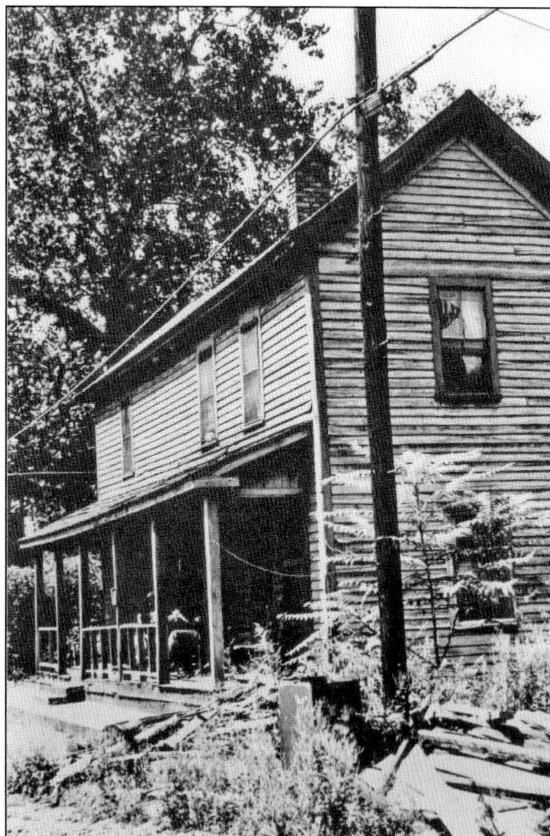

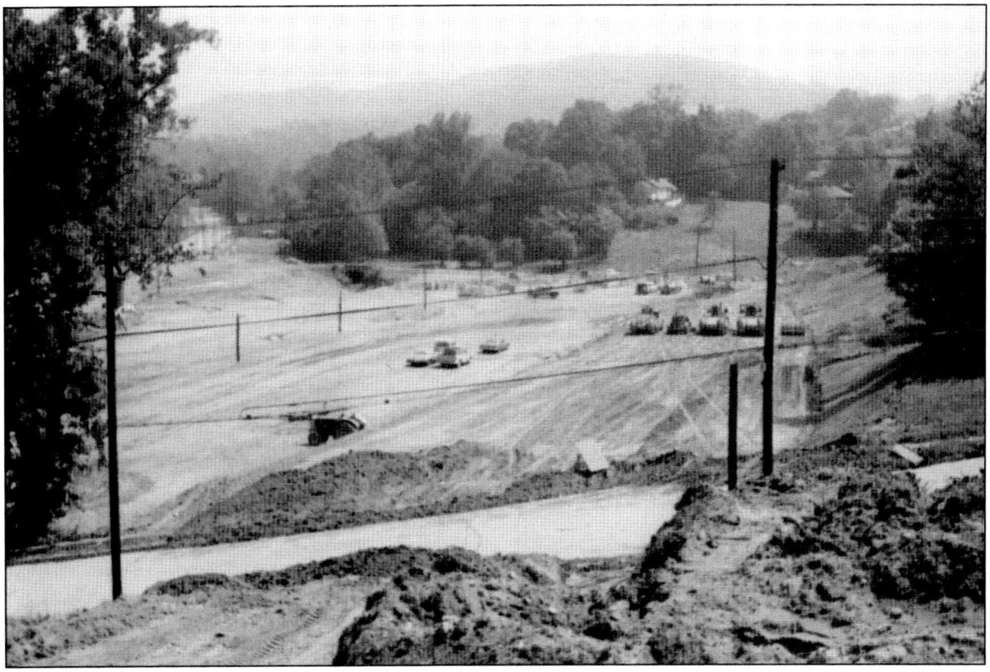

BULLDOZED. Urban renewal removed the architecture of community in favor or engineered high-density housing. (Photograph from Asheville's East Riverside Project documentation.)

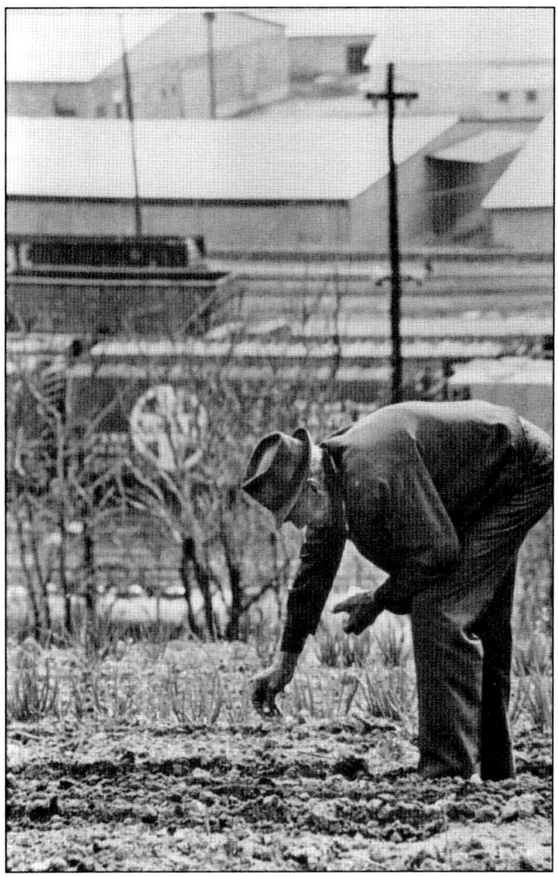

GARDENER NEAR TOBACCO HOUSE. Included in the photographs taken of Southside in the late 1960s before urban renewal is this one of a man gardening on a lot across the tracks from Day's Tobacco Warehouse on Lyman Street. City jobs and country gardens were a staple of life in these communities. Alstone Smith recalls, "The thing that strikes me the most was the amount of fruit trees [and vines, bushes, and patches] we had in our neighborhood. There were cherry trees—black, yellow, and red varieties—pears, plums, grapes, strawberries, blackberries, all kinds of apple trees, yours for the taking. But after urban renewal, there is less than a handful left. The free fruit being available then evened the score for us less fortunate." (Photograph from Asheville's East Riverside Project documentation.)

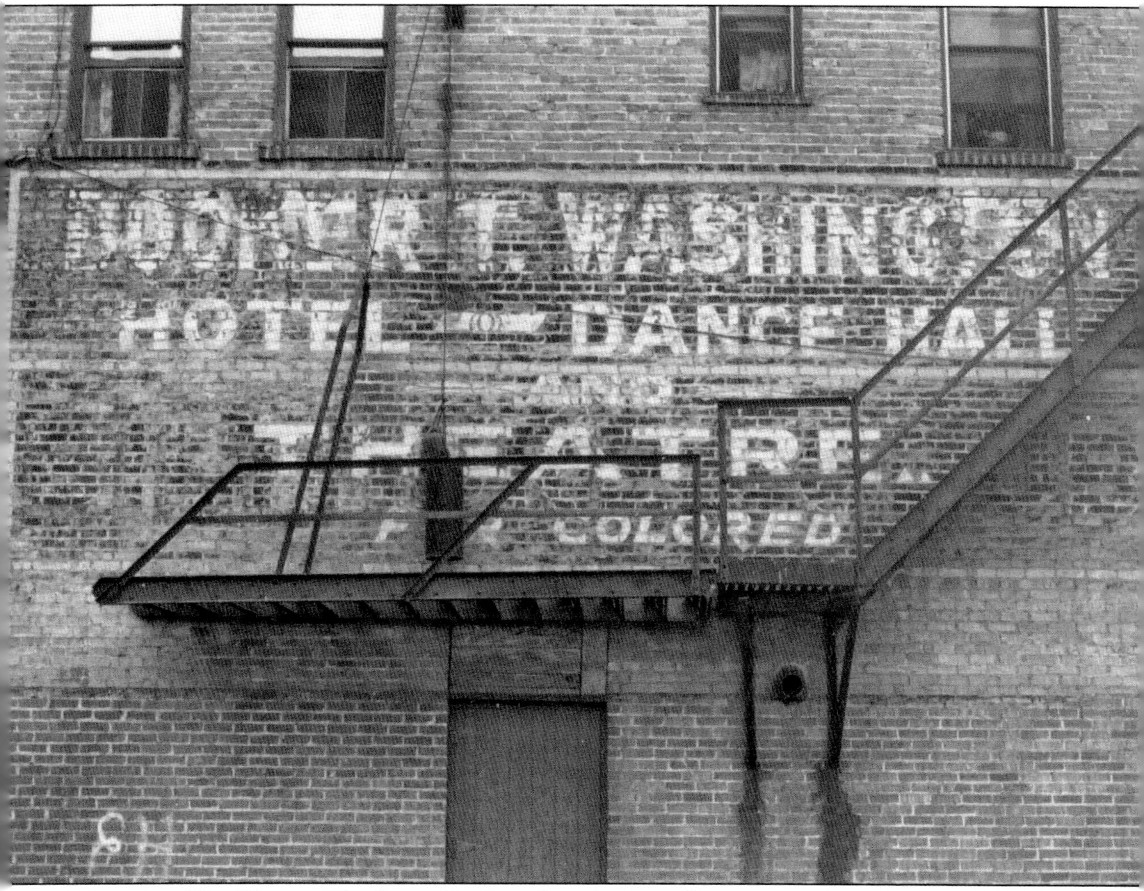

James Key Hotel. The James Key Hotel, with its Booker T. Washington Dance Hall located at 49 Southside Avenue, was one of the hot spots in the area. Built in the 1940s, it came under the ownership of Callie and Mason Washington James, who played host to many great African American celebrities. Performers and athletes touring the Jim Crow South had few classy spots in Western North Carolina at which to stop. The James Key Hotel was an oasis. Opera singer Marion Anderson, singer Nat King Cole, baseball star Jackie Robinson, and bandleader Count Basie all graced the place. The James also sponsored bands—the Eddie Crisp and Bull Moose Jackson bands, for example—that earned money on the "chitlin circuit." Guests had to be 21 to gain entrance to the dance hall. Benny Byrd, owner of Rabbit's Motel on McDowell Street, recalls as a child finding ways to enjoy the music. "We could hear the band," he said. The hotel "didn't have air conditioning, and had to open the windows and doors. We would sneak up the fire escape and peek in the window." Sam Camp, James' brother-in-law, became the owner of the hotel after he returned from the Korean War. When the city condemned it, he went to court to contest the low appraisal. He could not follow through because his family was afraid of the court system and of recriminations, Camp said. "I used to enjoy seeing people turn out for the dances, wearing evening gowns and heading up to the ballroom," Byrd reminisced. (Courtesy Andrea Clark.)

Nine

WEST END/CLINGMAN

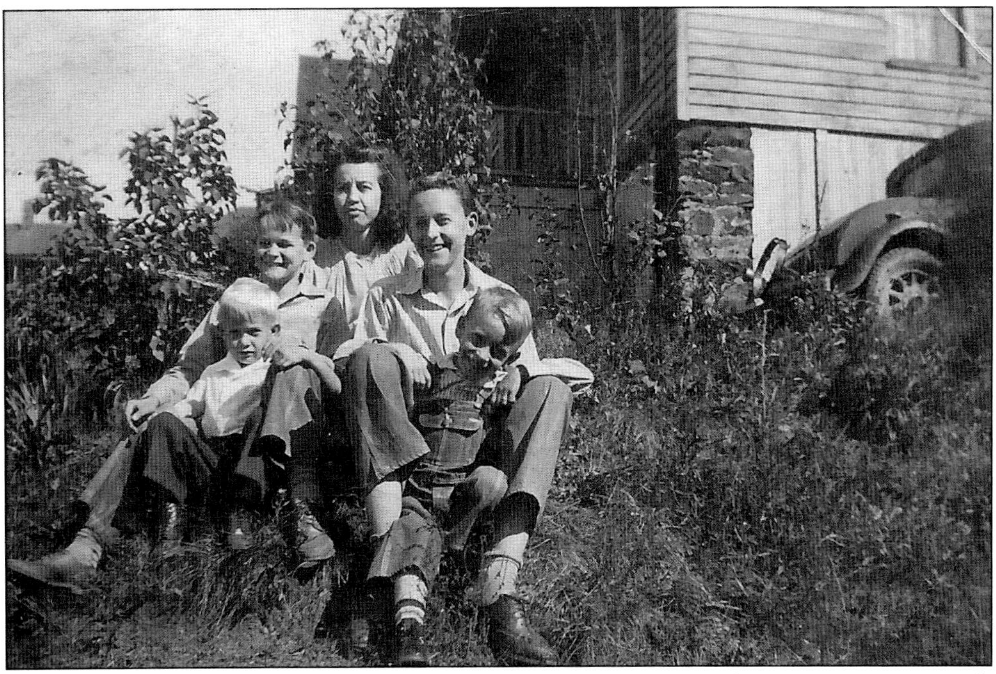

THE PRICE CHILDREN. Morris Charles and his children lived in a sturdy house at 7 Factory Hill. Factory Hill was the official name of the Asheville Cotton Mill village. People came to call it Chicken Hill because of the chickens that ran free or were associated later with the hatchery down below. Now much of village is gone, and there is disagreement over the continued use of the name Chicken Hill for the area. The West End/Clingman neighborhood—a bridging of former white and black communities—prefers the name they use and embraces the legacy of families who worked in the factories and struggled to better themselves. Pictured from left to right are Glenn, Don, Mildred, Ray, and Max Price. (Courtesy Max Price.)

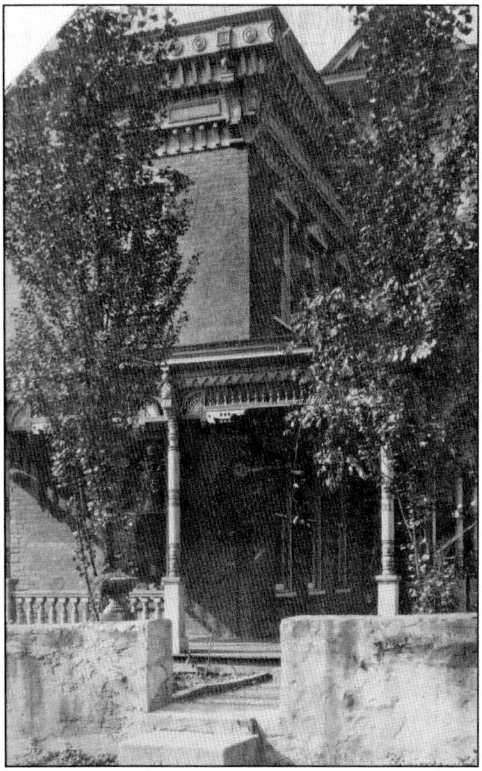

HANGAR HALL—THEN AND NOW. The mansion that Jubilee! minister Howard Hangar bought in 1973 had been built on Park Avenue in the 1880s by Peter Demens, who sold it to Col. and Mrs. James Rumbough, the owners of Mountain Park Hotel in Hot Springs, who later sold it to artist Ida Jolly Crawley. Hangar used a Corinthian capital salvaged from the former county courthouse to create landscape art. The renovated house is now home to a community of tenants. (Left, courtesy Howard Hangar; below, photographs by Henry Neufeld.)

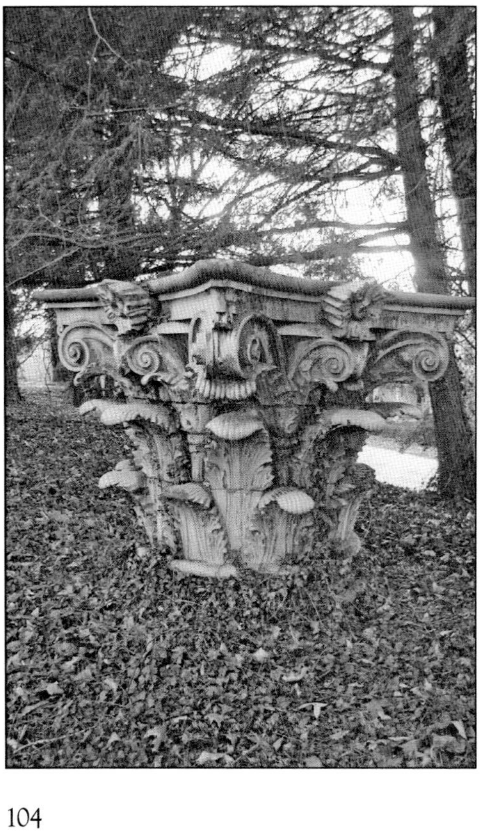

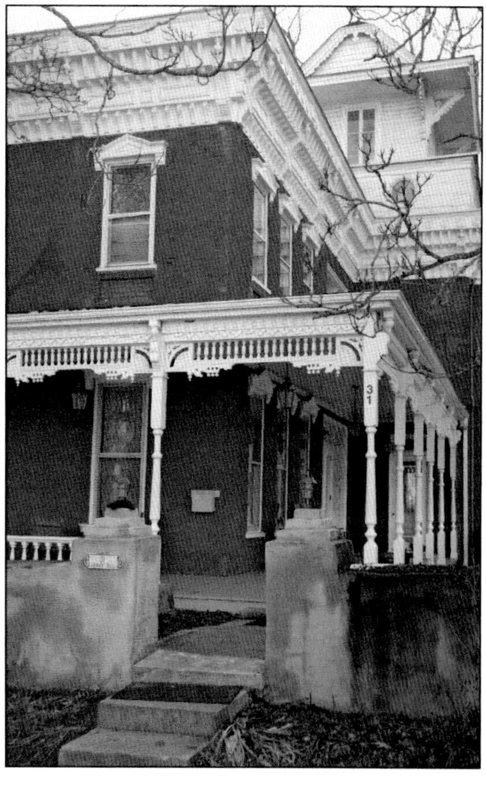

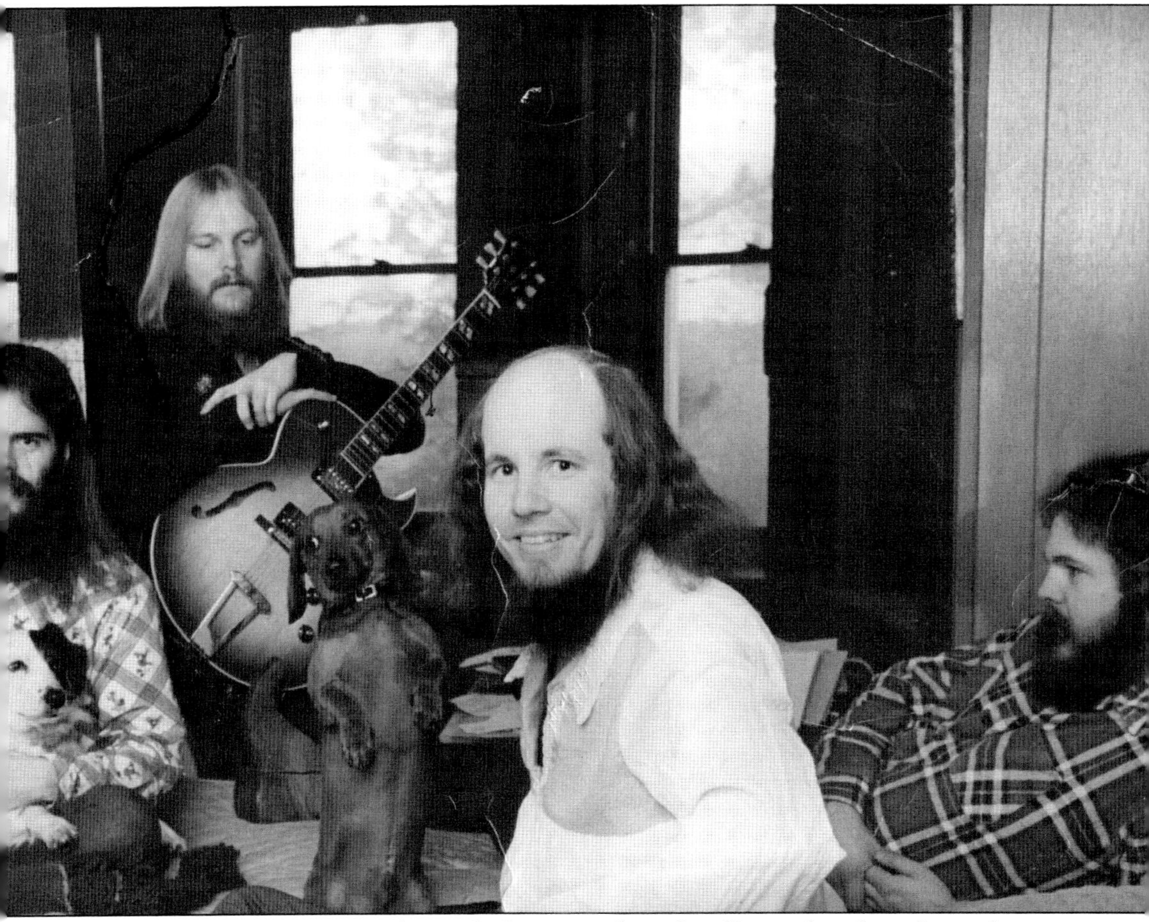

THE HOWARD HANGAR TRIO. The trio had grown to four when Hangar bought and moved into the old Rumbough house. They include, from left to right, A. D. Anderson, Ric McCarthur, Howard Hangar, and Martin Parker. Hangar Hall is the showpiece residence in the West End/Clingman Avenue neighborhood, which includes historic houses of many sizes. In October 2002, North Carolina's National Register Advisory Committee endorsed West End's nomination for national historic district status. Three weeks later, Asheville's Planning and Development Department opposed it, citing lack of historical integrity in West End. The planners also noted, "the proposed district is located in a neighborhood for which extensive redevelopment is anticipated"—namely, a newly devised option for an I-26 connector. On April 10, 2003, the National Park Service rejected the nomination "because the district has lost integrity." However, within the approximately 700-by-900-foot district bounded by Roberts Street, Park Avenue, and Club Street, there are 37 historic structures versus only 10 vacant lots where buildings had once stood. (Courtesy Howard Hangar.)

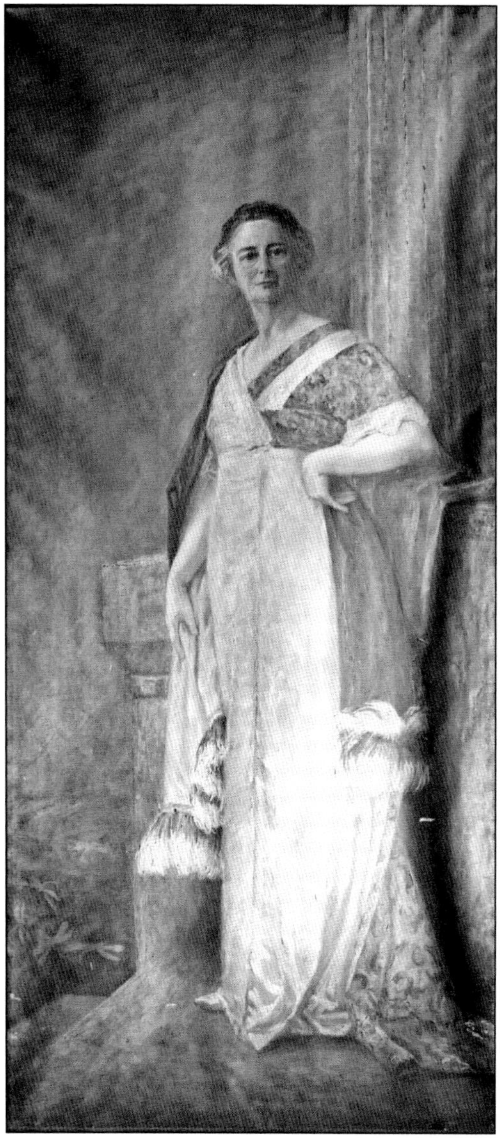

IDA CRAWLEY PORTRAIT. One day in the 1950s, Peggy Guest-Totherow and her friends looked across the street from Queen Carson School and saw a ghost. A movement on the second floor balcony of the Ida Jolly Crawley house had caught their attention. "I looked up," Peggy recalled in a 2005 interview conducted by West End residents, "and there was a woman with a long white dress on, and she had long white hair. I'm getting chills just thinking about it. And I said, 'Kids, who is that?' And those kids got so scared, they screamed and ran." Peggy warned the lady to be wary of the edge of the roof, which had no railing. The specter smiled and shook her head no. Peggy did some investigating. She knocked on the door of the house and was shown the portrait of painter Ida Crawley (pictured here). "That's her!" Peggy exclaimed. "Today is the anniversary of her death," her host said. Perhaps the genial spirit was a sign. Her confident demeanor on the precipice of the rooftop speaks of the history of the community. After taking hits—the 1916 flood, the Depression, industrial closings, urban renewal, and highway cut-throughs—West End/ Clingman has climbed back from the precipice to become a model of neighborhood improvement. (Photograph by Henry Neufeld.)

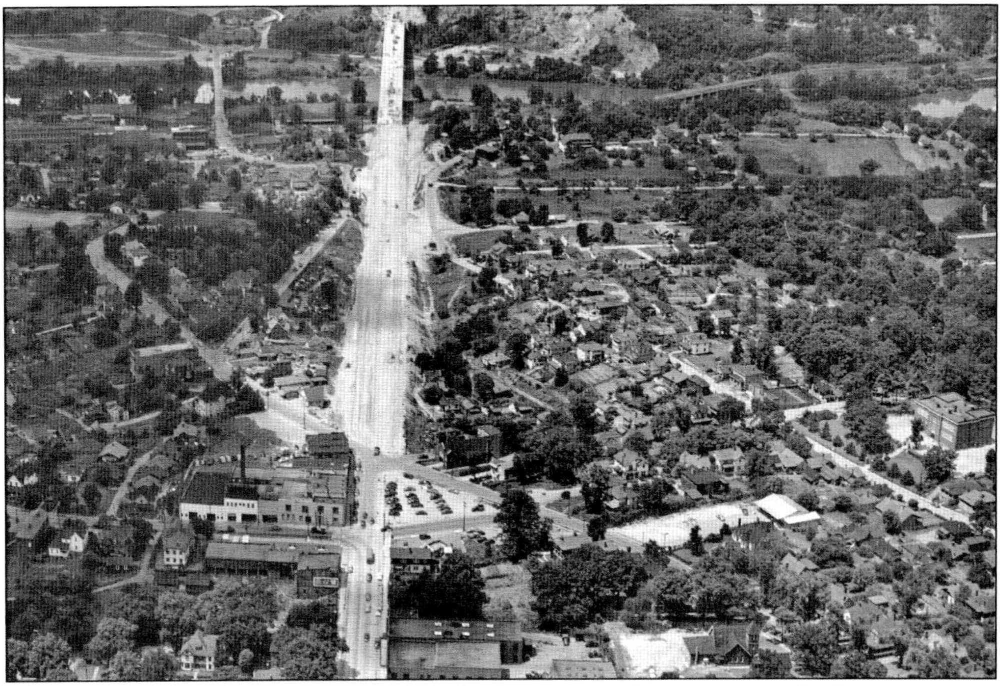

EXPRESSWAY COMING THROUGH. In 1952, the department of transportation built an expressway connecting Asheville to West Asheville. It eliminated and cut off the West End/Clingman neighborhoods. (Courtesy Asheville *Citizen-Times*.)

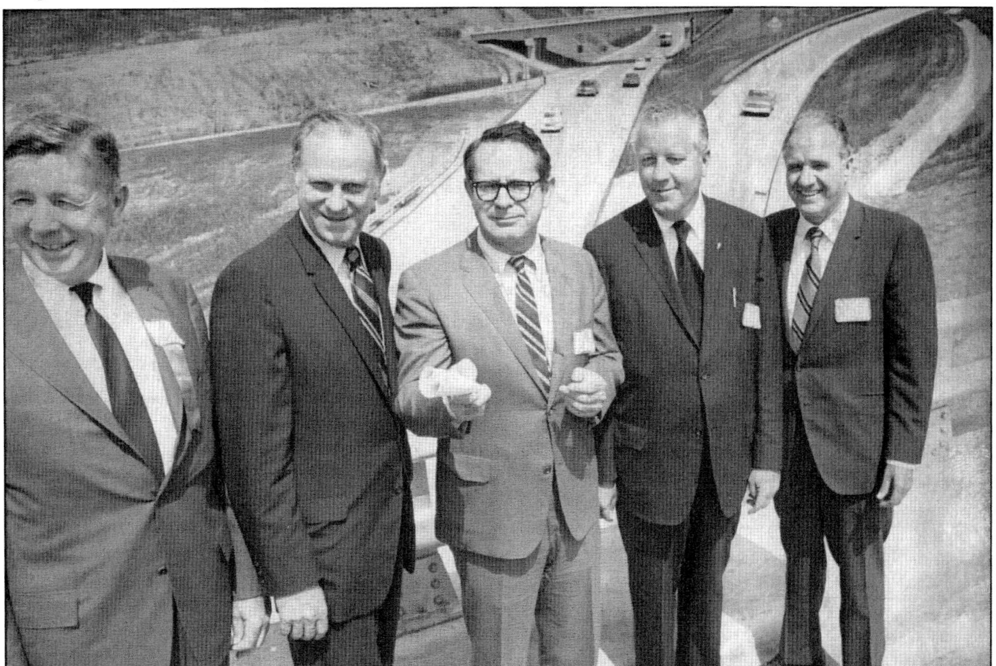

I-240 INTERCHANGE OPENING, SEPTEMBER 2, 1970. From left to right, Rep. Roy Taylor, Jack B. Kirksey, Lauch Faircloth, John Erichson, and James Stikeleather Jr. pose for the historic event. (Courtesy Asheville *Citizen-Times*.)

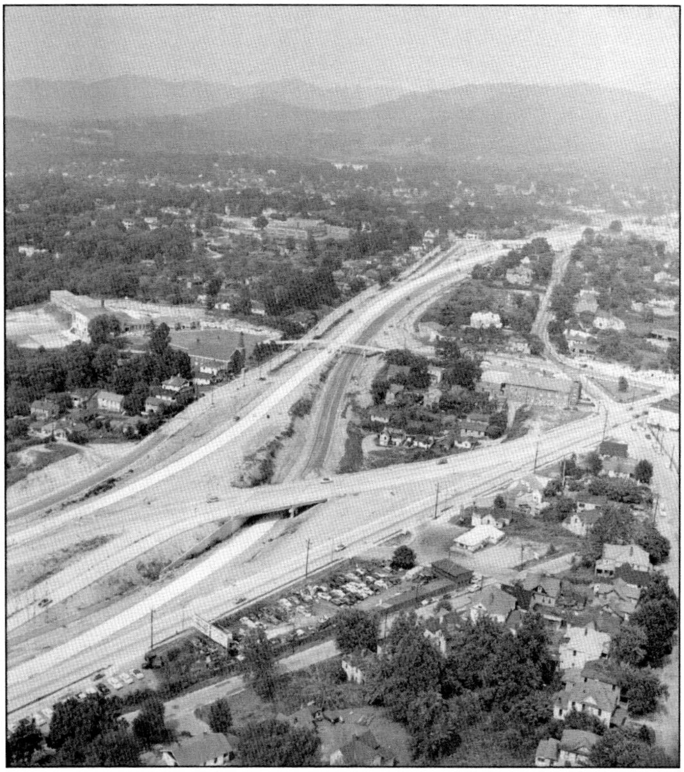

The Interstate. Clingman Avenue comes out of the West End community on the bottom right to cross Patton Avenue, where it feeds into I-240. The homes and businesses displaced by the highway, as well as those on the other side, had once been part of one community. In the triangle of land formed by Patton Avenue and the interstate is Haywood United Methodist Church, attended by many West End old-timers, and the site of WECAN's organizational meeting for national historic status. (Photograph by Malcolm Gamble, 1960, courtesy North Carolina Collection, Pack Memorial Library.)

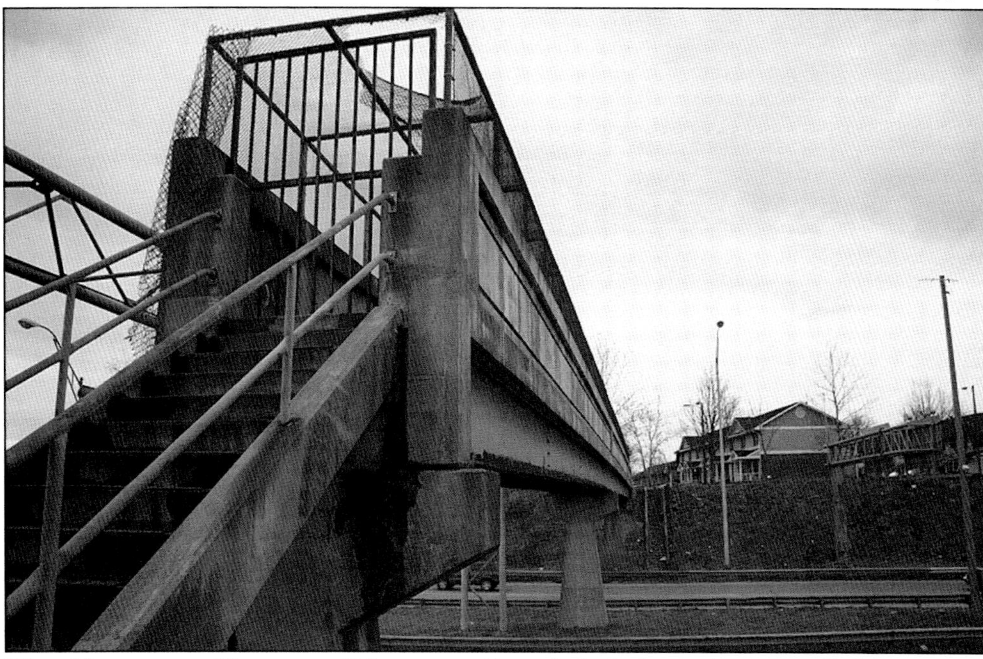

West Haywood to Hillcrest. Urban renewal brought high-density housing, called the Hillcrest Apartments, to what is now the north side of I-240. The pedestrian bridge, built to enable safe crossing, has been gated off. Hillcrest residents can still take the long way around off their hill and cross on a dirt path under the highway to Roberts Street. (Photograph by Henry Neufeld.)

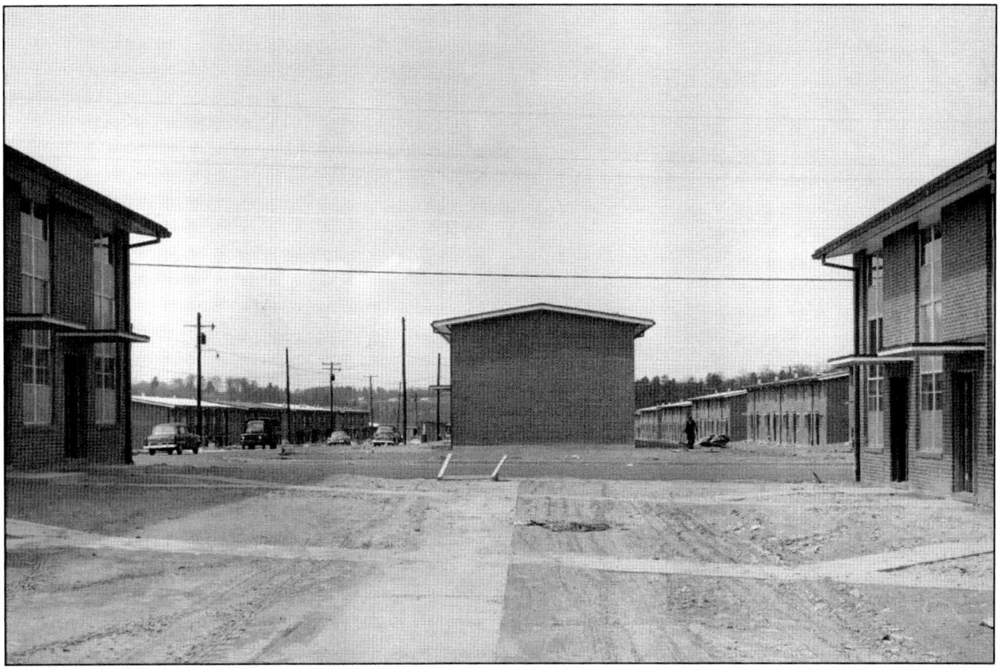

HILLCREST APARTMENTS. The Hillcrest Apartments, built in 1959, were called the West End Housing Development for Negroes in newspaper reports. (Courtesy Asheville *Citizen-Times*.)

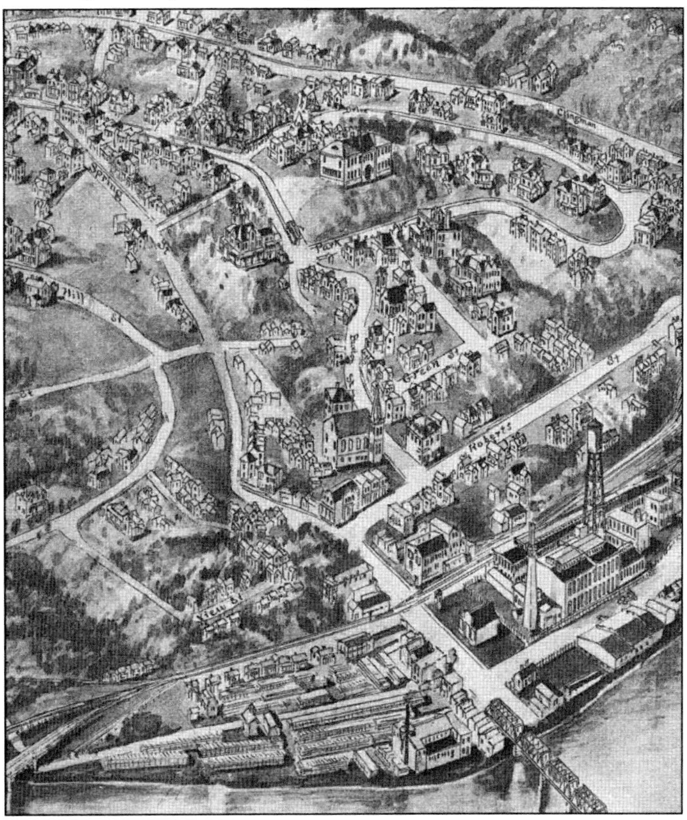

WEST END, 1912. At the top of the map is the sock-shaped neighborhood that C. E. Graham, a cotton mill owner, built around the Rumbough house on the steep ridge. He called it Prospect Park. Today, at the bottom of Girdwood Avenue, is a group of modest houses arranged down a hill on a circular road called Park Square. It gives a good idea of the kind of homes Graham built for his workers. On the left side of the map is Hill Street. (Courtesy North Carolina Collection, Pack Memorial Library.)

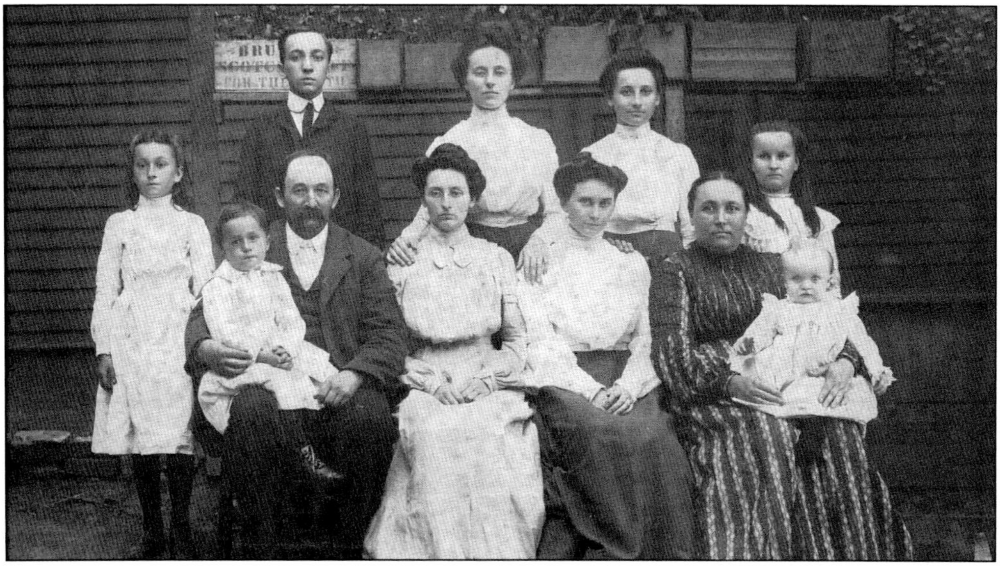

WESTMORELAND FAMILY. "The biggest irony," said Byron Ballard, a fourth-generation West End resident, "of it now being a place where you can buy a half million dollar condominium is that the [original residents] lived rough, they made do the best they could." Ballard's great-grandparents Benjamin Franklin and Lillian Moore Westmoreland moved to West End in the late 1890s for two reasons: to be near his place of work, the Biltmore Estate, where he was a laborer; and to escape his in-laws, a large, overwhelming family in Canton. B. F., who lived a long life with one lung, established one of the first stores in post-railroad West End. He also concocted get-rich schemes and inventions, and acted as a middleman in a bootlegging operation. "My mother remembered those bottles being around the house," Ballard related and recalled her parents "hiding bottles of illegal moonshine in her crib when she was little." Pictured are, from left to right, (first row) Allie, Roy, Benjamin Franklin (B.F.), Retta, Ora, Lillian, and Walter Westmoreland; (second row) Carl, Luna, Irene, and Freda Westmoreland. (Courtesy Byron Ballard.)

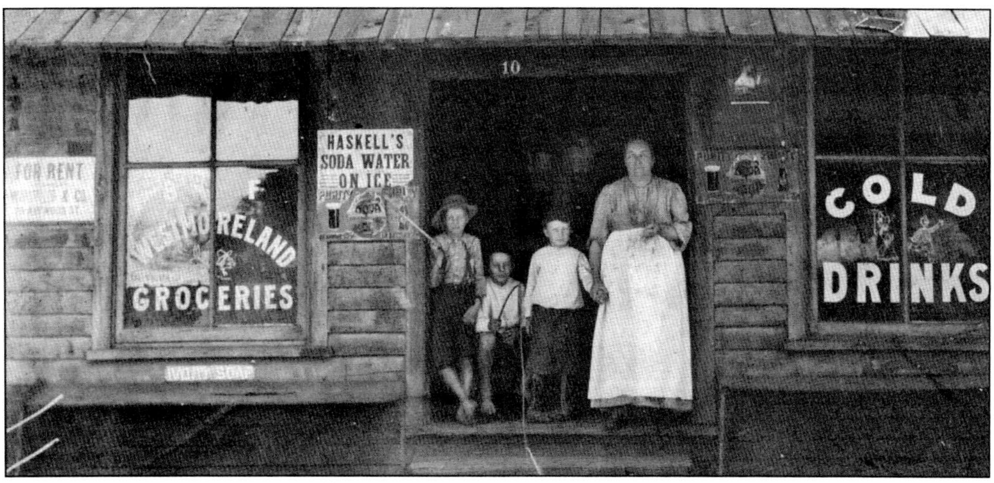

WESTMORELAND GROCERY. Lillian Moore Westmoreland poses in her ever-present apron in the doorway of Westmoreland Grocery at 10 Roberts Street in West End in April 1902. Lillian was both a welcoming mother and stern moral guide to all children. Pictured from left to right are family friend Ralph Robinson and Lillian's two sons, Ray and Walter Westmoreland. (Courtesy Byron Ballard.)

HELEN ON ROBERTS STREET. When Byron Ballard's grandmother Helen Westmoreland (later Boyd) applied for a job in the Asheville Cotton Mill, her brother Roy stepped in. He got her a job at Green's Hardware on Pack Square instead. Ottis Green, the hardware store owner, had been a mayor of Asheville and was part of the prominent Green family that had grown up in West End. "Roy was familiar with the cotton mill," Ballard recounts, "and he said the conditions were just hellish, and he didn't want his baby sister working there. The workers couldn't breathe. There were neighbors all around who had brown lung." (Courtesy Byron Ballard.)

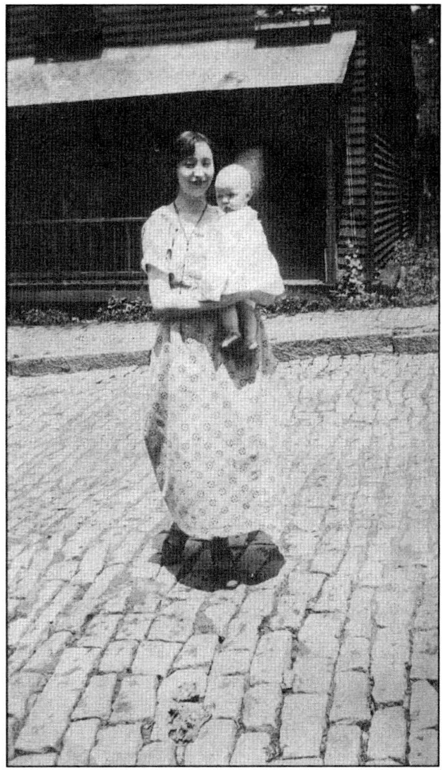

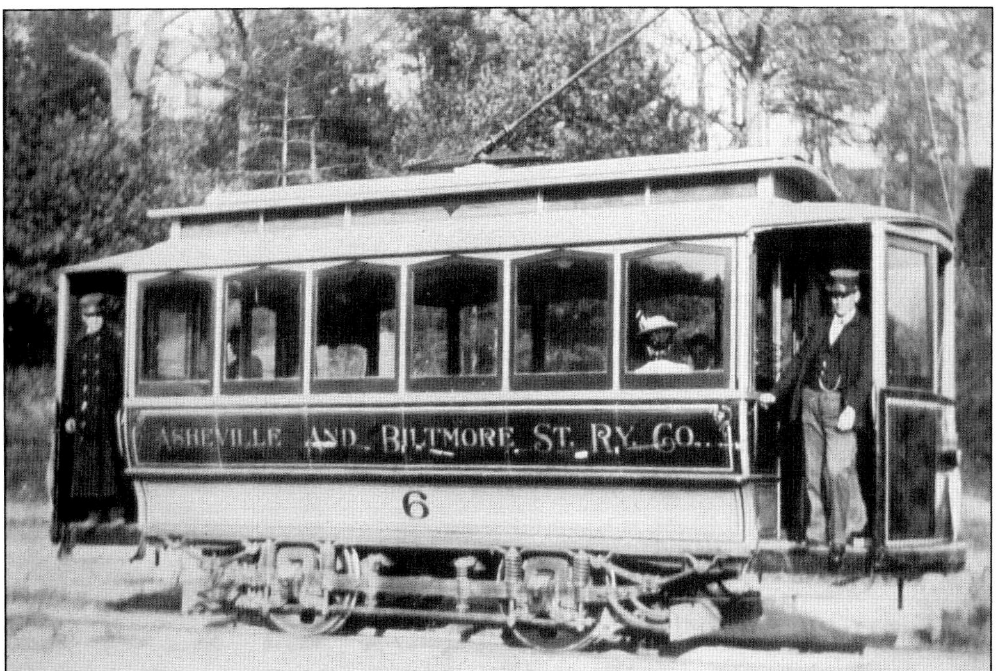

ELECTRIC STREETCAR. Asheville's electric streetcar served the riverside neighborhoods at a few points until buses replaced them and the tracks were torn up in 1934. Ida Jolly Crowley was known to take the trolley downtown. (Photograph from author's collection.)

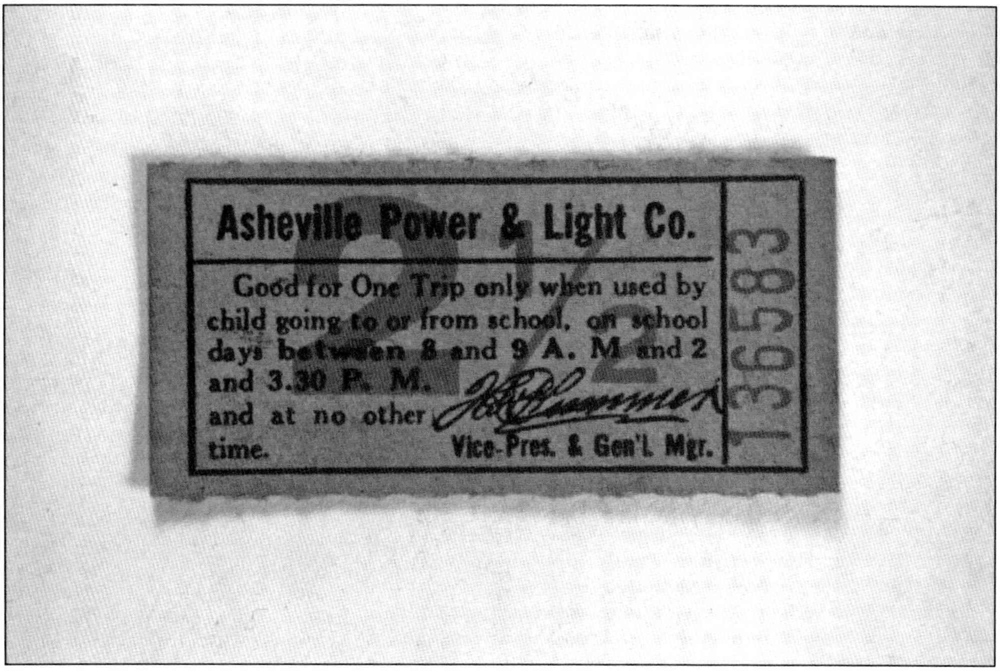

STUDENT FREEBIES. Asheville Power and Light provided free streetcar tickets to students. Students could stop downtown before going home. (Courtesy the author's collection.)

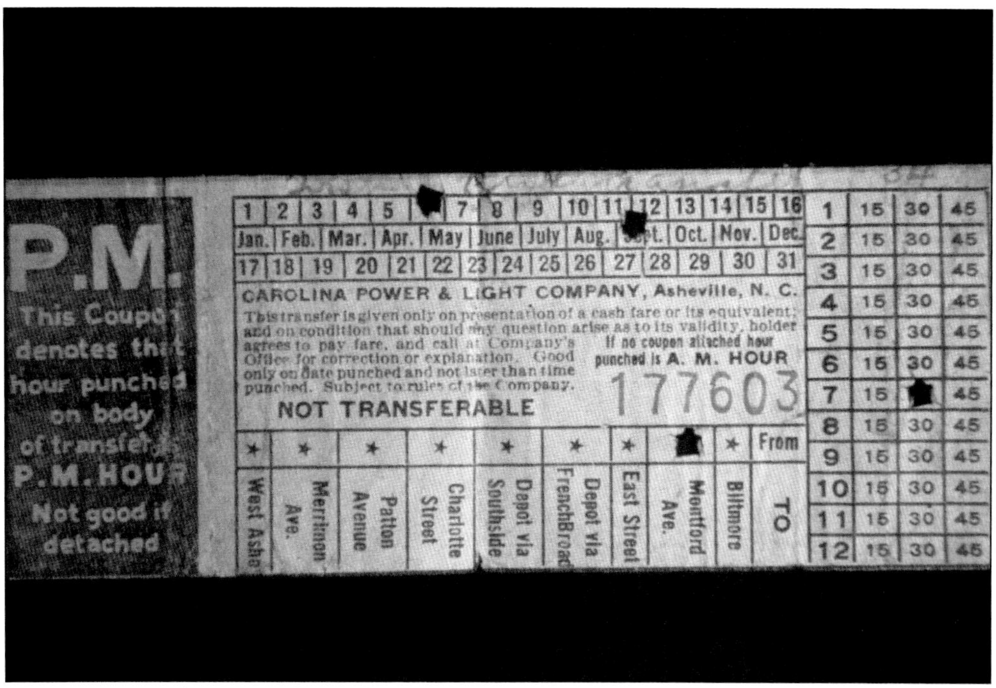

TRANSFERS. This transfer ticket shows the stops on the Biltmore line. It went down Depot Street. (Courtesy the author's collection.)

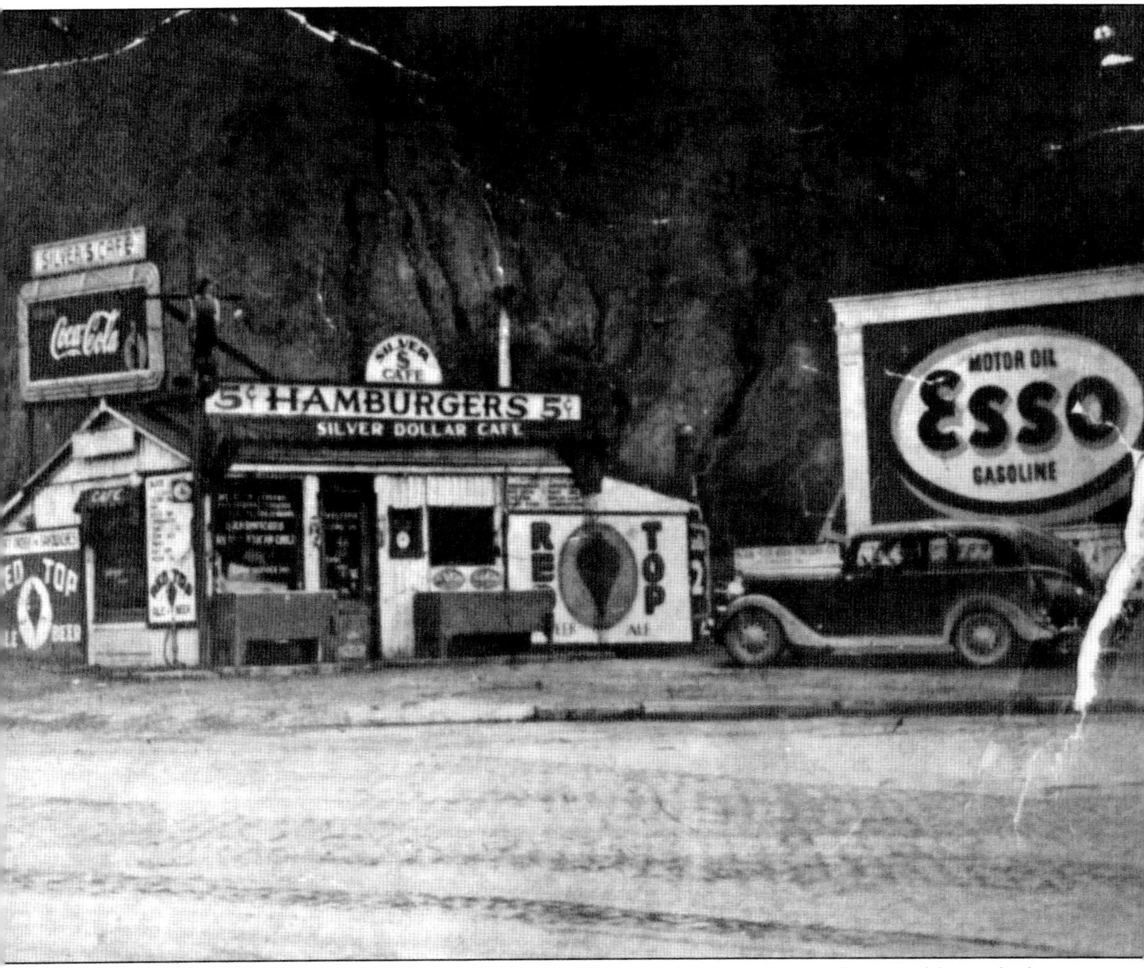

ROADSIDE CAFÉ. In the 1940s and 1950s, the era of blue highways (secondary roads), roadside cafés were popular stops. The walls of the Silver Dollar are decorated with mementos, including this photograph of an earlier incarnation. (Courtesy the Mitslos family.)

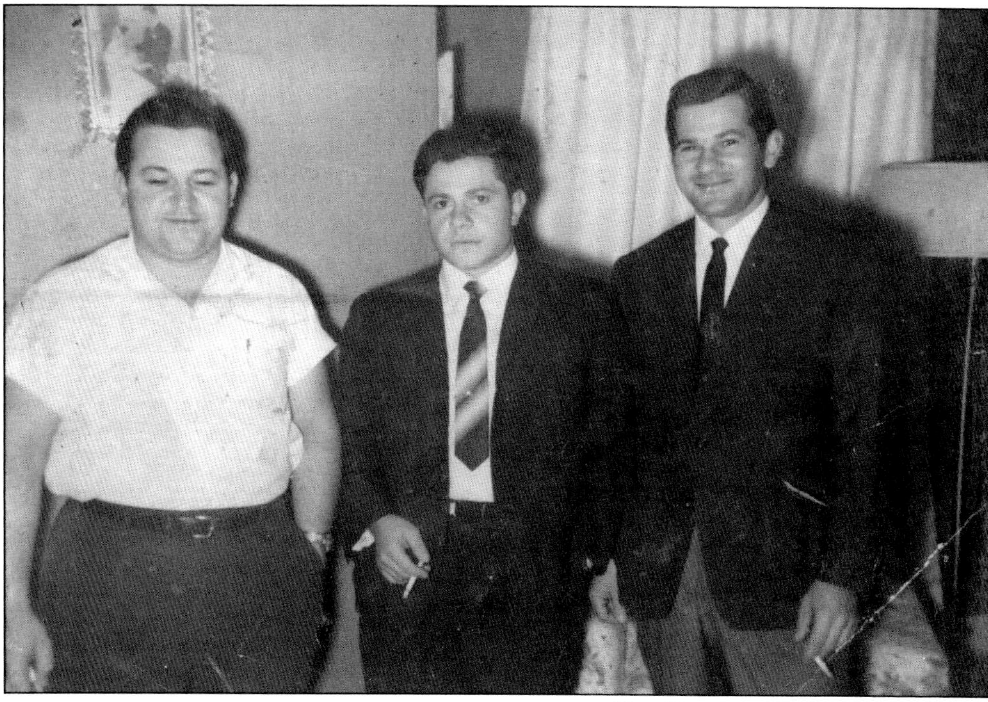

The Dotsikas Brothers. Pictured from left to right, Theodore, Jimmy, and Angelo Dotsikas bought the Silver Dollar Cafe in 1966. (Courtesy the Mitslos family.).

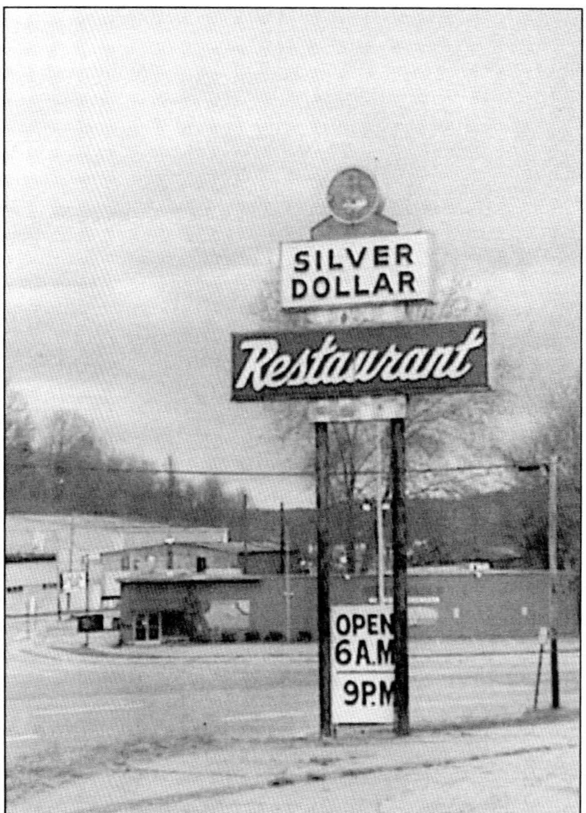

Silver Dollar Restaurant. The Silver Dollar Café had been located further west originally. The Mitslos brothers presided over the move to its present location, when Clingman Avenue was widened for the new West Asheville Bridge. In 2008, the brothers and Angelo's wife, Catherine, continued 42 years of service without having an heir apparent. (Courtesy the Mitslos family.)

Ten

West Asheville

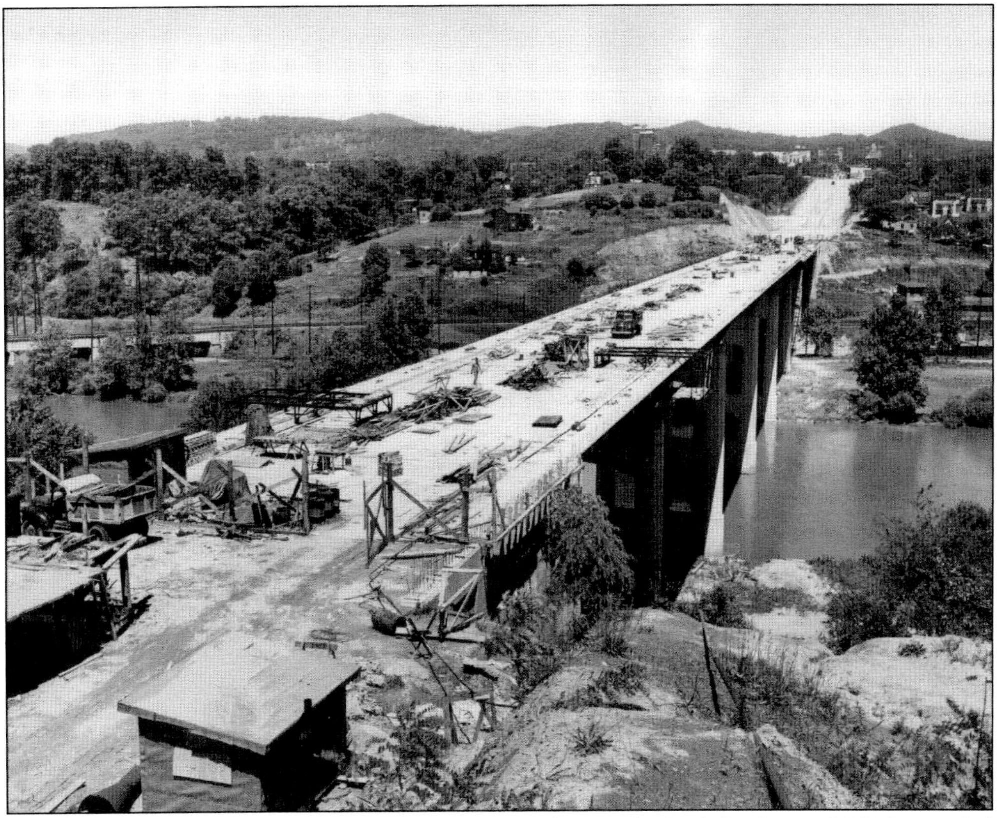

Smoky Park Bridge Construction, c. 1950. The Smoky Park Bridge and I-240 provided an alternate route to West Asheville from what had been the customary path down Haywood Road and the old West Asheville Bridge. The highway bridge led to the construction of Patton Avenue in West Asheville. With it came the pioneering Westgate Mall and a new business district that skirted West Asheville's main street. George Coggins, the Westgate Mall developer, invited longtime Haywood Road merchants Albert Fortune and John Lawrence to move to the mall, but they refused. Fortune recalls that Coggins predicted that there would be grass growing down the middle of Haywood Road soon. Within the last several years, West Asheville along Haywood Road has come back with new small businesses and home buyers interested in neighborhoods that are within walking distance of shops. (Courtesy North Carolina Collection, Pack Memorial Library.)

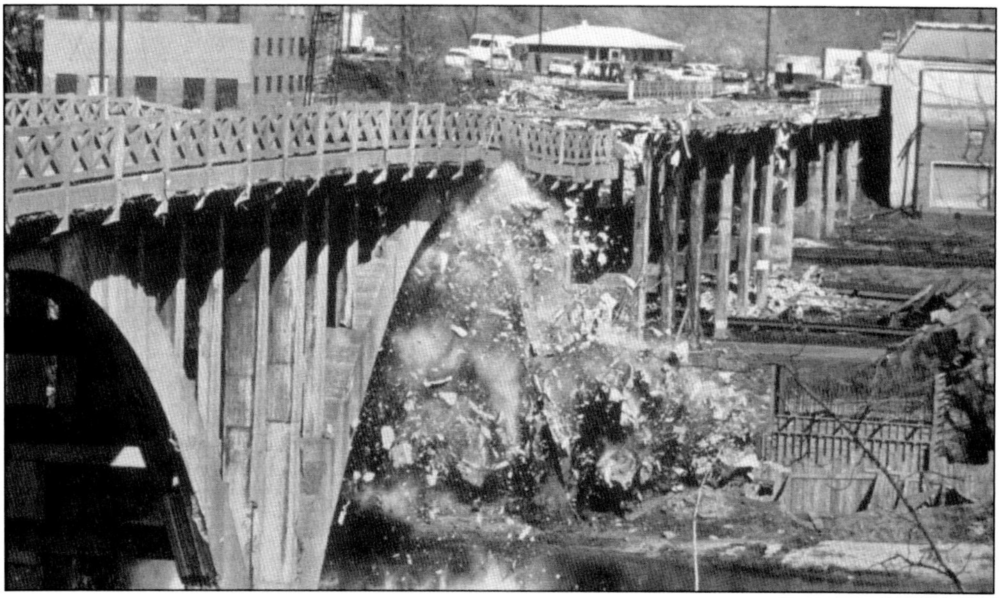

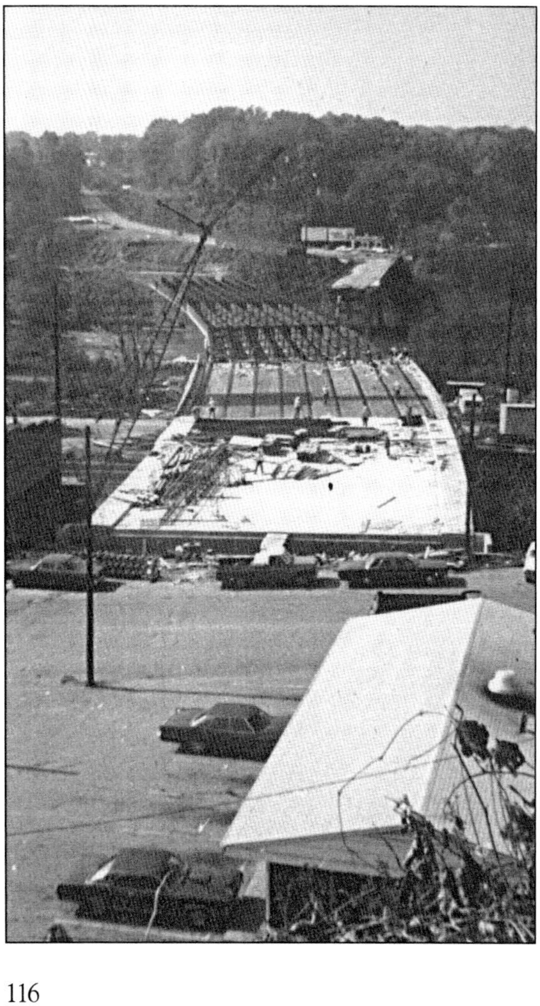

WEST ASHEVILLE BRIDGE DEMOLITION. A state engineer noticed that the old West Haywood Bridge was crumbling and proposed its demolition. The West Asheville Business Association mobilized and secured a promise that a new bridge leading to the head of the West Asheville commercial district would be built in about the same place. The old bridge was sturdier than it looked, and its destruction involved cost overruns. The new West Asheville Bridge, completed in 1972, involved widening Clingman Avenue and Haywood Road. The grading removed the winding *S*-shaped portion of Park Avenue that had crossed over Haywood Road and fed back into it. The resulting landscape includes a chopped hill across from the Phil Mechanic Building on Roberts Street and, on the other side of the bridge, an artistically landscaped welcome to West Asheville. (Courtesy North Carolina Collection, Pack Memorial Library.)

SILVER DOLLAR MOVE. The new West Asheville Bridge required moving the Silver Dollar Café, located in the bottom right of the photograph. (Courtesy North Carolina Collection, Pack Memorial Library.)

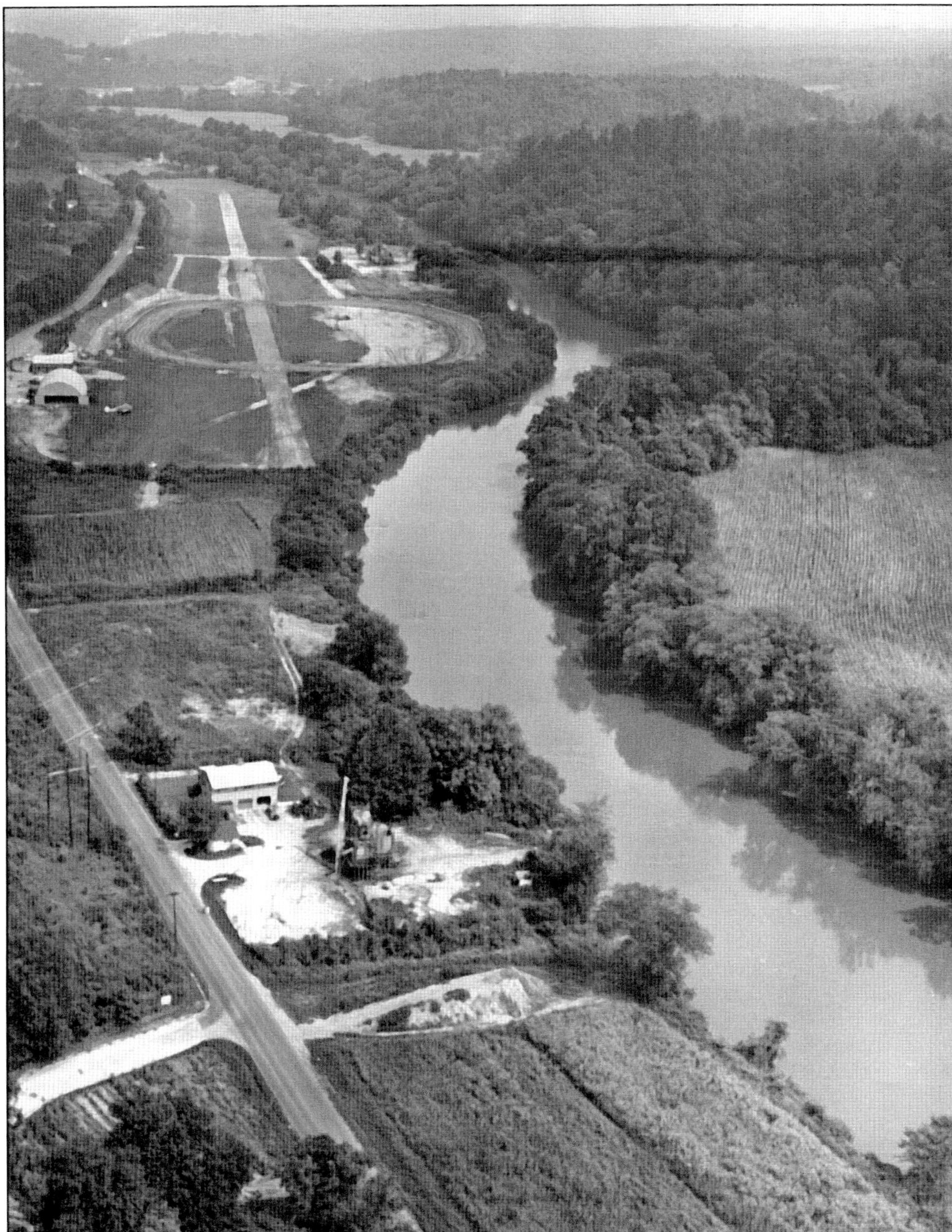

The River at Carrier Field. Forty years ago, there was little development along this stretch except for the Asheville Speedway, which has been replaced by a park, and a sand production company, now inactive. (Courtesy Asheville *Citizen-Times*.)

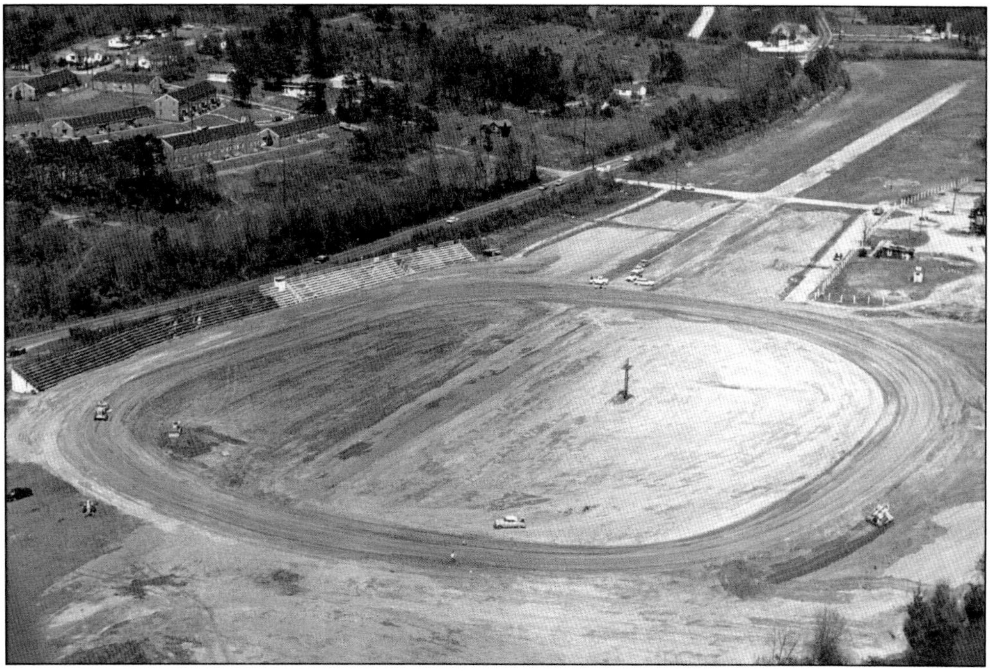

ASHEVILLE MOTOR SPEEDWAY. From 1962 through 1968 and again in 1971, the new Asheville Speedway hosted an annual NASCAR race. The track had been paved by that time. On Friday nights, four other divisions of cars raced, disturbing some neighbors with their noise. (Courtesy North Carolina Collection, Pack Memorial Library.)

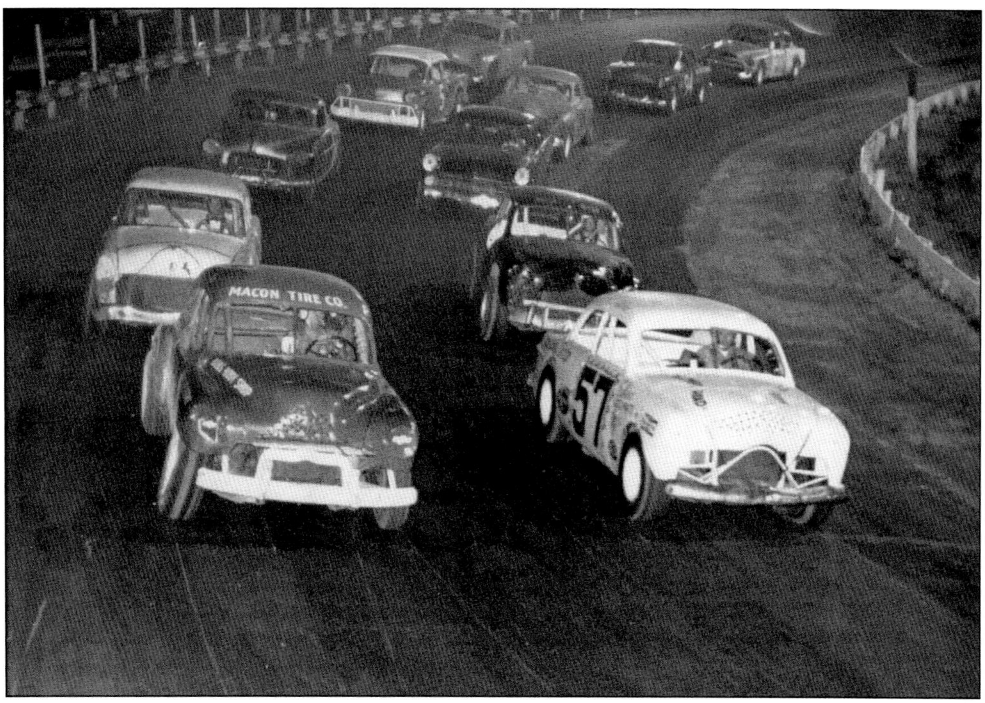

ASHEVILLE SPEEDWAY RACE. Cars in the Hobby Stock Division take a turn at the New Asheville Speedway. (Courtesy North Carolina Collection, Pack Memorial Library.)

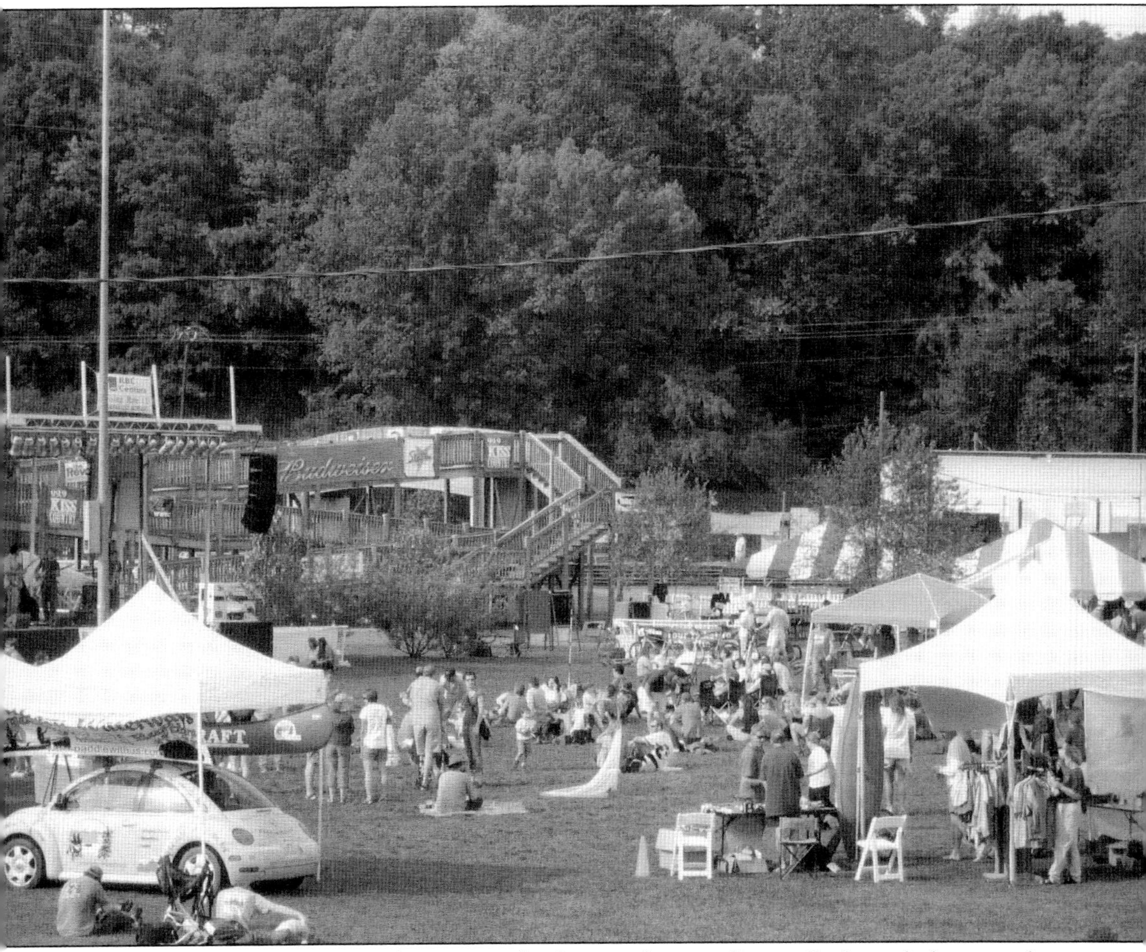

RIVERLINK RECREATION. Bicycles now circle the speedway at Carrier Park, and playgrounds enliven other parts of the 50-acre property, which was purchased by RiverLink in 1999 after a $1.6-million capital campaign. RiverLink donated the park to the city for its operation and maintenance. Starting in 2001, the Asheville Bicycle Racing Club has run a summer race series for fixed-gear and road bicycles on what has come to be called the Mellowdrome. The Asheville Mellowdrome is a member track of the American Track Racing Association and hosts the North and South Carolina State Track Championships. (Courtesy RiverLink.)

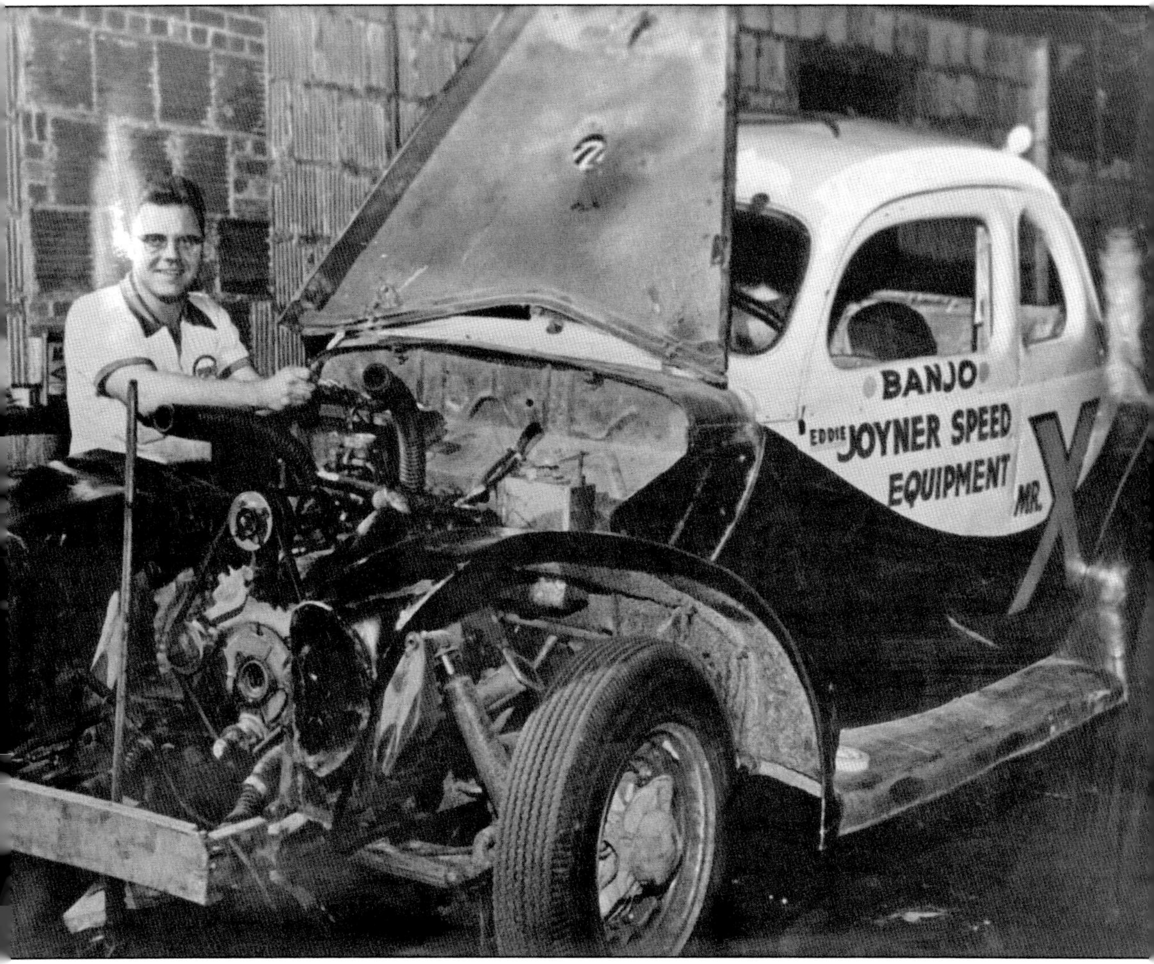

BANJO'S X CAR. Banjo Matthews, a legendary Asheville NASCAR driver, poses with his car, "Mr. X," which he had bought from Eddie Joyner and Toy Jones. Matthews was also famous for the cars he built and fixed for other drivers. Here he is outfitting the Mr. X with a seven-gallon tank to get it within NASCAR regulations. His 500-lap victory at McCormick Field Speedway, two miles northeast of the river, had been disqualified for his use of an oversize gas tank. He lost $961 in prize money that night. Matthews was also familiar with the New Asheville Speedway and had worked with transmission expert John Bell, whose Main Auto Parts shop is behind the Western Carolina Stockyard on the site of the former scrap yard. (Courtesy John Bell.)

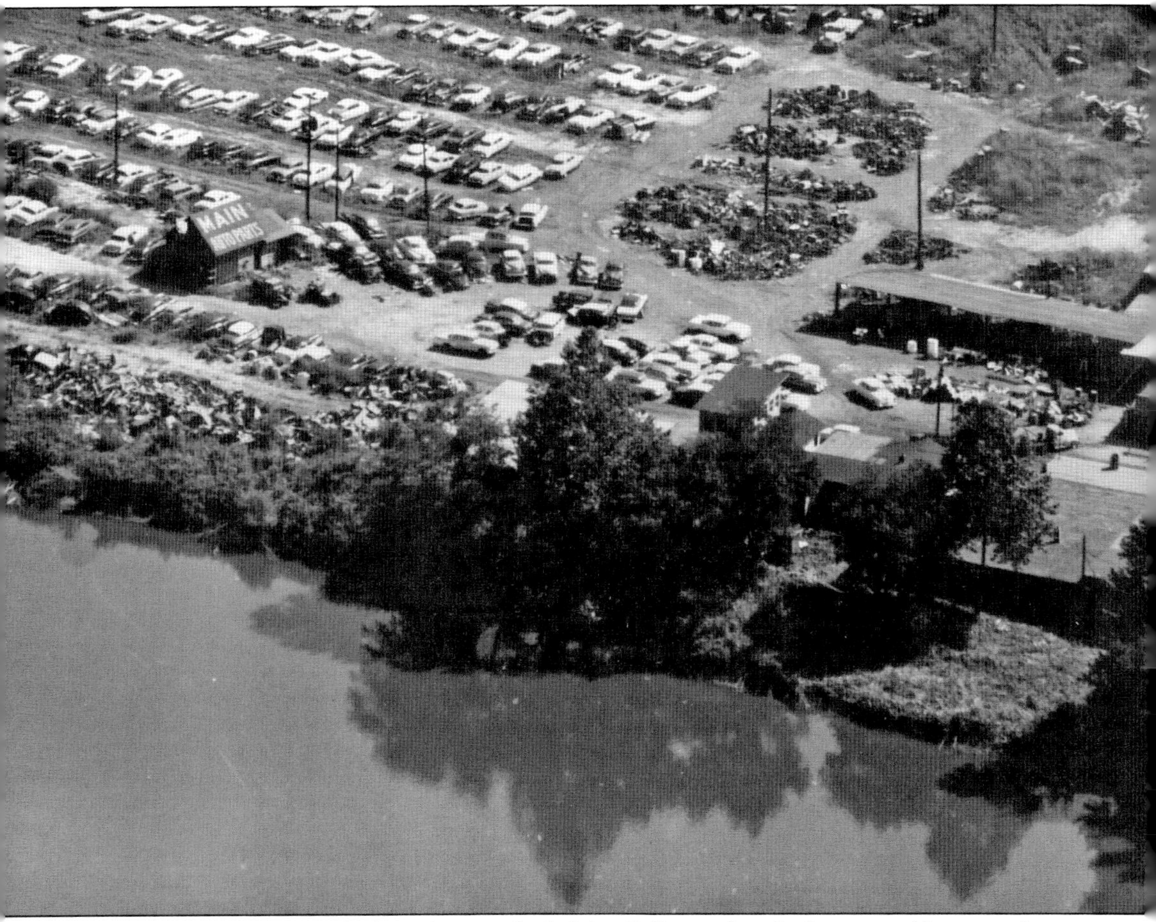

MAIN AUTO PARTS LOT. The large lot on which John Bell stored junked cars, used by many for auto parts, no longer exists. Over several years, the City of Asheville filled it in with the debris of buildings it demolished. Main Auto Parts is now the graveyard of many defunct and dismembered neighborhood school buildings. (Courtesy John Bell.)

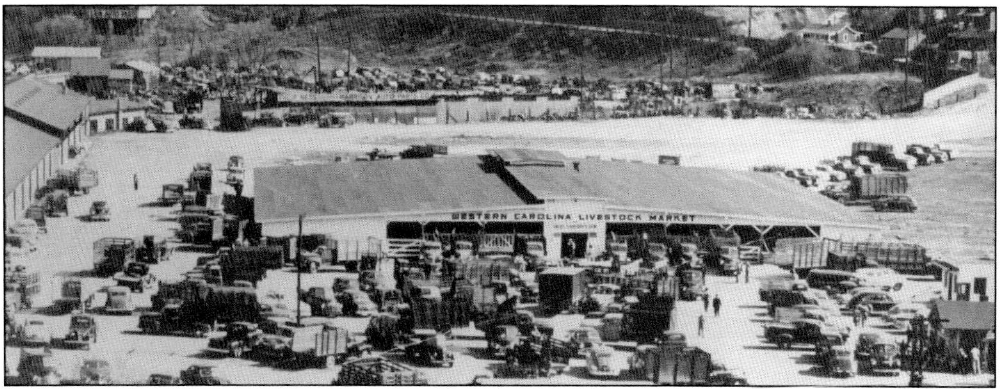

WESTERN CAROLINA STOCKYARD. Asheville's stockyard had once been on the other side of the river, and the West Asheville site had been the staging ground for traveling circuses. Steer and heifer sales took place at the livestock market for half a century. In 1999, it hosted the livestock auctioneers' world championship. The livestock market closed down in 2005. (Courtesy Willie Plemmons.)

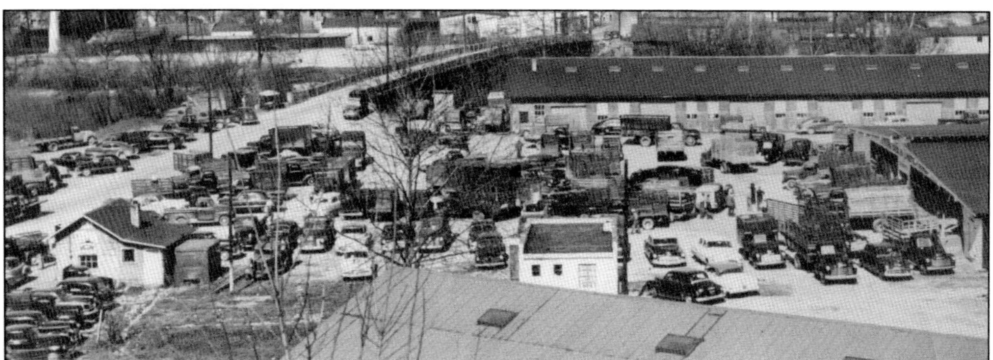

STOCKYARD GARAGE. The long garage building in the background burned down in the early 1990s. The small building on the left is the Stockyard Café, which is still in operation. (Courtesy Willie Plemmons.)

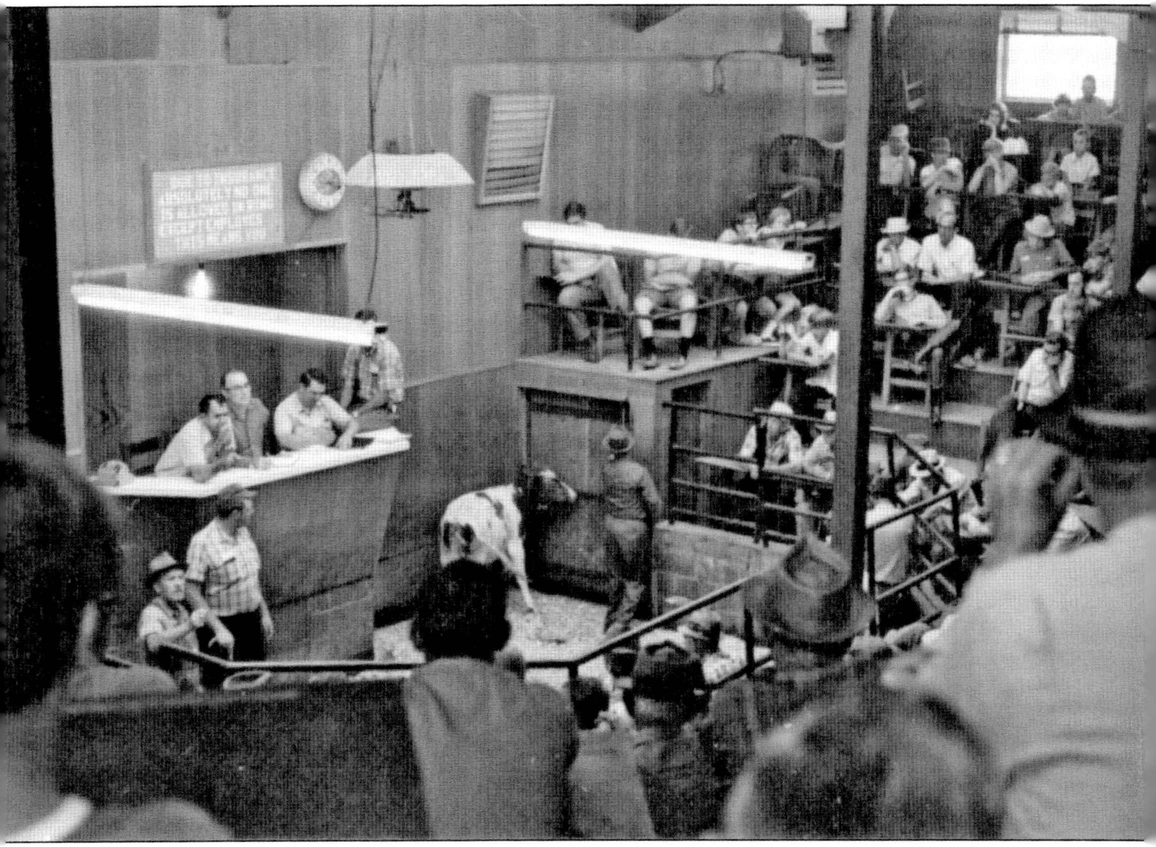

COWS AND MEN. The year 1950 was a peak one for livestock sales. In the Asheville stockyard alone, located on Riverside Drive until it moved across the river in 1953, sales topped $5 million. The livestock yard had a staff of 24 who weighed, identified, and classified cattle brought in by farmers from a 100-mile radius. Their trucks jammed the parking space around the yard. This photograph was taken in the late 1960s by Andrea Clarke.

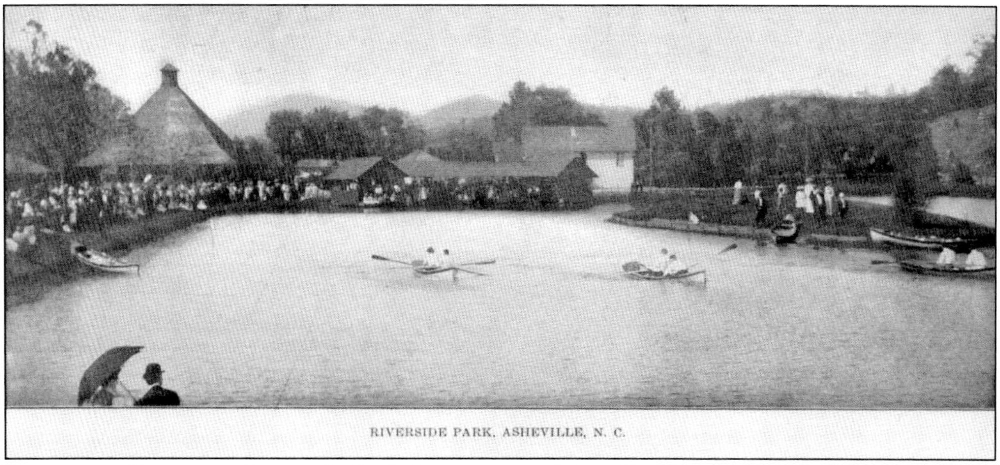

RIVERSIDE BOATING. Riverside Park downriver in Montford featured a lake for boating, an outdoor movie theater, and accommodations for horse shows and picnics. The flood of 1916 destroyed the park, and it never came back into use. (Courtesy North Carolina Collection, Pack Memorial Library.)

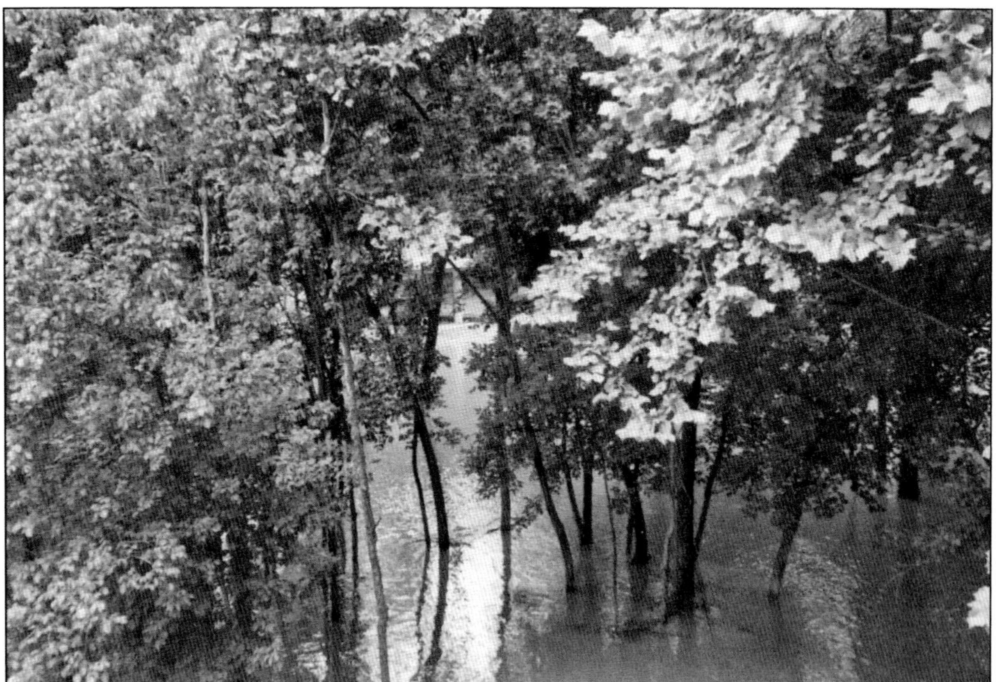

PARK IN FLOOD. RiverLink's French Broad River Park flooded in 2004, creating this scenic image. The park was not damaged. Many riverside enterprises have failed or been badly hurt throughout the years because of the river's unpredictable behavior. What would the district be like if it revered the river in all its forms? (Courtesy RiverLink.)

PENLAND'S AUCTION. Johnny Penland made his auction house a fixture next to the livestock market in 1966. His son-in-law, Tommy Tuten, now runs it with him. (Photograph by Henry Neufeld.)

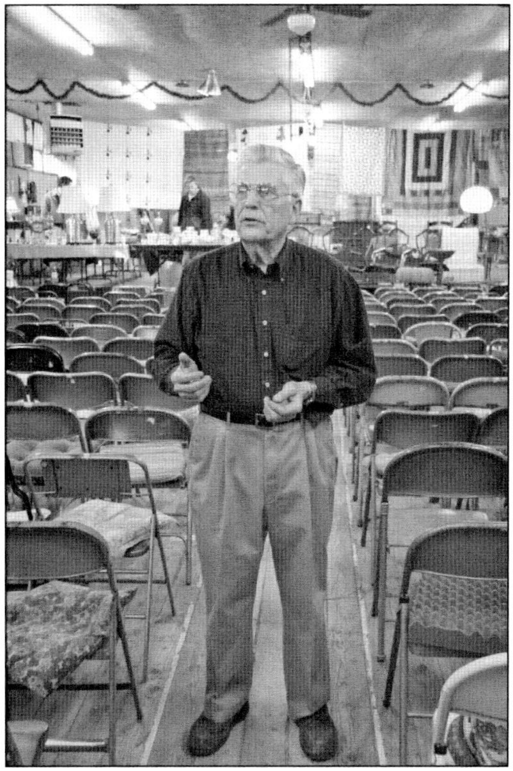

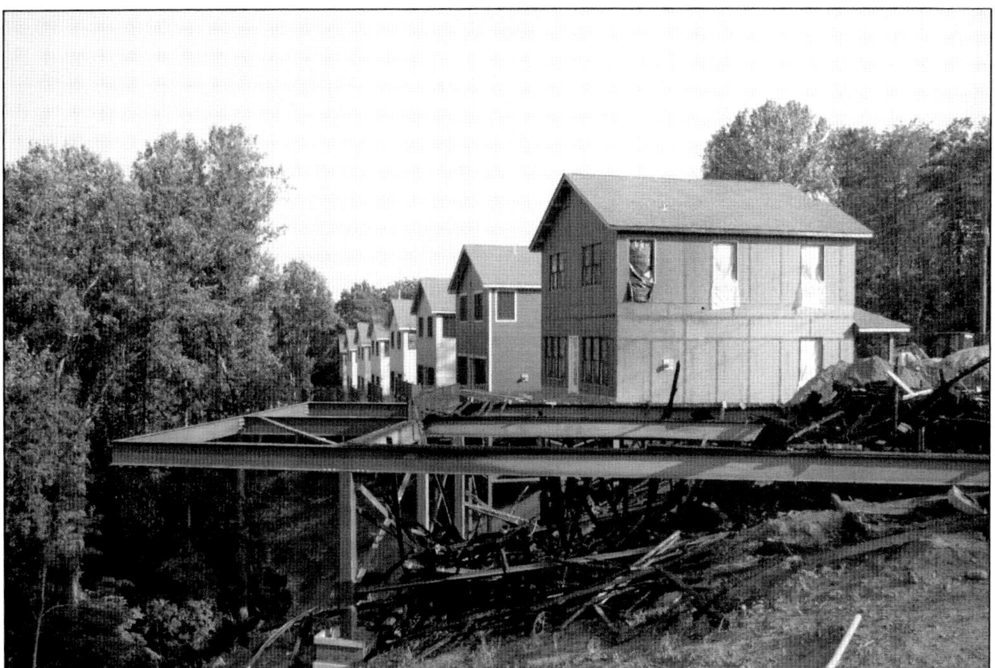

RIVERVIEW PERCHES. Homes built on the ledge overlooking the river from the west side have had to make use of metal stilts. In the foreground is a new construction that burned down in a suspicious fire. (Courtesy Henry Neufeld.)

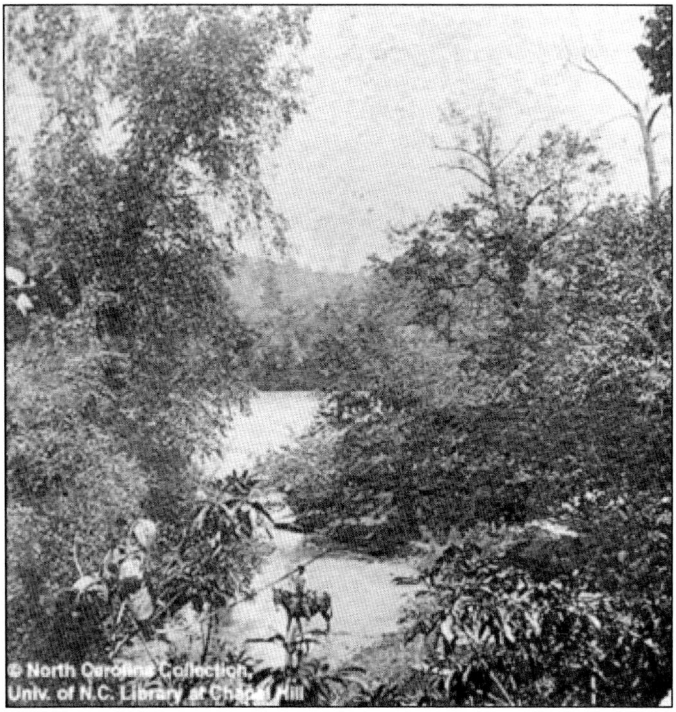

SMITH'S CREEK OF YORE. Smith's Creek runs through West Asheville into the French Broad River. It used to be a wild and romantic setting, as witnessed by this c. 1900 photograph of the junction of the creek and river. (Courtesy North Carolina Collection, Pack Memorial Library.)

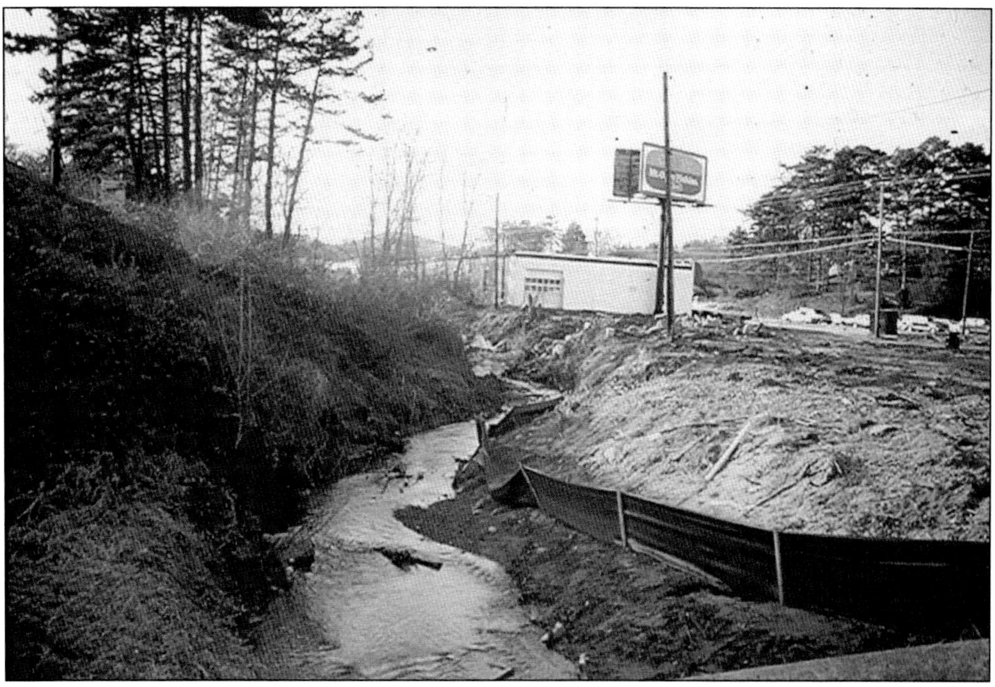

SMITH'S CREEK. The author took this photograph of Smith's Creek in 2000 while exploring the headwaters of streams that feed into the French Broad River. With the construction of Patton Avenue—an extension of the Smoky Park Bridge and highway—the creek was reduced to a culvert. Just up Patton at the Burger King, elders in the community related that there had been a few productive springs. (Courtesy the author's collection.)

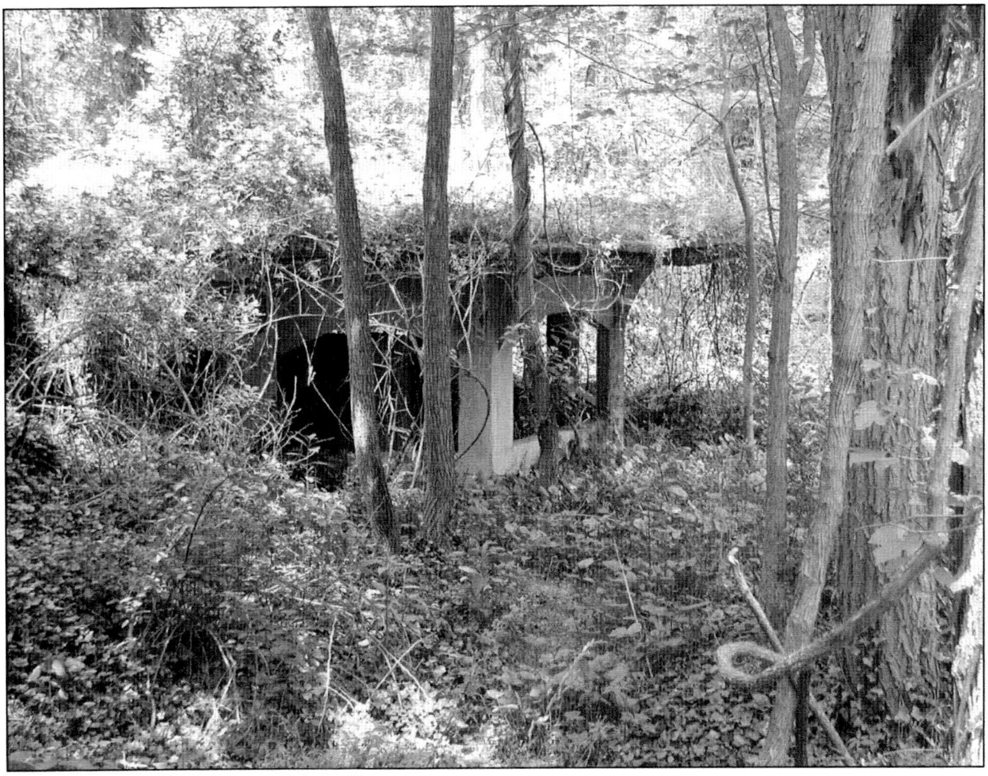

SULPHUR SPRINGS. West Asheville is the site of what had been the county's first health-related resort, Sulphur Springs Hotel, which was established by Robert Henry in 1830 and rebuilt by E. G. Carrier in 1887. The only remnant of the hotel is the springhouse (pictured above), neglected among the overgrowth in Malvern Hills. Asheville, like many cities, has buried its springs and channeled its streams. (Photograph by Rob Neufeld.)

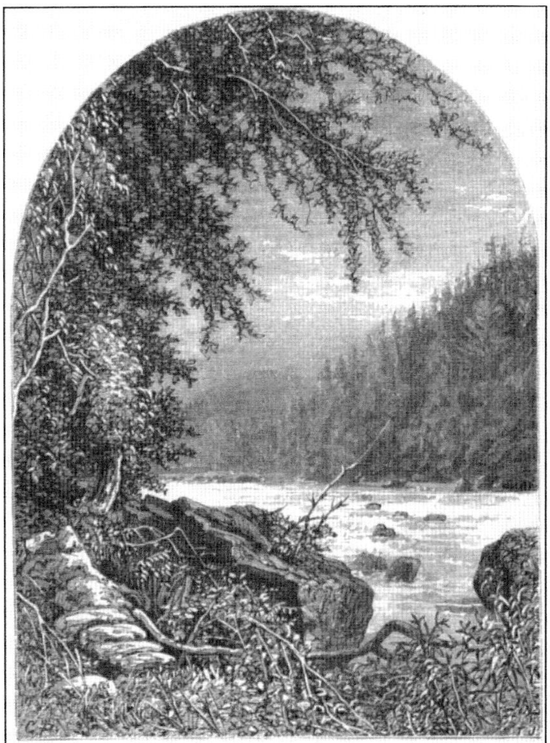

"WILDLY BEAUTIFUL."

WILDLY BEAUTIFUL. This etching from the April 1875 edition of *Harper's New Monthly Magazine* accompanied a romance that used the French Broad River for local color.